Dilemmas of
Masculinity

Books by Mirra Komarovsky

LEISURE, A SUBURBAN STUDY, *Co-Author*

THE UNEMPLOYED MAN AND HIS FAMILY

WOMEN IN THE MODERN WORLD

COMMON FRONTIERS OF THE SOCIAL SCIENCES, *Editor*

BLUE-COLLAR MARRIAGE

SOCIOLOGY AND PUBLIC POLICY, *Editor*

DILEMMAS OF MASCULINITY

Dilemmas of Masculinity

A Study of College Youth

MIRRA KOMAROVSKY

BARNARD COLLEGE, COLUMBIA UNIVERSITY

W·W·Norton & Company·Inc·

NEW YORK

Library of Congress Cataloging in Publication Data

Komarovsky, Mirra, 1906–
    Dilemmas of masculinity.

    Bibliography: p.
    Includes index.
    1. Masculinity (Psychology)   2. College students—United
States—Sexual behavior.   3. Sex role.   I. Title.
HQ28.K64 1976   301.41′1   76–166

ISBN–0–393–01125–9

To the Memory of *Mark*

CONTENTS

TABLES

ACKNOWLEDGMENTS

The financial support for this study was provided by Grant 14618 of the National Institute of Mental Health. As on previous occasions, the staff of the N.I.M.H. facilitated my work in numerous ways, serving as a model of an unbureaucratic governmental agency.

I am grateful to the Bureau of Applied Social Research for providing research facilities and wish to thank especially its administrative director, Miss Phyllis Sheridan, and Mrs. Madeline Simonson, administrative aide.

Chapter 9, the theoretical summary, was written at Villa Serbelloni, Bellagio, Italy, and I express my gratitude to the Rockefeller Foundation.

Miss Martha Peterson, president of Barnard College at the time this book was written, has been unfailingly understanding and generous in her help.

Associated with the author in the interviewing were Mr. Wesley Fisher, Ms. Susanne Riveles, and Dr. Edith Sanders. Dr. Ana Cheser Silbert analyzed the psychological tests and prepared the sixty-two psychological profiles.

Finally, I am indebted to Ms. Janet Price of W.W. Norton for her skillful editorial help.

Dilemmas of
Masculinity

INTRODUCTION

Hardly any segment of the population has been subjected to the scrutiny directed at college students. Researchers have studied their religious and political views, their emotional problems, dating patterns, sexual behavior, their alienation as well as their activism. More broadly, every book in the vast literature of concern or lament about the human condition not only includes but, no doubt, emphasizes the problems of the male of the species. This literature singles out the dominant economic, political, and cultural institutions and these, in turn, are dominated by men. One might conclude, therefore, that no problem of contemporary man, from childhood to old age and in every sector of his life, could have escaped recognition and study.

This much is true, but it is not the whole truth. The distinguishing feature of the present study is its explicit focus upon those strains that the male experiences precisely because he is a male and not a female, living in a particular social milieu. The emphasis, then, is upon distinctively male attitudes, roles, and problems. Viewed in this manner, the paucity of studies of masculine role strains (with some exceptions to be noted presently) contrasts strikingly with the ceaseless flow of publications on the changing roles of women. This contrast is not surprising. The preocupation with women's problems reflects women's discontent and their movement for equality. Change in power relationships between two groups generally begins with concentration on the weaker party in its struggle for power. Gradually, as the struggle achieves some public recognition, attention tends to shift from the weaker party to the relationship between the two. It is in a similar fashion, perhaps, that "labor problems" became in time "labor-management" problems. There are signs that we may have reached the point when the upheaval in women's roles must be seen for what it is, a process of change in both feminine and masculine social roles in our society. The signs in question are the books with the word "male" in the title that began to appear in the early 1970s. Contrary to the apprehension about a possible masculine backlash in the wake of the Women's Liberation Movement, only a few of the books have an antifeminist slant. Those few attempt to show that genetically rooted sex differences set limits to women's quest for equality.[1] However, the dominant message of the recent "men's" books is a plea for men's liberation from the allegedly oppressive and constricting traditional masculine roles. The authors claim that men reap dubious rewards for the alleged advantages of masculine superiority.[2]

This emerging concern with the masculine role may portend new trends, but for the time being the literature on men does not compare in sheer volume or in quality of research with the writings on women.

I became interested in the masculine side of intersexual relationships having been concerned for many years with the changing roles of women. This background dictated both the research and the selection of the sample. Since much of my own work and that of other investigators was centered on female undergraduates, a comparable group of men was chosen in the interests of a parallel and continuous study. Obviously, other strata of society and other stages of the life cycle remain to be investigated from a similar point of view. Indeed, the findings of this study, conducted on a single campus, cannot be assumed to represent male undergraduates in other types of institutions and in other regions of the country. In order to offset these limitations, relevant studies, whenever available, are cited throughout the book.

As the Table of Contents indicates, the male senior was considered in several of his roles, for example: as son, student, potential family provider, and male friend. But the emphasis is on his emotional, sexual, power, and intellectual relationships with women. This focus may created the unwarranted impression that women constitute the major source of men's woes. One other unintended implication of the selective concern of the study calls for a warning. My primary purpose was to locate and interpret

1. See, for example, Lionel Tiger (1969) and Steven Goldberg (1973).
2. E.g., Myron Brenton (1966); Warren Farrell (1974); Marc Feigen Fasteau (1974); Joseph H. Pleck and Jack Sawyer, eds. (1974); Helen Mayer Hacker (1957); Joel Knox, et al. (1972).

strains in masculine roles. Occasionally, the absence of some expectable difficulty turned out to be the more intriguing finding. The proportion of well-adjusted individuals is scrupulously reported for each sector of life. Nonetheless, the reader must be reminded that, if the portrayal appears unduly pessimistic, it is because the aim was precisely to uncover the disturbed areas of life. We shall return in the final chapter to the theme of role strain underlying this book. Suffice it to state here that these strains are not measured against a vision of some perfectly integrated society composed of members free of all tensions. Some degree of strain is inescapable and there are strains that are functional for personal or social goals in given societies. Even Durkheim, so troubled by anomie and its consequences, conceded that some degree of anomie is the inescapable price complex societies may have to pay for flexibility and individualism. Public policy could attain at best only some alleviation of the problem.

The masculine role strains receiving special attention in this book are those perceived to be potentially remediable. Were the purpose of the book to set forth the inherent dilemmas and pain of the human condition, other issues would have been emphasized. The moral impetus of the study, apart from scientific curiosity, lies in the hope that fuller understanding of the social roots of current strains may play a constructive part in public policy. Few would deny that gender roles today reflect massive institutional and cultural disorganization. The images of masculinity and femininity, the division of labor between the sexes in the worlds of work, home, and other institutional sectors present inconsistencies that adversely affect individual and social welfare. The author hopes that understanding and rationality may contribute to a redefinition of gender roles so as to bring them in greater harmony with the realities and central values of our society.

THE SAMPLE AND THE INTERVIEW

This book reports the attitudes and experiences of a sample of college males, randomly selected from the senior class of an Ivy League male college. In order to ensure representation of various groups, the sample was stratified by race, religion (Catholics, Jews, and Protestants), and education of father (twelve years of schooling or less and over twelve years of schooling). The lists of all white seniors containing the above information were compiled in alphabetical order and every third name was drawn from each category. Because of the small number of black students, each successive name was drawn from the alphabetized list of black seniors.

Having selected the prospective respondents, we sent each a letter, explaining briefly the nature of the study, giving the names of the principal investigator and her associate interviewers, and preparing them for a follow-up telephone call or visit. The great majority of the students could be reached by telephone. Sixty-two seniors consented to participate in the study, representing the response rate of 78 percent (the original sample consisted of 79 names). A few students refused to be interviewed but the 22 percent of refusals included several students who lived off campus and had no telephones, and whom we could not reach after repeated follow-up letters. Each student received ten dollars for his participation in the study.

The fieldwork was done in 1969–1970. In order to bring the materials up to date, relevant publications between 1970 and 1975 are cited throughout the book, reflecting both continuities and changes in specific areas.

Each of the sixty-two students contributed a minimum of three two-hour interviews and filled out a set of five schedules and two personality tests: the Gough Adjective Check List for "my real self" and "my ideal man," and the California Psychological Inventory. The schedules were completed by the students between the interviews, giving us an opportunity to discuss their answers. The psychological tests were scored by a computer service and the scores interpreted by a clinical psychologist, employed for that specific task. The Interview Guide was pretested by the principal investigator in experimental interviews with five male undergraduates.

A sample of sixty-two seniors obviously sacrifices the advantages of a large survey. Our findings remain to be tested with larger numbers. This holds especially when findings pertain not to the whole sample but to subgroups within it. But many hypotheses of this study are buttressed by, in addition to statistical tables, the internal evidence of case studies—the motives respondents expressed, corroborated by the succession of events.[3] A statistical

3. See "discerning" in Mirra Komarovsky, 1940, pp. 135–46, also Mirra Komarovsky, 1967, pp. 5–6.

correlation that was a mere accident of sampling would not be supported by such further evidence.

The case-study method had its unique advantages. It provided a check on schedules adopted from previous studies or developed by us. For example, some men who gave affirmative answers to a proposition, "It is appropriate for a mother of a preschool child to take a full-time job," upon further probing, qualified their assent by reservations that virtually nullified it. The opportunity to discuss the schedules enabled us to correct some incomplete or misleading questions.

The schedules served also as starting points for an inquiry into uncharted areas. Chapter 6 on self-disclosure illustrates the combined use of a schedule and open-ended questions. The seniors rated on a schedule their extent of self-disclosure to various persons in several areas. With this schedule in hand, the interviewer proceeded to inquire into motives for disclosure, reserve, or outright deceit. The schedule enabled us to rank various role partners in terms of psychological intimacy, but the explanation of the ranking order was supplied by the open-ended probing. "I tell my girl friend," one man explained, "that I want to be a great writer and go on about style, structure, imagery like a pompous ass. She listens and encourages me. . . . With my male friends, I'd feel silly and conceited to go on the way I do with her." Classifying the varieties of such comments helped to account for both the dominant patterns of disclosure and the exceptions to the rule. Put more generally, the case-study method in this instance supplied the intervening variables (or explanations) for empirical generalization derived by quantitative techniques.

Some sections of the Interview Guide depended wholly upon open-ended questions. For example, the respondent was asked to review what might be termed, "the natural history" of his relationship with his closest woman friend. Though the narrative was guided by our theoretical concerns, the net was wide enough to catch unanticipated remarks bearing on strains or their absence. Similarly, experiences and attitudes in the sexual sphere were ascertained by means of flexible interviewing. In contrast to questionaires which channel answers into predetermined categories, the interview caught the unanticipated qualifications of some expressed attitude, the link with other attitudes, the embarrassment, guilt, humor, indignation, and the depth of these and other feelings. Excerpts from interviews abound throughout this book. Such excerpts are frequently referred to as illustrations, but they do more than illustrate—they convey additional knowledge. For example, Chapter 4 describes the seniors who were still virgins at the time of the interview. The majority, though not all, of the virgins expressed distress over their lack of sexual experience. Case studies of the virgins, presented in Chapter 4, classify several reactions and adaptations to what the virgins perceived as a deviant pattern for their age group. The anxiety experienced by the majority of the virgins may be illustrated by an excerpt from one case study. This senior had a platonic relationship with a woman friend who attended an out-of-town college. In accordance with accepted practices of their social circle, she had stayed overnight in his apartment on several visits to the campus. After one such visit, the young man became "fantastically upset" because he had not made love to her. On the night following her departure he had three beers (he explained that as a rule he did not drink) and phoned the young woman at 2 A.M. to apologize: "Are you upset that I didn't make love to you?" he inquired.

Case studies may, in the fashion just illustrated, convey something of the flavor of life in its totality and uniqueness but the primary purpose of this study was not artistic. The qualitative materials were analyzed from a sociological perspective and the attempt was made to abstract, compare, and generalize. A hypothesis suggested by a single observation was checked by examination and a comparison of all cases. Thus, within the limits of our sample, the analysis was systematic.

The bewildering complexity of the world as it is presented to our experience requires the existence of specialized academic disciplines. They provide us with manageable fields of study. But there is no gainsaying the fact that we pay a price for the analytical selectivity of a given discipline. Although this is primarily a sociological study, the use of two standard psychological tests enabled us to investigate the interplay of sociological and psychological perspectives in both role strains and adjustments. One of the major concerns of the study was to explore the added understanding that comes with the joint use of the two perspectives. As will be illustrated throughout the book and summarized in the final chapter (see pp. 245–48), this double perspective has yielded several kinds of results. The psychological tests occasionally explained the meaning of a correlation between two sociological variables, by supplying the intervening psychological nexus. In addition to thus providing a fuller explanation of some dominant relationship, the psychological tests also illuminated the deviant cases, that is, the exceptions to the prevalent relationships.

Quite a different role was played by psychological data when they supplied additional, independent variables increasing the explanatory power of the analysis to account for the observed behavior (see Mirra Komarovsky, 1973b).

Finally, the summaries prepared by the clinical psychologist, on the basis of the two psychological tests, often revealed psychodynamic processes, which in a given case appeared to explain either the nature of the strain an individual experienced, or his mode of coping with it. Thus, the psychological information enabled us to deal with the "man behind the mask" and the "intrusion of self into the role" allegedly lacking in works emphasizing role analysis (Malcolm Bradbury, et al., 1972, cited in Komarovsky, 1973b).

SOME CONCEPTUAL DEFINITIONS

Most of the concepts used in this book constitute the generally accepted arsenal of sociological conceptual tools. I shall review them briefly for a reader unfamiliar with sociological terminology but shall devote more attention to our special use of the concept of role strain.

A social norm is a socially sanctioned rule of behavior, one implying "should" or "should not." A value is an approved standard which is more general than a norm. Thus, the traditional Chinese value of "filial piety" was reflected in a great variety of specific rules of behavior or norms, e.g., "the father should be served first at a meal." Similarly, the norm that an interested judge should disqualify himself from the case is but one manifestation of the more general standard of fair play.

A social role is a set of social norms (normative expectations about appropriate behavior, attitudes, and beliefs towards designated others) associated with a given status. Social roles often entail clusters of expectations or subroles. For example, the role of the husband includes a member of subroles, e.g., provider, companion, sexual partner.

A status (or position) is a location in a social system associated with a set of social roles. The concept of the role-set now generally denotes the cluster of roles towards various categories of role partners, linked to one status. The status of a nurse implies a set of roles to patients, doctors, families of patients, fellow nurses, and hospital administrators. The status-set is the cluster of statuses occupied by a given individual who is a worker, a son, a male friend, a union member, and so on.[4]

Turning to the concept of role strain we note that the term has been used to denote a variety of phenomena presently to be distinguished. For one thing, role strain is generally used synonymously with role conflict, whereas we propose to treat the term "strain" as the genus of which "conflict" is but one species. The existing formal definitions fail to encompass this wide range of usage. For example, role conflict was defined by Parsons as "the exposure of the actor to conflicting sets of legitimized role expectations such that complete fulfillment of both is realistically impossible" (Talcott Parsons, 1951: 280). This surely covers a large variety of role conflicts but does not cover them all. Among the excluded cases are those involving lack of congruence between personality and social role, or the conflict between obligations and pressures. William J. Goode's definition, "felt difficulties in fulfilling role obligations" (1960: 483ff.), would appear to subsume both the "malfit" between personality and role as well as the conflict between legitimate expectations. Moreover, this definition has the virtue of including also conflicts between legitimate and illegitimate expectations as well as role strain which does not stem from any conflict but is caused by situational obstacles to role performance. But the language of role strains, for better or worse, has not in fact been confined to "felt difficulties in fulfilling role obligations."

---

4. The objection raised by Frederick L. Bates (1956) that the continued use of the term "position" discourages adequate description of its internal structure does not appear critical if the position is recognized for the label that it is.

It is useful to keep the term "position" or "status" recognizing, of course, that the full description of a given position is nothing else than the detailing of the roles associated with it. We thus avoid the awkward reference to "occupants of roles" equally improper whether the reference be to role expectations or actual role performance. There is something to be said in favor of Linton's well-known distinction between the static "status" and the dynamic process of role enactment, though the proposed usage is not identical with Linton's. We simply recognize the heuristic usefulness of keeping the label of a social category. The individual is or is not a father, a judge, a stranger. Beginning with the mere occupancy of the social space we can proceed to describe the social roles associated with this position or the degree of conformity to them on the part of a particular status occupant.

The phrase carries the connotation of consciously felt difficulties, excluding those which remain below the level of awareness. Moreover, role strain has been implied by some writers to be present when conformity to a role, in itself not problematic for the actor, nevertheless generates latent strains in the role, because, for one thing, the rewards of conformity are felt to be inadequate. We propose that the generic definition of role strain include felt and latent (not fully recognized by the person) difficulty in role performance and perceived paucity of rewards for role conformity.

1

IMAGES OF FEMININITY AND MASCULINITY: Beliefs, Norms, and Preferences

The seniors of this study were growing up at a time when traditional sex roles were beginning to be questioned and images of femininity and masculinity were beginning to change. The seniors were more or less aware of these changes even when they could not describe them as explicitly as the one youth who said:

"I see two basic conflicting conceptions of masculinity within our culture, the dominant and the 'hip.' The dominant ideal pictures the man as physically strong, muscular, and athletic. He is intellectually able, possessed of a rational, logical mind, and psychological strength; he displays little emotion, for he is tough and allows very little to phase him. In his relations with women, the masculine male is always dominant. He is the woman's physical superior. Most importantly, he is dominant psychologically, providing the rock strength of the relationship, someone for the woman to lean on and look up to for support.

"Opposed to this ideal is the hip counterculture, which finds its roots in the Women's Liberation Movement. In this subculture man and woman are supposed to be intellectual equals, the woman no less rational or logical than the man. Most important of all, the counterculture dictates that men and women are equal partners in a relationship—eliminating the stereotype of the submissive, weak woman dependent upon the support of the cool, hard will of the man she idolizes. Women no longer surrender their decision-making power to males."

To be sure, comparable data on male conceptions of femininity and masculinity for the early decades of this century are scarce and we do not know the precise extent of changing views. In the absence of firm evidence, values held by commentators frequently affect their perception of change. Those who oppose any further convergence in the social roles of the sexes are alarmed by recent changes and tend to exaggerate their extent. (See, for example, Charles E. Winick, 1968.) The advocates of radical reconstruction, on the other hand, either stress the persistence of traditional stereotypes or, alternately, celebrate the spread of new attitudes. Theirs is the dilemma of all reformers: how to summon rage against the powerful enemy and yet sustain the hope of ultimate victory.

For all the scarcity of comparable historical data, there is no denying a number of trends. For example, in comparison with college students in the 1930s, the seniors in this study began interacting with girls at an earlier age. Documenting the trend towards earlier cross-sex interaction and dating, J. Richard Udry (1966) writes: "Studies done in the 1930's show little cross-sex interaction among grammar school children, and few cross-sex sociometric choices. . . . Today the pattern is changing. . . . A recent national survey of fourth, fifth, and sixth grade teachers indicates that in most communities there is considerable interaction at these age levels (much more, in fact, than was found in earlier studies). Sociometric choices in late elementary school show nearly half the children included at least one cross-sex friend in the top four. For activities such as 'taking a walk,' and 'going to a movie,' fifty per cent of the fifth graders preferred a cross-sex companion to one of the same sex." (see also J. Joel Moss, et al., 1971, and Carlfred D. Broderick, 1966.)

The trend toward earlier heterosexual interaction may be expected to affect male attitudes towards women in several respects. For middle-class, college-bound youth, female associates, in all likelihood, increasingly serve as a source of self-validation and a reference group—perhaps at the expense of male cliques. To the extent that the cross-sex interaction takes place within more equalitarian relationships, it should lead to some convergence in the ideals of femininity and masculinity and some weakening of stereotypical beliefs.

There are other examples of changing trends. Although differences between male and female undergraduates in attitudes toward premarital sex and in incidence of premarital coitus still exist, these differences are not as great as they were a decade or so ago. The proportion of female undergraduates who indicate that they have sexual relations has increased since 1960. In Chapter 3 we describe the sexual experiences and attitudes of male seniors and cite the evidence for recent changes. (See, for example, K. L. Cannon and R. Long, 1971.) Here we only wish to record a certain convergence in premarital sex patterns of female and male undergraduates.

Cultural currents in the wider society, in some degree, also modify traditional ideals of masculinity. The counterculture, referred to by the senior cited earlier, in its condemnation of competitive striving for success, of militarism, and "machismo," challenges some basic elements of traditional masculinity. So does the feminist movement and the stirrings of the men's liberation movement.

Such shifts as we have sketched do not take place in an orderly fashion, nor do they occur without strain for the individual. What is involved is not merely changes in dating practices or even in sexual norms. Changing images of masculinity and femininity reach to the deepest core of personality. It would not be surprising if college seniors were still searching for a model in the welter of diverse values and amid the din of contradictory injunctions from various reference groups. Even those who are sure of their goals may find the obstacles from within and from without difficult to overcome.

BELIEFS ABOUT FEMININE AND MASCULINE PERSONALITY TRAITS

How do young men perceive masculine and feminine personalities—as widely divergent or as relatively similar? Is there a consensus as to traits attributed characteristically to each sex? Does the negative stereotyping of the female, found in earlier studies, persist? (See, for example, P. M. Kitay, 1940; J. P. McKee and A. C. Sherriffs, 1957; Paul Rosenkrantz, et al., 1968; Inge K. Broverman, et al., 1970; and bibliography cited by Broverman.) The answers to these questions to be presented here were derived from structured questionnaires which, no doubt, tapped largely the conscious and socially acceptable attitudes. Other chapters, specifically those dealing with emotional and sexual relationships with women, based on descriptions of ongoing experiences, brought to light less stereotypical images of women, the products of longing, love, fear, or hostility.

The seniors' perceptions of psychological sex differences were sought for their intrinsic interest but also as a clue to possible role strains. In the past, the ideological support for the polarities in sex roles was rooted in the belief that males and females differed radically in innate psychological traits. Any erosion of this ideological rationale would make it more difficult for modern men to defend the differentiation in the social roles of the sexes. Put in other words, we sought to ascertain the degree of consistency between cognitive beliefs about psychological differences and norms of sex roles, with the expectation that inconsistency between those elements might lead to strain.

Data as to cognitive beliefs came from answers to sixteen propositions regarding psychological sex differences. The seniors were asked to check one of five possible answers: "agree," "agree somewhat," "uncertain," "disagree somewhat," and "disagree."[1] The interviewer explained that the statements did not necessarily imply that the sex differences were genetically determined, and that disagreement with a proposition implied no endorsement of a contrary statement.

Table 1.1. Beliefs about Feminine and Masculine Personality Traits (Percentage of sample holding specified beliefs)

Traits	Agree or Agree Somewhat	Uncertain	Disagree or Disagree Somewhat	N
1. Women are more sympathetic than men	49	23	28	(61)
2. Women are more emotional than men	79	8	13	(61)
3. Women are more sensitive than men	44	18	38	(61)

1. The author is indebted to Kenneth Kammeyer (1964) and to Kathryn P. Johnson (1969) for their permission to use elements of their scales.

Traits	Agree or Agree Somewhat	Uncertain	Disagree or Disagree Somewhat	N
4. Men are more aggressive than women	69	10	21	(61)
5. Men are more ambitious than women	45	21	34	(61)
6. Women have a higher moral character than men	15	25	60	(60)
7. The reasoning ability of men is greater than of women	34	20	46	(61)
8. Women are more artistically inclined than men	23	20	57	(61)
9. It probably goes against basic needs of men or women to place women in a position of authority over men	41	23	36	(61)
10. Men are more straightforward, less devious devious than women	35	25	40	(60)
11. Women tend to be pettier than men	65	15	20	(59)
12. Men are more original than women	20	32	48	(60)
13. Women are more insecure than men	41	18	41	(44)
14. Women are more superficial than men	26	16	58	(43)
15. Women are more artificial than men	26	16	58	(43)
16. Women are more easily offended than men	35	23	42	(43)*

*An earlier study of the beliefs held by college women about female personality traits used methods similar to ours (Kenneth Kammeyer, 1966). A random sample of 232 women attending a state university filled out the questionnaires in 1961.

Apart from a few traits, Table 1.1 does not show a consensus concerning sex differences. Of the sixteen propositions, nine received so scattered a vote that no majority opinion emerged either endorsing or opposing a particular statement. Conversely only seven received a majority vote. Combining "agree" and "agree somewhat" (also "disagree" and "disagree somewhat") the seven opinions are cited in the order of magnitude:

"Women are more emotional than men"	79 percent agreed
"Men are more aggressive than women"	69 percent agreed
"Women tend to be pettier than men"	69 percent agreed
"Women have a higher moral character than men"	60 percent disagreed
"Women are more superficial than men"	58 percent disagreed
"Women are more artificial than men"	58 percent disagreed
"Women are more artistically inclined than men"	57 percent disagreed

Not only is there no strong consensus as to sex differences, the seniors were somewhat tentative about the judgments they did express. The most confidently held beliefs were those indicated by the answers "agree" or "disagree" rather than answers qualified by "somewhat." Of 904 individual judgments, only one-third (34 percent) consisted of "agree" or "disagree" responses. The reply "uncertain" constituted 22 percent of the responses with the remaining 44 percent containing the more tentative qualifier of "somewhat" (agree or disagree).

Apart from three traits confidently sex-linked, i.e., "men are more aggressive," "women are more emotional," and "women are pettier," these young men, we conclude, were far from certain that the sexes differed significantly with respect to traits included in the test.

When it came to evaluating the psychological profiles of the sexes, the seniors were somewhat less inclined to stereotype women negatively than previous studies might have led us to expect.[2]

These women were quite traditional on some crucial items of the scale. For example, 75 percent agreed that "women are more emotional than men," 66 percent agreed that "men are better leaders than women," 39 percent that "men are better able to reason logically than women," and 56 percent that "men are more aggressive than women." On these items, at least, the female undergraduates of a western state university in 1961 were not too far apart from the seniors of our 1970 sample.

2. See K. Johnson (1969).

Taking as standards the dominant values of our society, the negative traits attributed to women by a considerable proportion of the men were deviousness, insecurity, and touchiness. We had the impression that "emotionality" attributed to women by 79 percent of the men was also used in the pejorative sense of emotional instability. Moreover, the men refused to concede to women some traditional equalities: only 23 percent judged women to be more artistically inclined and only 15 percent attributed to women a higher moral quality.

Offsetting these negative judgments was the refusal to claim for themselves a superiority with regard to traditionally masculine strengths. Only 20 percent "agreed" (or "agreed somewhat") that men were more original than women, though another 32 percent were "uncertain." As to "reasoning ability," 34 percent thought men were superior and 20 percent were "uncertain."

In the overall assessment of sixteen traits, some tendency to stereotype women negatively did persist. Excluding two traits, ambition and aggressiveness, the evaluation of which may be questionable, we added up the total number of judgments on the remaining fourteen traits. Using the general standards of our society in classifying traits, of the 782 total judgments, 28 percent attributed to women an excess of negative characteristics and only 11 percent gave women a superior rating over men on positive qualities. The remainder consisted of judgments that disagreed with the alleged superiority or inferiority of either sex or expressed uncertainty.

The tendency to stereotype women negatively was not affected by religious affiliations, as seen in Table 1.2. As an index of negative stereotyping, the table used unfavorable judgments as percentages of total judgments made by each religious group. Contrary to a plausible hypothesis that college seniors from less-educated families may be more traditional and hence more prone to negatively stereotype women, Table 1.2 does not reveal such a tendency.

The conceptions of psychological sex differences held by the seniors were not related to their personality profiles. For example, seniors who believed in male superiority in reasoning ability had almost identical scores on the two personality tests as those who did not uphold this view. (See Tables 1.3 and 1.4.) The only exceptions would suggest that the belief in male intellectual superiority

Table 1.2   Tendency to Stereotype Women Negatively by Religion and Education of Father

	Unfavorable judgments as percentage of total judgments made by specified groups	
*Religion**	*Education of Father*	
	12 YEARS OF SCHOOLING OR LESS	OVER 12 YEARS OF SCHOOLING
Protestants	(N = 120) 26	(N = 240) 24
Jews	(N = 88) 26	(N = 192) 30
Catholics	(N = 140) 27	(N = 124) 31

*The three religious groups did not differ in specific beliefs concerning sex differences with one or two exceptions. Of the twenty-four Protestants, only 25 percent "agreed" or "agreed somewhat" that "male reasoning ability was superior to women's." The corresponding endorsement of male superiority were 44 percent on the part of nineteen Jews and 35 percent of the seventeen Catholics. On the other hand, 71 percent of the Protestants and only 56 percent of the Jews asserted that women were pettier than men. The corresponding figure for the Catholics was 82 percent. The proposition "It probably goes against the basic needs of men and women to place women in positions of authority over men" was endorsed ("agree" or "agree somewhat") by approximately equal proportions of Protestants (45 percent), Jews (40 percent), and Catholics (35 percent).

was associated with lower Well-Being and Lower Intellectual Efficiency on the California Psychological Inventory. On the Adjective Check List the male supremacists were lower in Heterosexuality and higher in Autonomy.

In subsequent chapters that deal with actual relationships with women, we shall find a higher association between patterns of relationships and personality profiles. Perhaps cognitive beliefs are not as closely linked to the deeper layers of personality as is actual behavior. In Chapter 5, pp. 149–51, we shall return to this issue and illustrate the complex interplay between behavior (or experience), cognitive beliefs, and values. It is likely that a much larger sample would be required to discern dominant directions in what is frequently a set of circular relationships.

How do these seniors compare with men whose beliefs concerning psychological sex differences were studied by other authors? The search for comparable data is handicapped by the variety of methods used by past and contemporary investigators. The considerable skepticism about the validity of traditional sex stereotypes, expressed by the seniors, contrasts sharply, for example, with the findings of two studies: Paul Rosenkrantz, et al., 1968 and Inge K.

Dilemmas of Masculinity

Table 1.3. Seniors Who Agreed That Male Reasoning Ability Was Superior to Women's Compared with Those Who Were Uncertain or Disagreed (ACL)

| Traits | Percentage of scores falling at standard mean score or above | |
	Males are superior* (N = 18)	Others* (N = 38)
Self-Confidence	50.0	50.0
Self-Control	33.3	42.1
Personal Adjustment	38.9	39.5
Achievement	55.6	55.2
Dominance	50.0	55.2
Intraception	72.2	76.3
Affiliation	33.3	36.8
Heterosexuality	33.3	52.6
Autonomy	72.2	52.6
Aggression	61.1	60.5
Succorance	44.4	34.5
Self-Abasement	50.0	47.4
Counseling Readiness	44.4	44.8

*The total of 56 falls below 62 because personality tests were missing from a few case studies.

Table 1.4. Seniors Who Agreed That Male Reasoning Ability Was Superior to Women's Compared with Those Who Were Uncertain or Disagreed (CPI)

| Traits | Percentage of scores falling at standard mean score or above | |
	Males are superior* (N = 18)	Others* (N = 38)
Dominance	72.2	69.2
Self-Acceptance	88.9	82.1
Well-Being	22.2	38.5
Socialization	44.4	35.9
Self-Control	33.3	33.3
Achievement via Conformity	55.6	48.7
Achievement via Independence	100.0	89.7
Intellectual Efficiency	61.1	71.8
Psychological-Mindedness	83.3	84.6
Femininity	72.2	69.2

*The total of 56 falls below 62 because personality tests were missing from a few case studies.

Broverman, et al., 1972. Broverman concludes that "a strong consensus about differing characteristics of men and women exists across groups which differ in sex, age, religion, marital status, and educational level" (Broverman, 1972: 61). The disparity of results may be attributable to the exceptional "liberality" of the campus of our study or to the differences in methods. Both Rosenkrantz and Broverman used bipolar items, with poles separated by sixty points, e.g., "not at all aggressive . . . , "very aggressive," "very gentle . . . ," "very rough." An item was declared sex-linked or stereotypic if 75 percent or more of college subjects agreed that it was "more masculine" or "more feminine." Of the 122 items, 41 were selected by Broverman as "stereotypic" because 75 percent or more of the respondents agreed in their allocation of the trait to the more masculine or the more feminine direction. Of the sixteen sex differences presented to our seniors (see Table 1.1) on only one item did the agreement reach 75 percent. Conceivably, the seniors in our study, presented with such psychological polarities as "very rough," and "very gentle" might have also shown higher agreement as to which items represent "femininity" or "masculinity." Other variations in the formulation of questions affect results: Anne Steinmann and David Fox (1966: 275) noted, as we did, that "global" or general questions evoke one set of answers, whereas basically identical questions expressed more specifically resulted in contradictory answers. A person may easily affirm some accepted moral principle or a stereotypical belief when the question is posed in general terms. But the same principle or belief tapped by more specific questions may evoke qualifications or, indeed, an outright denial of the original answer. General questions may only reveal the respondent's familiarity with the prevailing stereotype. Concrete questions, on the other hand, are more likely to call forth "operative" rather than ideal norms and a wider range of attitudes responsive to particular circumstances.

This difference in responses to general and specific questions may have accounted in part for another of Rosenkrantz's findings concerning self-concepts of the sexes. The self-concepts of both men and women in the Rosenkrantz study were less "masculine" and "feminine," respectively, than were their responses about masculinity and femininity in general. This may mean that respondents felt themselves deviant and deficient. But the discrepancy between a general answer and the self-concept may be explained otherwise. The first may show familiarity with the conventional stereotype. A question posed in the context of actual experience, on the other hand, evokes less rigid images of masculinity and femininity.

In an earlier attempt to tap psychological sex stereotypes (S. W. Fernburger, 1948), the respondents were undergraduate and graduate students in psychology, with undergraduates exhibiting a greater tendency to support the traditional stereotypes. This was the case notwithstanding the lectures, preceding the test, which emphasized the lack of reliable evidence concerning psychological sex differences. Once again, methods of the 1948 and the present study were not identical. A recalculation of Fernberger's tables, however, enables us to compare the results in two respects. Of the 143 undergraduate and graduate males, 45 percent endorsed male superiority in intelligence as against our 34 percent. Again, of the 143 respondents in the 1948 study, 67 percent felt that women were more sensitive than men. Only 44 percent of our seniors agreed with this proposition.

Whether the explanation lies in the difference in samples or in the methods of the various studies, the seniors expressed somewhat greater uncertainty about the traditional beliefs as to psychological sex differences than was the case in the other studies.[3]

Turning from beliefs to ideal preferences, the focus shifted to the question: "What are for you, personally, the three or four most desirable characteristics in a woman (or man) who is to be close to you?"

IDEALS OF FEMININITY AND MASCULINITY

The qualities desired in female and male friends were classified into six clusters. "Sexual compatibility and love," which understandably appeared frequently among the desiderata in a female friend, were excluded for obvious reasons from this classification. The first cluster, "social amenities," consisted of such items as poised, tactful, pleasant, attractive appearance, sociable, and the

---

3. We are not concerned here with the validity of the beliefs expressed by the seniors. The latest assessment of the body of evidence concerning the psychology of sex differences is to be found in Eleanor E. Maccoby and Carol N. Jacklin (1974).

like. The second cluster included self-assurance, independence, confidence, energetic, decisive—all termed, "ascendancy traits." Stimulating, intelligent, well-informed, clear-thinking, socially concerned, were the attributes of the "intellectual cluster." Supportive, warm, understanding, sensitive, and kind were items classified as "expressive." "Intimacy" dealt with openness in communication. "Health" included emotional as well as physical well-being. Table 1.5 presents the results for the four hundred traits desired in closest male and female friends.

Only two clusters show a marked divergence in the desiderata for female and male close friends; these are "social amenities" (which included attractive appearance) for women and the relatively higher frequency of intellectual qualities desired in male friends. One might conclude that men still want good looks in a female and brains in a male friend but this would exaggerate the revealed differences. The relative ranking of clusters is nearly identical for both friends. The most impressive finding would appear to be the convergence in the qualities sought in the two relationships.

Table 1.5. Traits Desired in Closest Female and Male Friends by Selected Clusters (Exclusive of "Sexual Compatibility and Love")

	Female Friend		Male Friend	
Cluster	*Number*	*Percent*	*Number*	*Percent*
Social Amenities	49	21.3	9	5.5
Expressive	55	24.0	35	20.6
Ascendancy	14	6.0	11	6.5
Intellectual	68	29.6	67	39.4
Health	7	3.1	7	4.1
Intimacy	22	9.5	19	11.2
Similar Interests	–	–	5	2.9
Miscellaneous	15	6.5	17	10.0
Total	230	100.0	170	100.0

The traits desired in female and male friends were classified in still another manner. Earlier studies (McKee and Sherriffs, 1957; Johnson, 1969) presented lists of adjectives which their college subjects assigned more frequently to one rather than the other sex. For example, modest, warm, sensitive, religious, emotional, sympathetic, and others are attributed by one or both groups of men in the above studies more frequently to women than to men. The "masculine" adjectives, those that the men defined as more typically male, were intelligent, ambitious, independent, aggressive, wide interests, and others. Using only the adjectives so sex-linked on the McKee and Sherriffs and the Johnson studies, we reclassified our data.

Of the 117 traits the seniors desired in a close female friend, 53 percent fell into the "masculine" stereotype as defined in those studies and only 47 percent were "feminine" traits. Of the 89 traits ideally expected in a male friend, 29 percent were part of the "feminine" cluster and 71 percent were "masculine." The residue of negative perception of femininity is apparent in the fact that even in female friends men desired many qualities identified with the traditionally "masculine" profile.

The seniors also filled out an Adjective Check List for "my ideal man." Of all the traits attributed to the ideal man, about 30 percent were "feminine" as defined by the two studies cited above. Considering the higher evaluation of typically "masculine" traits on the part of college men (and women), it is significant that nearly one out of every three traits seniors deemed admirable in a man should fall into the "feminine" cluster. This is not to obscure another of our findings that the ideal man for these seniors was still an "assertive," "strong," "courageous," "aggressive," and "masculine" man. In Chapter 5 we shall compare their perception of ideal masculinity with their self-concepts.

Some convergence in the ideals of femininity and masculinity has been reported in several studies. McKee and Sherriffs (1959) found that male undergraduates believed that "in the eyes of women the ideal male is one who exemplifies not only much that society alleges to be masculine but also much that society alleges to be feminine."

Inge K. Broverman, et al. (1972), using different and not strictly comparable methods, arrived at conclusions similar to ours in one respect. Certain traits, previously defined by male college students as stereotypically feminine (the "warmth-expressiveness" cluster), were subsequently considered by them as desirable for men as well. But of the twenty-nine male-valued stereotypical items (the "competency" cluster), twenty-eight items were considered by the same men to be more desirable in a male than in a female. Of all traits our seniors ideally desired in a close female friend, 53 percent fell into the masculine stereotype, as we defined it.

In sum, a degree of stereotyping of masculine and feminine personalities remained among the seniors as does a somewhat

negative relative evaluation of women. We were surprised, however, by the considerable skepticism expressed by the men about
the existence of psychological sex differences and by the considerable convergence in the ideals of masculinity and femininity.
Though, to the best of our knowledge, comparable studies for the
1930s are not available, our findings are consistent with the expected consequences of the trend towards earlier cross-sex interaction. Moreover, Chapter 3, on intellectual relationships with
women friends, will describe the desire of the majority for full
intellectual companionship with women friends. The chapter on
self-disclosure, Chapter 6, will demonstrate the predominance of
the closest female friend over other role partners in communication concerning interests as well as feelings.

The skepticism with regard to sex differences and the considerable convergence in ideals of masculinity and femininity might be
expected to create a strain towards consistency. The greater the
perceived similarity between the sexes, the more universalistic the
principles in terms of which they are appraised and treated. For
example, one senior had this to say about his former girl friend: "I
would have liked her to be more ambitious, to be able to set a goal
for herself and strive to achieve it. She kept changing majors. I
don't like to see *people slacking off*" [emphasis ours]. Given this
perception of the common humanity of men and women, it
becomes increasingly difficult to view such American values as
freedom of choice, fair play, full development of one's potential,
and achievement, as exclusively male privileges.

The matter does not rest here. The earlier cross-sex companionship would appear to generate some mutual empathy. For example, the senior might feel less sure now than in the past that women
are constituted so differently from men as to find complete fulfillment in a kind of domesticity that would repel men. As one senior
put it bluntly: "Girls will not, unless they are really stupid, get
satisfaction out of just keeping house for the rest of their lives."

The following sections of this chapter deal with male attitudes
towards women's occupational roles in general, and the preferred
roles for their future wives in particular. To anticipate one finding,
consensus is high with regard to postcollege roles. The seniors
expected their wives to play the role of homemaker and child-rearer
of young children and they themselves expected to be the principal
achievers in the outside world. One senior's remarks illustrate the
inconsistencies of attitudes. He "disagreed" with thirteen out of the

sixteen propositions asserting sex differences. He endorsed enthusiastically the proposal to counsel qualified high school girls to "train for occupations which are now held mainly by men." In fact, he termed "sick" the current practice of influencing girls to enter only feminine occupations. But describing his preferences for the future, he wanted his wife to stay home to rear their children. In the interview, in answer to our standard question: "List three most favorable qualities of your mother as a mother in relation to you," he said: "She was completely devoted to me. She was a very bright and a very intelligent woman and she stayed home till I was grown. I mean, she didn't go to work until I went to high school; she then took a job till three o'clock so that she could be home to cook dinner." He hoped his future wife would be as good a mother to their children.

Having first described male attitudes towards postcollege sex roles, we shall consider how the seniors coped with the inconsistencies between their belief that the sexes may not differ radically in psychological traits, on the one hand, and, on the other, the expectation that they will play sharply different roles after marriage.

The implication that such "inconsistencies" create a problem for the individual may be challenged, since discrepancies between one's beliefs, norms, and values are so widespread as to constitute the rule rather than the exception. Inconsistencies vary in kind and Chapter 9, pp. 238–41, will consider both their varieties and their potential for stress. Suffice it to say here, that if human beings are not wholly rational and consistent, they do exhibit a strain towards cognitive and moral congruence. Their very rationalizations, evasions, and suppressions are a testimony to such a tendency. Leon Festinger and Elliot Aronson (1968) assemble an impressive body of evidence about efforts of human beings to reduce cognitive dissonance ("simultaneous existence of cognitions which . . . do not fit together . . . " [p. 125]).[4]

4. A study by Kenneth Kammeyer (1964) of female attitudes on a state university campus found less consistency than he expected between, on the one hand, some beliefs about sex differences in personality traits and women's attitudes towards sex roles, on the other. "About one-third of the girls," states the author, "were found to be traditional on one scale while at the same time modern on the other" (p. 304). Analysis indicated that the degree of consistency increased with the extent of social interaction of the respondent. The author surmises that communication and feedback tend to alert the person to her inconsistencies and create some pressure to modify attitudes. The females in the Kammeyer sample, studied in 1960, were, if anything, somewhat more traditional than our seniors in their beliefs about psychological sex differences.

ARE SOME COLLEGE MAJORS
UNFEMININE?

Women undergraduates in the 1940s who majored in physics, mathematics, and other "nonfeminine" fields were known to conceal this fact from their dates on initial acquaintance fearing that the truth would antagonize the men. We attempted to elicit the attitudes of the seniors towards the suitability or unsuitability of various majors for women. Since the major in college has implications for postcollege occupations we shall be dealing here with matters that extend beyond suitable courses of study.

We might designate as "liberal" or "feminist" the respondents who declared that there were no "unfeminine" college majors and that pioneering choices did not affect adversely their attitude towards a date. In fact, some of these feminist men claimed that such unusual choices made the girl doubly interesting. A senior, a Greek major, explained: "If a girl majored in physics and was able to explain to me what it was all about, it would be exciting!" Another youth remarked that he would be flattered to date a career-oriented girl because "a girl so dedicated to her work must think an awful lot of you if she wants to spend time with you."

Possibly some seniors voiced these modern ideals without having tested them in actual experience. Taking at face value their assertion that an unfeminine choice of a major would not prejudice them against a date places about one-half of the sample (48 percent) in the feminist category.

The "traditionalists" comprised 39 percent of the group. These men opposed pioneering choices and, conversely, endorsed only the traditionally feminine subjects and occupations. Finally, 13 percent were ambivalent.

Six traditionalists based their opposition upon pragmatic grounds, e.g., the difficulty of combining such demanding careers as medicine or law with homemaking or the prejudice against women in the men's world. "If I had to choose whom to go to or whom to employ [in the unfeminine occupations]," declared one senior, "I'd choose the guy anytime." The allegedly high rate of attrition of professional women because of marriage and motherhood and the consequent waste of graduate training were also mentioned. But the most frequent arguments against pioneering choices were based upon other grounds. First, the traditionalists felt that the prerequisites for success in masculine occupations—i.e., competitiveness, backbiting, aggression, "cold intellectuality"—while tolerable in a man, would be highly objectionable in a woman. The only way a businesswoman could escape turning into an aggressive competitor would be to use "feminine wiles" on the job, but this would put her male competitors at a disadvantage. Some men, unabashedly resentful towards women, insisted that women did in fact tend to take advantage of male chivalry. Apart from the incompatibility between traits required for success and the ideal of femininity, the entry of women into the pioneering occupations clearly posed a direct threat to the men. A prelaw male senior objected: "When I went to take the law boards, I felt shocked to see all those girls. I didn't think I would feel that way, but I did. Any girl has to be pretty smart and aggressive to go into a field where she has to compete with men. It's a threat to the security of all men in the profession." Another senior spoke with sympathy about his friends: "I know several premed guys who are really bugged that girls take the place of a man [in medical schools]." "She would be crowding my field," said another respondent.

Finally, the traditionalists worried about the deleterious effects of demanding careers upon the husbands of such women. "A chick who is premed is a pretty serious person," remarked a senior. "If you get involved with her there may be a hassle between the marriage and her going to medical school. A girl with another major can change her plans more easily." Again: "It would mean competition with one's wife even if her career were different. Suppose her job turned out to be more important than her husband's?"

One senior gave an eloquent example of the traditional attitudes. He had met a co-ed in a history class, liked her, and began dating her. She never mentioned her major although they frequently discussed his. Whenever asked, she explained that she hadn't quite made up her mind. He finally discovered by accident that she was premed. She told him that she had to go to summer school in order to take organic chemistry. "Why in the world would you want to take such a course?" he asked her, and then he learned that she was premed. "It was a real shock," he recalled. "She was too nice a girl to go for a thing like this." He lost interest and did not take her out anymore. He explained that her ambition might have "challenged my superiority."

The third small group (13 percent of the sample) was too ambivalent to fit into either of the first two categories. For example, one senior asserted that women in engineering lost their femininity: "They put their intellect before their heart and get hardened." But no sooner did he express this view than he caught himself: "Hell, if I can play the violin why can't a girl go into physics? There should be no limitation on her choice of a major." As to careers for mothers, he felt that a girl should have a field of her own and if his wife's career was worthwhile, he would not object to assisting her with their children. But he would certainly expect her to stay home with preschool children and work only part-time as long as the children were in school. Even as he was expounding his views, he exclaimed with exasperation: "Oh, I don't know, the whole thing is unfair to women."

This youth and others like him were aware of the mixture of admiration and apprehension aroused in them by career-oriented women, and of their conflicts between values and sentiments. They punctuated their replies with such apologetic remarks as, "I shouldn't resent it but I do." Given current values and their skepticism concerning psychological sex differences, they judged their own sentiments to be irrational.

In contrast to such self-conscious ambivalence, other men, apparently unaware of their own inconsistencies, expressed incompatible desires or endorsed goals for women while censuring the means necessary for their attainment. One such senior upheld the principle of free choice of profession for women, specifically including medicine. In a subsequent interview, in answer to our standard question about unfeminine behavior, he cited "too great a concern with grades." He found such concern repugnant also in a man. But he made allowances for a male premed student, anxious about admission to a good medical school, who would go to see a professor about a C on a chemistry test. In a girl, such an act would be "obnoxious" and he would be completely "turned off" by a girl who was similarly concerned about a poor grade.

The traditionalism of the men concerning sex-linked occupations became apparent in their attitudes towards certain proposed reforms. "How much need is there," we asked, "to have high school counselors urge qualified girls to train for occupations which are now held mainly by men?" Only 30 percent of the sample checked "very great" and "great" and, conversely, 70 percent replied "some" and "no need." Thus, whereas 48 percent accepted or admired pioneering choices on the part of college girls, only 30 percent felt such choices should be stimulated by high school counseling.

THE WAGE-EARNING WIFE OF A STUDENT-HUSBAND

Male attitudes towards being supported in graduate school by a wage-earning wife tell us something about the process of social change. The comparison of students who were untroubled by this reversal of traditional roles with those who opposed it is instructive. It confirms the hypothesis that in a period of change, new norms will be the more readily accepted if they serve the interests of the individual. Self-interest, in other words, is solvent of traditional attitudes.

Underlying the diversity of attitudes, to be presently described, one finds the nearly universal assumption that the young husband's graduate education takes priority over that of the wife's, should a choice have to be made. Fellowships, loans, parental support, part-time jobs were all suggested to enable both to pursue graduate study if both so desired. However, if all fails, it is the wife's education that has to be sacrificed or postponed. Of the sixty-two seniors, only one man conceived the possibility that certain circumstances, such as, for example, the duration of graduate study, might dictate a temporary postponement of the husband's education to enable the wife to get on with hers.

If this extreme feminist position was endorsed by only one vote, several men were ready to make some compromises in the interest of the women's graduate plans. One recently married senior and his wife applied to many graduate schools. He was fully prepared to enter the school of his second or third choice if it turned out to be the university that also accepted his wife.

To return to an overview of the group, only about a third were traditionalists, opposing this reversal of roles on traditional grounds and claiming that it would undermine male self-esteem, and give the wife "a leverage on the husband," getting the marriage off to a bad start. The working wife was bound, it was said, to exact a high price for this sacrifice: "I have given you the best years of my life." One of these traditionalists, his principle tested by experience, refused the offer of his fiancée to drop out of college in order to support him through law school. Clearly, these men would prefer continued economic dependence upon parents to the dependence upon the wife, if fellowships, loans, or part-time jobs were not available.

The majority of the seniors, however, accepted the idea of the wife's support. This majority was divided. About one-third of the sample found nothing objectionable or threatening in such temporary dependence upon a working wife. These men said in effect, "After all, I'll be supporting my wife and children throughout my life. There is nothing wrong in her contributing to our common goal for a limited period of time." Among these were men who, in other respects, adhered to a traditional view of sex roles. For example, one engaged senior, admitting that his attitudes might be "antediluvian," did not think it appropriate for a woman to aspire to a Ph.D. His sensitivity to sex roles was seen in his remark that, if his head happened to be lower than his fiancée's on the pillow, he readjusted his position. But all this traditionalism did not stand in the way of his plan to be supported by his future wife through his medical training. His wife would also manage the budget because, as he explained, "women are better at it than men." His last remark hints at some redefinition of sex roles in order to make the desired allocation of tasks congruent with his traditional outlook.

Some 20 percent of the sample also accepted the idea of a temporary dependence upon a wage-earning wife but they qualified their acceptance by a concern for the wife's interests. For this 20 percent the wife's support was acceptable provided she herself had no desire to pursue graduate education or provided her job was not below her capabilities and was otherwise satisfactory to her. There was some hint of selective perception in the kind of cases each group cited in support of its position.

One man concerned about the wife's interests in such a situation told of a friend of his who married a brilliant student. She had wanted to go to graduate school. But her husband was accepted by a university that admitted very few women. The young wife ended up taking a routine job and supporting her husband through graduate school. Our respondent knew that his friend was con-cerned about his wife's disappointment and feared that this might put a strain on their marriage.

Finally, the remaining 14 percent revealed conflicting feelings. The vacillation of one ambivalent student is illustrated in the following excerpt from his interview. This was a student whose family would be unable to finance his graduate training. "I might have to marry someone to put me through graduate school," he admitted, "but then I won't be able ever to divorce her. Perhaps it is all right if my wife had no plans of her own for graduate study—all the same even though love is greater than money, the provider has the control and it would probably cut my masculinity and my freedom of action to have to depend upon my wife."

We suggested at the outset that self-interest acts to undermine the allegiance to the old norms and to facilitate the acceptance of the new. The comparison between the traditionalists and the others supports this hypothesis. The latter group was closer to marriage, with one-third either engaged or married, whereas only one of the twenty-one traditionalists was engaged. Those confronted with the reality of marriage were thus more willing to accept the wife's support. Not only does a working wife make an early marriage economically feasible; in a few cases it promised a welcome escape from the economic dependence upon parents. The testimony of one engaged senior exemplifies the process of change. A senior, whose fiancée expected to work and support him through the school of dentistry, described the change in his feelings: "The idea of being supported by my wife hurt my ego at the beginning, but it doesn't bother me now. I had felt I was supposed to be the bread-winner and all that, but then I realized that my attitude was sort of archaic, childish, and ridiculous, and that it doesn't apply to our situation since we are both young and starting off entirely unestab-lished."

Forty percent of the traditionalists turned out to be virgins. In contrast, only 18 percent of those who did not object to working wives were virgins. The virgins were especially anxious about their lack of dominance and inadequate masculinity. Not only was the idea of marriage and its economic problems remote; their anxieties may have made the prospect of economic dependence upon a wife particularly threatening.

Finally, did the traditionalists suffer from being "the last to give up the old" in a period of shifting norms? This could be the case if the young man, wishing to marry while still in graduate school and having no economic resources of his own, could not countenance the economic dependence upon his wife. One black senior broke up with his "steady" because he was not ready for marriage. He intended to go to graduate school and was determined to begin married life as the sole provider. Though he occasionally missed his former girl friend and sometimes wondered whether he would ever meet "so nice a girl," he gave the impression of optimism on this score.

The interviews suggest that the traditionalists did not generally pay a high price for their refusal to accept the economic assistance of a wage-earning wife; this for the simple reason that in the face of a desire to marry and economic need their attitudes tended to change. A small minority remained ambivalent, partly out of concern for the wife's interests and partly in defense of their masculine self-esteem.

WORKING WIVES AND WORKING MOTHERS[5]

The ethos on this eastern Ivy League campus clearly demanded that men pay at least lip service to liberal attitudes toward working wives. If the initial responses to structured questions were accepted as final, the majority would have been described as quite feminist in ideology. But further probing revealed qualifications which occasionally almost negated the original response. For example, an affirmative answer to the proposition, "It is appropriate for a mother of a preschool child to take a full-time job," was, upon further questioning, conditioned by such restrictions as, "provided, of course, that the home was run smoothly, the children did not suffer, and the wife's job did not interfere with her husband's career." The interview provided an opportunity to get an assessment of normative expectations, ideal and operative, as well as of actual preferences. The classification of attitudes to be presented in this report is based on the total interview. Preferences reported here

5. See Komarovsky, 1973a. The author is indebted to the *American Journal of Sociology* for permission to reprint sections of this article, in this and the following chapter.

assume that a wife's paycheck will not be an economic necessity. The overwhelming majority in the pre-Recession year of 1970 appeared confident that their own earnings would be adequate to support the family. Throughout the discussion of working, only two or three seniors mentioned the temptation of a second paycheck.

Four types of response to the question of wives' working may be identified. The traditionalists, 24 percent of the men, said outright that they intended to marry women who would find sufficient fulfillment in domestic, civic, and cultural pursuits without ever seeking outside jobs.

Who are these traditional men, the "last to give up the old" on this liberal campus? An analysis of "sexist" students based upon the 1972 survey of entering freshmen, conducted by the American Council on Education, was provided by Alan E. Bayer (1975). One of the criteria of male sexist attitudes was the agreement with the statement, "the activities of married women are best confined to the home and the family." Though, as we shall point out on p. 34, reaction to such a statement and an expression of a personal preference are not strictly comparable, we shall examine our traditionalists against Bayer's results. Similar to the national survey was the high proportion of black students among the traditionalists, 33 percent, as against only 15 percent of blacks in our total sample. On the other hand, neither the religious affiliation nor the father's education was related in our sample to traditional preferences. Possibly four years of college have modified the attitudes brought to college by these subgroups whereas the traditionalism of the black student on the subject of being the sole provider has deeper roots.

We compared the traditionalists with the rest of the sample on psychological tests. The only differences which appeared striking on the California Psychological Inventory were that the traditionalists were lower on Well-Being (only 15.4 percent scoring at the mean or above as against 38.6 percent of the remainder of the group) and on Intellectual Efficiency (53.8 percent at or above the mean as against 72.7 percent of the rest). The traditionalists were lower on Femininity (only 53.8 percent as against 75 percent for the nontraditionalists). The low scorers are described as ". . . hard-headed, ambitious, masculine, restless . . . impatient with delay, indecision, and reflection."

The Adjective Check List also portrays the traditionalists as low in Personal Adjustment with only 20 percent at the mean score or above as against 46.3 percent of the nontraditionalists.

The lower Intellectual Efficiency of traditional seniors is consistent with Bayer's finding that academically sexist students were relatively less likely to have been highly successful in high school.

Why should the traditional seniors be lower in Personal Adjustment and Well-Being? Is it that both the innovators and ideological laggards pay the price of deviating from the dominant pattern? Case analyses suggest that in this instance, apart perhaps from perceiving themselves as being old-fashioned the traditionalists were not penalized for their views. Possibly, later in life with their attitudes unchanged, they may have to forego the advantages of a second paycheck in married life.

It is more likely that a variety of personal problems gave rise to patriarchal attitudes as defensive reactions. Significantly, out of ten white traditionalists, seven had been classified as "troubled" on the score of power vis-à-vis women. In the total sample, 45 percent were so troubled. (See Chapter 5 on Emotional and Power Relationships with Women.)

To return to the remaining three types of preferences on the subject of working wives. In addition to the traditionalists we termed 16 percent "pseudofeminists." These men favored having their wives work, at least when the question was at a high level of abstraction, but their approval was hedged with qualifications that few woman could meet.

The third and dominant response included almost half (48 percent) of the respondents. These men took a "modified liberal" position which favored a sequential pattern: work, withdrawal from work for child rearing, and eventual return to work. They varied as to the timing of these stages and as to the aid they were prepared to give their wives with domestic and child-rearing functions. The majority saw no substitute for the mother during her child's preschool years. Even the mother of school-age children, were she to work, should preferably be at home when the children return from school. Though they were willing to aid their wives in varying degrees, they frequently excluded specific tasks, for instance, "not the laundry," "not the cleaning," "not the diapers," and so on. Many hoped that they would be "able to assist" their wives by hiring maids. The greater the importance of the wife's work, the more willing they were to help her. (One senior, however, would help only if his wife's work were "peripheral," that is, not as impoitant to her as her home.)

The last, the "feminist" type, was the smallest, only 7 percent of the total. These men were willing to modify their own roles significantly to facilitate their future wives' careers. Some recommended a symmetrical allocation of tasks—"as long as it is not a complete reversal of roles." In the remaining 5 percent of the cases, marriage was so remote that the respondents were reluctant to venture any views on this matter.[6]

The foregoing summary of types of male attitudes toward working wives fails to reveal the tangled web of contradictory values and sentiments associated with these attitudes. We shall presently illustrate a variety of inconsistencies. But underlying them is one basic problem. The ideological support for the belief in sharp sex-role differentiation in marriage has weakened, but the belief itself has not been relinquished. Earlier cross-sex association in childhood and early adolescence was accompanied by raised male expectation of enjoying an emotional and intellectual companionship with women. These expectations, however, coexist with the deeply rooted norm that the husband should be the superior achiever in the occupational world and the wife, the primary child rearer.

One manifestation of this basic dilemma is the familiar conflict between a value and a preference. "It is only fair," declared one senior, "to let a woman do her own thing, if she wants a career. Personally, though, I would want my wife at home."

More interesting are the ambivalent attitudes manifested toward both the full-time homemaker and the career wife. The image of

6. Some liberalization of attitudes of college freshmen was reported by Alan E. Bayer (1975) on the basis of annual studies of entering college freshmen published by the American Council on Education. In 1967, at the time of entry to college, a national sample of freshmen were asked their position with respect to the statement "the activities of married women are best confined to the home and family." Sixty-six percent of them agreed "strongly" or "somewhat." This percentage dropped to 40.9 for the freshmen in 1973. There is additional evidence of liberalization of attitudes between the freshman and senior years. The entering freshmen in 1967 became more liberal in a re-survey in 1971; only 30 percent of the men agreed with the traditional statement cited above (Bayer, 1975: 391).

Although on the face of it, the proportion of traditional students among our seniors appears close to the national average, the results are not quite comparable. There is a strong suggestion in the interviews that the seniors would be liberal in response to a general statement, since they repeatedly endorsed free choice as to working wives. But this section describes their personal preferences rather than ideal norms.

each contained both attractive and repellent traits. Deprecating remarks about housewifery were not uncommon, even among men with traditional views of women's roles. A conservative senior declared, "A woman who works is more interesting than a house-wife." "If I were a woman," remarked another senior, "I would want a career. It must be boring sitting around the house doing the same thing day in, day out. I don't have much respect for the type of woman whom I see doing the detergent commercials on TV."

But the low esteem attached by some of the men to full-time homemaking coexisted with other sentiments and convictions which required just such a pattern for one's wife. For example, asked about the disadvantages of being a woman, one senior re-plied: "Life ends at forty. The woman raised her children and all that remains is garden clubs and that sort of thing—unless, of course, she has a profession." In another part of the interview, this young man explained that he enjoyed shyness in a girl and detested aggressive and ambitious women. He could never be attracted to a career woman. It is no exaggeration to conclude that this man could not countenance in a woman who was to be his wife the qualities that he himself felt were necessary for a fulfilling middle age.

If the image of the full-time homemaker contained some alienat-ing features, the main threat of a career wife was that of occupa-tional rivalry, as illustrated in the following excerpt from the interviews. A senior speaks:

"I believe that it is good for mothers to return to full-time work when the children are grown, provided the work is important and worthwhile. Otherwise, housewives get hung up with tranquilizers, because they have no outlet for their abilities. . . . Of course, it may be difficult if a wife becomes successful in her own right. A woman should want her husband's success more than he should want hers. Her work shouldn't interfere with or hurt his career in any way. He should not sacrifice his career to hers. For example, if he is transferred, his wife should follow—and not vice versa."

Work for married women with grown children is approved by this young man, provided that the occupation is of some impor-tance. But such an occupation is precisely one which carries a threat to the husband's pride.

The expectation that the husband should be the superior achiever appears still to be deeply rooted. Even equality in achievement of husband and wife is interpreted as a defeat for the man. The prospect of occupational rivalry with one's wife seems intolerable to contemplate. "My girl friend often beats me in tennis," explained one senior. "Now, losing the game doesn't worry me. It in no way reduces my manhood. But being in a lower position than a woman in a job would hurt my self-esteem."

Another youth explained why he could not be happy with a professional wife: "The wife should be home when a guy gets there. She should be intelligent and educated and have as much right as her husband to make family decisions, but there should be no question as to which one of the two is the superior achiever." He wants his future wife to look up to him and say, "isn't he fine!" The young woman he was dating at the time of the interview had at first attracted him because she was intelligent and a major in his own field. But she decided to go to graduate school to train for a career in public service. Her recent plans were "turning him off"—he would not want to face competition within his own family.

Still another senior, having declared his full support for equal opportunities for women in the occupational world, added a qualification: "A woman should not be in a position of firing an employee. It is an unpleasant thing to do. Besides, it is unfair to the man who is to be fired. He may be a very poor employee, but he is still a human being and it may be just compounding his unhappiness to be fired by a woman."

An engaged man and his working fiancée, who shared his apartment, presented a vivid case of ambivalent expectations. His major strain came from the excessive dependency of his fiancée. He pictured clearly the person he would have liked her to be but failed to recognize the likely implications of the desired traits for his other requirements.

This was an energetic and determined senior who combined scholarly interests with active civic and political activities on the campus. His fiancée was not self-sufficient enough and needed to have him around evenings, whereas he felt the pull of his various responsibilities. He wished she were more deeply involved in her major and would go on to get a doctorate in her field. Since he hoped to teach in college they would thus have free summers and share the same life styles. Moreover, such a professional commitment would ensure continued growth in his future wife. He did not admire his mother, a full-time homemaker, who, he felt, failed to develop with the years. Indeed, he could not imagine how any woman could be satisfied with housewifery as a lifetime career. "If I wanted a maid, I would get one," he added sarcastically.

Would he wish, the interviewer asked, that his fiancée were as deeply committed to a professional career as he was to his? "Definitely not," was his answer. For one thing, he would expect her to follow him if he were accepted at the university of *his* first choice. Furthermore, he wanted his children to have a "full-time mother" until they go to school.

This young man wanted his fiancée to be self-sufficient enough to free him for his varied interests. He, also, admired professional commitment in a married woman and held lifelong domesticity in some disdain. But nowhere in the interview did he appear to have an inkling of the problems such a professionally committed wife might have in making the expected adjustments to his and their children's interests.

Finally, another senior, describing characteristics he wanted most in a wife, said: "I want her to be alive, to have something in her life that makes life worth living apart from me and our children." But in another part of the interview, he praised his sister-in-law for the full-time attention she was giving his little niece. A mother of preschool children, he thought, should not take even a part-time job. This should wait until the children are in school. When they are in college, a full-time job may even be of benefit to the children because, at that stage of life, a working mother would give her children more emotional independence.

Some of the revealed inconsistencies are, thus: the right of an able woman to a career of her choice; the admiration for women who measure up in terms of the dominant values of our society; the lure but also the threat that such women present; the low status attached to housewifery but the conviction that there is no substitute for the mother's care of young children; the deeply internalized norm of male occupational superiority pitted against the principle of equal opportunity irrespective of sex.

Such ambivalences on the part of college men are bound to exacerbate role conflicts in women. The latter must sense that even the men who pay lip service to the creativity of child rearing and domesticity reserve their admiration (if occasionally tinged with ambivalence) for female achievers who measure up in terms of the dominant values of our society. It is becoming increasingly difficult to maintain a system of values for women only (Komarovsky, 1953).[7]

7. It is no doubt, equally true that role conflicts of women create confusion and uncertainty for men.

Nevertheless, to infer from this account of male inconsistencies that this is an area of great stress for them would be a mistake. It is not. By and large, the respondents assumed that the women's "career and marriage" issue was solved by the sequential pattern of withdrawal and return to work. If this condemned women to second-class citizenship in the occupational world, the outcome was consistent with the conviction that the husband should be the superior achiever.

Men who momentarily worried about the fate of able women found moral anchorage in their conviction that today no satisfactory alternative to the mother's care of young children can be found. Many respondents expressed their willingness to help with child care and household duties. Similarly, many hoped to spend more time with their own children than their fathers had spent with them. But such domestic participation was defined as assistance to the wife, who was to carry the major responsibility. Only two or three of the men approved a symmetrical, rather than a complementary, allocation of domestic and occupational roles. An articulate senior sums up the dominant view:

"I would not want to marry a woman whose only goal is to become a housewife. This type of woman would not have enough bounce and zest in her. I don't think a girl has much imagination if she just wants to settle down and raise a family from the very beginning. Moreover, I want an independent girl, one who has her own interests and does not always have to depend on me for stimulation and diversion. However, when we both agree to have children, my wife must be the one to raise them. She'll have to forfeit her freedom for the children. I believe that, when a woman wants a child, she must also accept the full responsibility of child care."

When he was asked why it was necessarily the woman who had to be fully responsible for the children, he replied:

"Biology makes equality impossible. Besides, the person I'll marry will want the child and will want to care for the child. Ideally, I would hope I'm not forcing her to assume responsibility for raising the children. I would hope that this is her desire and that it is the happiest thing she can do. After we have children, it will be her career that will end, while mine will support us. I believe that women should have equal opportunities in business and the professions, but I still insist that a woman who is a mother should devote herself entirely to her children."

The lack of concern about the issue of working wives may also be attributed to another factor. The female partners of our respondents, at this particular stage of life, did not, with a few exceptions, force the men to confront their inconsistencies. Apparently, enough women have freely made the traditional-for-women adjustments—whether scaling down their own ambitions or in other ways acknowledging the prior claims of the man's career.[8] This judgment is supported by the results of three studies of female undergraduates done on the same campus in 1943, 1971, and 1972 (Table 1.6). The big shift in postcollege preferences since 1943 was in the decline of women undergraduates who opted for full-time homemaking and volunteer activities. In 1971 and 1972, the majority chose the sequential pattern, involving withdrawal from employment for child rearing.

The attitudes of the seniors' female associates, gleaned from the men's descriptions, were liberal but not militantly feminist. Women are likely to shift to the feminist direction in the coming years. At least one study of female undergraduates at Douglass College, a state-supported women's college in New Jersey (Ann P. Parelius, 1975) reports a striking rise in feminist attitudes between 1969 and 1973. The author describes the college as "especially sensitive to the Women's Liberation Movement." In the 1973 Douglass sample 81 percent of females believed that "a wife's career is of equal importance to her husband's" and 60 percent intended to work all their adult life. To the best of my knowledge, these are the most feminist responses of all the existing studies. The college women in the 1970 national sample, cited in Chapter 10, p. 250, were more traditional. The national sample differed in composition (age, regions, types of colleges) from the Douglass College sample.

Though feminist in their occupational aspirations, the Douglass College women hoped to marry and have children. Moreover, they believed that men prefer more traditional women and would not want to marry "women like themselves" (p. 152). Parelius surmises that, in consequence, "many were probably experiencing considerable anxiety about their futures."

The Douglass College women were probably justified in their belief that most men would be more traditional as to sex roles. However, Anne Steinmann and David J. Fox (1966) challenge the

---

8. Possibly, the interviewed men tended to select women with more traditional attitudes. We have cited a few cases of men who were "turned off" by the occupational ambitions of otherwise attractive female friends.

Table 1.6.   College Women's Attitudes toward Work and Family
Patterns

	Random sample of sophomore class at women's liberal arts college 1943 (N = 78) Percent	Class in introductory sociology, same college 1971 (N = 44) Percent	Two classes* on changing sex roles, same college 1972 (N = 59) Percent
Assume that you will marry and that your husband will make enough money so that you will not have to work unless you want to. Under these circumstances, would you prefer:			
1. Not to work at all, or stop after childbirth and decide later whether to go back.	50	18	13
2. To quit working after the birth of a child but definitely to go back to work.	30	62	51
3. To continue working with a minimum of interruption for childbearing (or not marry and/or not have children).	20	20	36
	(100)	(100)	(100)

SOURCE: Mirra Komarovsky, unpublished studies.

*These classes may have selected more upper-class and more feminist women than the two earlier samples. "Do not plan to marry" or "do not plan to have children" constituted 8 percent of the 1972 group and was included under option 3.

accuracy of perceptions women have of male attitudes. In their study men took a more liberal position on several items than women imagined. All the same, if men are more liberal than women imagine, men remain more conservative than women.

Whatever pressures college women have begun to exert upon male seniors since 1970, the interviewed men in our study did not view the problem of sex roles within marriage as a source of future strain.

The attitudes of the seniors in our study toward some proposed reforms throw light upon their lack of perception of changing sex roles as a social problem. The seniors were asked: "How great a need do you think there is for the following social changes?" The possible replies were: "very great need," "great need," "some need," "no need at all," "don't know." Table 1.7 lists four reforms and shows the percentage of the sixty-two men who checked "very great," or "great" need.

The men who favored child-care centers frequently added that the need for such facilities arose when economic exigencies forced mothers to work. Thus, this endorsement was not inconsistent with their prevailing conviction that mother's care of young children was preferable to group care.

The opposition of the majority to paid maternity leaves was

Table 1.7.   Male Attitudes to Feminist Reforms*

Question: "How great a need do you think, is there for the following social changes? Very great need, great need, some need, no need at all, don't know?"	Percent checking "very great" and "great" (N = 62)
"Have high school counselors urge qualified girls to train for occupations now held mainly by men."	30
"Paid maternity leave should be available for all working mothers who want or need it."	36
"The federal government should establish the principle of equal opportunity for women in hiring, training, and promotion in private employment."	65
"Make available professionally supervised child-care facilities for children of working mothers."	71

*The author is grateful to Dr. Alice Rossi for her permission to use this schedule.

explained on two grounds: the population explosion, and the view that neither industry nor government had any obligation to assume the cost of such private decisions.

The comments accompanying this schedule conveyed the impression that the majority perceived women's dilemmas as individual problems requiring individual adaptations rather than a social problem. By the same token, the seniors referred infrequently to any need for major institutional reorganization in this area of gender roles.

Without retracting any of the explanations of male attitudes towards postcollege sex roles offered so far, we shall return to this issue on pp. 251–57 to suggest what is, perhaps, the underlying structural cause of the inconsistencies detailed in this chapter.

How reliable are the attitudes towards sex roles expressed by college seniors as predictors of their future behavior? We can only speculate in the absence of a follow-up study.[9]

That words and deeds are not always in accord has been recognized throughout history. This is all the more so when the words we recorded were spoken by young men at the ages of twenty-one or twenty-two about the future which, of necessity, they cannot perceive with full clarity and assurance.

On a liberal campus, with sanctions against old-fashioned attitudes, some seniors may have paid only lip service to the moderately liberal views they expressed. Given the opportunity in postcollege years to select preferred mates and a sustaining social milieu, they may revert to more traditional views and behavior. Apposite is Erik Erikson's statement, made in another connection, that "it takes a much longer time to emancipate what goes on deep down inside us—that is, whatever . . . [has] become part of our impulse life and our identity formation—than the time it takes to re-define professed values . . ." (1965). Presumably those deeper layers of identity affect our actual behavior even as we learn to mouth the fashionable new beliefs.

That much is in accord with the popular idea that young adults tend to revert to more conventional attitudes with the assumption

9. The most exhaustive examination to date of relationships between verbal statements and actual behavior is to be found in Irwin Deutscher (1973). The disjunctions and consistencies in studies assembled by Deutscher involved short-range relationships. The experimental studies, particularly, tested verbal statements and behavior within a limited time period. By contrast, we are, in effect, asking whether the behavior of the seniors in the decades following graduation would be consistent with attitudes expressed in their senior year. Our problem is closer in its logical structure to the theme of Theodore M. Newcomb, et al. (1967).

of adult responsibilities. Though we have no way of estimating its prevalence, the reverse pattern cannot be excluded from our speculation. Depending upon economic and cultural changes and the continued spread of women's and men's liberation movements, men who were traditional in college may assume more feminist sex roles in their adult years. In some cases, it may be merely a surrender to the superior power of the wives they marry. But ideological changes and situational pressures may make for more equalitarian marriages than some men had anticipated in college. Even in our college sample there were a few men more egalitarian in behavior than in ideology. They have made a variety of novel egalitarian adjustments in "steady" relationships, seemingly unaware that they had departed from their professed traditional beliefs. The emotionally-charged stereotype of masculinity endured in the face of their contrary new adaptations.[10] It is likely that in our case this discrepant combination of "modern" behavior and traditional ideology presupposed a satisfactory relationship with the woman. The reason is twofold. A satisfactory relationship both increases the motivation to serve the interests of the mate and tends to conceal the full significance of these accommodations. A man adhering to traditional ideology is likely to view the egalitarian male as emasculated and defeated. Hence, the very self-esteem that the traditional man enjoys in a satisfactory relationship helps maintain the fiction that his egalitarian adjustments are minor changes, dictated by practical exigencies, which in no way violate masculine leadership. Erikson's insight about the resistant feelings of identity must, hence, be qualified by the human capacity to redefine situations and to maintain fictions. One is reminded of Sumner's insight that mores tend to be changed by ritual, by small variations in behavior and habit and, eventually, by changes in attitudes (Mirra Komarovsky, 1973b).

Liberalization of sex-role attitudes need not, of course, always take the form of such sub rosa, unconscious adjustments. The influences we cited, economic as well as cultural, the expectations brought to marriage by their wives, and a supportive social environment may eventuate in consistent and conscious liberalization of attitudes and behavior in comparison with views held at age twenty-one.

10. This phenomenon is well recognized in studies of prejudice. Unfavorable stereotypes of minority groups or of older workers have been known to persist despite favorable encounters with members of these groups, who were defined as exceptions to the rule.

2

RELATIONSHIPS WITH WOMEN:
Intellectual Aspects

The preceding chapter was based largely on schedules and "pencil and paper" tests. It may be assumed that such methods tend to evoke normative statements and stereotypical, or at least, conscious attitudes. This chapter and Chapters 3 through 5, on the other hand, draw upon descriptions of actual relationships with women friends, past and current. In the case of the few respondents who dated very infrequently, if at all, preferences, insecurities, and other attitudes expressed toward women were used as the basis of classifications, though, admittedly, these attitudes were not tested by experience.

The descriptions of the actual relationships come closer to the reality of male-female interaction than the normative account presented in Chapter 1. Occasionally, situational pressures are strong enough to modify behavior in such a manner that individuals are more radical in practice than in professed beliefs. In other cases, social sanctions require at least lip service to newer values, while the individual continues traditional practices. Besides revealing discrepancies between ideal norms and actual behavior, the descriptions of relationships with women friends will illuminate the interplay of psychological and social factors in role strains.

We shall begin with an account of the dating status of the seniors at the time of the interview. The results are nearly identical with the findings of a larger survey done on the same campus in 1965 (see Table 2.1).

CURRENT DATING STATUS: AN OVERVIEW

For one out of four seniors the search for a mate was over. This group included three married and seven engaged seniors with an additional five men, though not formally engaged, fully committed to marrying their current sexual partners.

Another group (18 percent of the sample) maintained an exclusive relationship with a young woman but with no commitment to marriage. Of these eleven men, ten had regular sexual relations with their steadies, and, the one who did not, was a Catholic youth who had continued dating his high school steady, also a Catholic, after he left for a metropolitan college. He explained with some resentment that, after one episode of sexual intercourse during his freshman year at college, his girl friend refused to continue sexual relations during their meetings on holidays.[1]

The largest single group, nineteen (31 percent) were playing the field, in the sense that at the time of the interview they were not having an exclusive relationship with any one woman. These men had some sexual experience in the past and were currently dating, with or without sexual relations, a succession of women or, more casually, several at the same time.

Table 2.1. Dating Status in 1965 and the 1969–70 Studies*

Status	1969–70		1965	
	Number	Percent	Number	Percent
Engaged	7	12	15	17
Exclusive dating	16	27	24	27
Playing the field	29	49	39	43
No dating	7	12	12	13
Totals	59	100	90	100

*The author is indebted to Dr. David Caplovitz and Harry Levy for making available these data of their unpublished manuscript.

1. See pp. 136–37 for fuller analysis of this case.

The remaining sixteen seniors (26 percent) were virgins. Of these, seven were nondaters— so designated because they had fewer then ten social dates throughout their college years. The other nine virgins dated occasionally.

The relative proportions of exclusive daters, those playing the field, and nondaters corresponded closely to the findings of a study done on the same campus in 1965. That study excluded the married seniors. Eliminating the three married men in our sample, Table 2.1 presents the close agreement of the two surveys.

INTELLECTUAL COMPANIONSHIP WITH WOMEN

The description of past and current relationships with women friends, the findings on self-disclosure,[2] the qualities desired in close female friends,[3] all add up to an unmistakable conclusion: The feminine ideal of the men was a far cry from the legendary "dumb blonde." The majority of the seniors hoped to share whatever intellectual and academic interests they had with their female, as well as their male friends. To be sure, what some men meant by an intellectual rapport was having an appreciative listener. "I wouldn't go out with a girl," declared an intense youth, "who wasn't quick and perceptive enough to catch an intellectual subtlety." And another explained that he would not be able to confide in a girl who wasn't intelligent enough to understand his problems.

All the same, many expressed the desire for a true dialogue and a delight in intellectual rapport when they found it. "What I love about this girl," exclaimed one senior feelingly, "is that she is on my level, that I can never speak over her head." "Describe a typical evening with your fiancée," the interviewer asked of another student. He replied: "We talk a lot and we never run out of topics. We are both interested in politics, in people and we talk over what we read or saw on Channel 13 or how we could help a friend who has a problem." In answer to a further question, he added: "It's a funny thing, sometimes I think my fiancée is only as intelligent as I am and sometimes I know she is much more intelligent or at least more

2. See Chapter 6.
3. See pp. 20–22.

sensitive." "Does this bother you at all?" probed the interviewer. "Oh no, it's beautiful!" he exclaimed. "We can sit and talk for five, six hours. We each consider the other more intelligent." This young man is urging his fiancée to go to graduate school whereas she is still undecided about her plans.

"I want an intellectual partner in residence," was the way another respondent expressed himself. Still another said: "I am looking for an intelligent girl who has opinions about things like politics and social problems; someone I could talk to about things guys talk about." "A guy leaving a movie with his date," explained one youth, "wants her to make a stimulating comment of her own and not merely echo his ideas."

As many as 20 percent of the total group, when asked to list defects in former or current girl friends, included "isn't informed (or "intelligent," "stimulating," "intellectual") enough." His first girl friend, explained one senior, made him realize that he needed a woman with whom he "could talk on all levels and a girl with certain ambitions and goals of her own." Still another student never again took out a girl who on their first date "didn't have the slightest idea as to what went on in the movie" they had seen together.

The prevailing expectation of intellectual companionship is confirmed indirectly by the plight of the senior who, though intellectual himself, had in his own words "old-fashioned" ideas about girls. He had gone to an all-boys high school and learned "not to think of girls in an academic context." His beliefs concerning psychological sex differences indicated a strong tendency to stereotype women negatively.

This man's first sexual experience was in his junior year during a seven-months relationships with a co-ed. "It was very beautiful but basically we were two very confused people," he explained. He eventually realized that she was an extraordinarily bright girl who wanted not only to be loved physically but to be appreciated intellectually. But for him, at the time, the affair was just a wonderful physical release. One day, out of a clear blue sky, just as he was about to cancel a trip to Europe in order to remain with her during the summer, she decided that they should split up. He learned later that her decision was precipitated by meeting a man she had known in high school. "She talked to him about her interests and she realized how much she missed such talks in our relationship," the respondent reported ruefully. "We rarely discussed books and I was condescending when we did. Now I have changed and I am looking for a girl who would be close to me emotionally, intellectually, and physically, probably in that order."

This case attests to the costs of clinging to the past in the face of shifting norms. A few other respondents reported similar dissatisfactions on the part of their women friends.

Turning to strains, we attempted to ascertain whether the men experienced any intellectual rivalry and insecurity vis-à-vis women. This was a plausible expectation. In the past, when men enjoyed superior educational advantages, the traditional expectation of male superiority in reasoning ability, logic, originality, and knowledgeability must have been validated by experience. Moreover, to the extent that men limited certain spheres of communication to male associates, the segregation between the sexes served to cushion painful comparisons. But today, the female companions of our respondents are also college students, and, if anything, more rigorously selected in terms of academic performance. In a 1970 survey of 180,684 entering college freshmen in 274 public and private institutions, the American Council of Education found that 69 percent of the female, but only 59 percent of the male freshmen ranked in the top quarter of their high school class.[4] The likely persistence of the norm of masculine intellectual superiority, conditions which no longer give men their former educational advantages, the new value of cross-sex intellectual companionship—this conjuncture of factors suggests the probability of masculine strain in intellectual relationships with women.

Our findings indicate that such strain does exist, but it is not as prevalent as the foregoing hypothesis would have led one to expect. About one-third of the respondents experienced insecurity and ambivalence in this area and we shall describe this minority. More intriguing is the absence of strain among the majority, an issue to be considered presently.

The following excerpts from the interviews will illustrate intellectual rivalry with women. Some men acknowledged intellectual insecurity and wished they could have maintained masculine superiority. Others, equally troubled, protected their self-esteem by putting the onus of strained encounters upon "unfeminine," "bickering," "argumentative" women.

4. *Princeton Alumni Weekly*, February 23, 1971.

THE TROUBLED MEN: INTELLECTUAL
RIVALRY WITH WOMEN

Of the fifty-three seniors for whom this information was available,[5] sixteen (or 32 percent) admitted that intellectual rivalry with women had been in the past, or was currently, a more or less troubling issue for them. This number included men, who, having acknowledged the problem, sought to avoid it through selective dating and were successful in this strategy. One young man broke off a friendship with a bright girl, largely, he admitted, because she "bested me in arguments too often for comfort." Others took preventive measures. For example, one student volunteered the information that he would not date a girl in his class if he had observed that she performed better than he.

The following excerpts from the interviews were regarded as indications of intellectual rivalry with women:

"A brilliant girl would give me an inferiority complex; the girls I date are less smart than I."

"I make it a point never to take out a girl in my own field [economics], because I would resent possible competition with her. I would bail out quickly if in talking to me a girl made better points in my field."

"I resent bickering girls who always know something about everything. I think I feel more competitive toward them than I would toward a man."

"I enjoy talking to more intelligent girls, but I have no desire for a deep relationship with them. I guess I still believe that the man should be more intelligent."

"I may be a little frightened of a man who is superior to me in some field of knowledge, but if a girl knows more than I do, I resent her."

"Once I was seeing a philosophy major and we got along quite well. We shared a similar outlook on life and while we had some divergent opinions, I seemed better able to document my position. One day, by chance, I heard her discussing with another girl an aspect of Kant which just the night before she described to me as obscure and confusing. But now she was explaining it to a girl so clearly and matter-of-factly that I felt sort of hurt and foolish. Perhaps it was immature of me to react in this way."

"Girls have a Germanic self-confidence and arrogance," remarked another senior peevishly. He felt that he had a wider

5. Three cases contained no information on intellectual relationships and six others were nondaters who did not express any relevant attitudes.

perspective than most girls and was irked because they did not always recognize his superiority. With his male friends the problem did not arise, as he explained in answer to the interviewer's question, because the men were generally his classmates and, in case of disagreement, he felt sure his views would be eventually vindicated by a teacher. But with the argumentative and unyielding girls he met outside of school such ultimate vindication was not possible.

Another senior was equally irritated by "dumb" as by "overly intelligent" women. "It isn't the girl's place to talk about politics," he remarked. But the real source of his discomfort surfaced when he finally added: "I hate to admit it, but Jane [his current girl friend] is probably more intelligent than I. She always insists on making some intelligent comment after we see a movie. I'd rather be silent, otherwise it makes me feel 'on stage.' " Generally, when she makes those intelligent comments, he "puts her down" by responding in a dumb voice: "Gee gosh, I guess I didn't see that, ah duh!"

A few men reported that they changed the subject when they sensed that their dates knew *more* about it than they did. Women, if anything, would be more likely to drop a topic upon discovering that their dates were *less* informed about it than they were. (See p. 54 ff.)

Selective dating and the avoidance of threatening women did not solve the problem for some. Half a dozen seniors were caught in the dilemma of both yearning for intellectual challenge and fearing invidious comparisons with their dates. One nineteen year old, good-looking senior seeks a girl friend who "has some defined crystal of her own personality and can express a thought that is not merely an echo of my previously expressed ideas—a girl who is stimulating." But such a girl tends to make him feel "nervous and unsure of myself." At the time of the interview he was dating a girl who was "only moderately intelligent. I am beginning to feel that she is not sharp or perceptive enough. She never says anything that would make me sit up and say, 'Aha, that's interesting.' " He recently met a bright girl who impressed and fascinated him but with her he felt "nervous and humbled."

The effort to resolve a similar dilemma is apparent in the following excerpt:

"My fiancée was not more intelligent than I, but she knew a lot more about certain fields: art, music, and even politics, a 'masculine' field. I got a big kick out of her interests but our discussions often upset me. She was better informed on social issues and she could debate more logically. I always felt at the losing end of the argument. Instead of admitting I was wrong I wouldn't give in and she wouldn't give in just to pacify me. I was really in a dilemma. I expected her to be an individual and not just agree with all of my opinions, but I felt hurt when she disagreed. Now I am trying not to take each disagreement as a personal attack and a threat to my pride."

Finally, still another ambivalent senior pithily summed up his dilemma: "With security comes boredom, with enjoyment—a defensiveness." He went on to describe his plight: "My feeling of intellectual inferiority has caused me to avoid intellectual discussions with girls for fear that I'd appear politically or philosophically weak—a very terrible experience. The discussions I cannot avoid are transformed into defensive ego games rather than being serious, sincere considerations of ideas. At the same time, my feeling of security with girls who are not intellectually threatening is offset by the dullness of the relationship. This was the situation with a girl at school this year with whom I felt intellectually confident but who lacked wit, sharpness of mind, and creativity."

The problem of these youths was to seek the rewards of valued attributes in a woman without arousing in themselves feelings of inferiority. It may be argued that in a competitive society this conflict tends to characterize encounters with males as well. Nonetheless, if similar problems exist between two males, the utility curve is shaped differently by the norm of male superiority. As long as this norm exists, even equality with a woman may be interpreted as a defeat.

The ambivalence of the men occasionally surfaced in criticism that placed women in a double bind. The women were mocked for their passivity in class and their meticulous and compliant note taking. At the same time "aggressive," "opinionated," "argumentative," and "snobbishly intelligent" women students were resented. It is likely, and a few respondents admitted as much, that the tolerance threshhold for "aggressive" class participation was lower for a female than for a male fellow student.

So much for the 32 percent of the seniors who admitted that intellectual rivalry with women constituted a problem for them, even if some succeeded in avoiding it through selective dating.

The majority of 68 percent assured us that neither in the past nor in their current relationships have they experienced any intellectual insecurity.

THE ADJUSTED MAJORITY

The adjusted majority represented a variety of types. Eleven men felt either superior to their women friends or at any rate, very confident of their own intellectual abilities. In two or three cases the relationships were equalitarian with strong emphasis on the rewards of intellectual companionship. In contrast, several men—and their dates—evinced so little interest in academic or intellectual concerns that the denial of any intellectual insecurity may have bespoken the low saliency of the whole issue in their social circle. In a few instances the severity of other problems overwhelmed this one.

Finally, some eight men were happily adjusted despite the acknowledged superiority of their women friends. What makes for accommodation to this still deviant pattern?

By and large, the woman's intellectual superiority was acceptable because she had some weakness which offset it, such as emotional dependency, instability, or a plain appearance, giving the man a compensating advantage. For example, one senior has recently married a woman (one year older than he) who was a graduate engineer, earning a good salary at her first job while he was still dependent upon his parents. Neither her technical competence, nor her earnings presented a threat to her husband. His problem instead was caused by her excessive emotional dependence upon him. He also wished that she were better informed about current affairs. Moreover, whatever her competence, the wife had no permanent career ambitions that would in any way interfere with his projected business career and his vision of family life. The acceptance on her part of the priority of her husband's career and her dependency gave this man, on balance, a superior power in the relationship.

Again, a student, worried about his lack of motivation and poor academic record, was having an affair with a girl who was a superior student. "She studies a lot harder than I," he explained. As to changes he would have wished to make in her, he remarked: "She undervalues her capacities and has too low a self-image. This causes her to be always needlessly anxious about future performance." Having described these shortcomings, the young man mused, "I really don't know whether I would like her to be different."

The offsetting weakness in a third case was the girl's lack of organization and her self-destructive tendencies. Her fiancé forced her to attend to her studies, with the result that her academic average was higher than his own. This was a competitive man, striving hard for high grades. Nevertheless, far from being disturbed by his fiancée's academic superiority, he took pride in it because he saw himself as her mentor and protector.

A different process accounted for the adjustment of another man, engaged to a superior scholar. He was a bright youth and despite his good looks, surer of his intellectual skills than his ability to keep the loyalty of a sexually attractive and popular girl. His bright fiancée was plain looking and socially shy. Despite her intellectual distinction, the young man enjoyed some power over her. Given his vulnerabilities, an attractive and popular girl would have constituted more of a threat to him than the bluestocking scholar he had chosen.

In the cases cited so far, some redeeming strength of the man offset the threat of intellectual superiority. A different type is presented by a senior who had gone steady with the same young woman since their high school years. He described her as "actually a little smarter than I," also as more independent and less emotional. Unlike some other bright girls, however, she didn't make him "feel like a dunce." The superiority of this girl was tolerable not because of any compensating defects but rather because she put her strength devotedly at his service in a supportive relationship which he both needed and could accept, with only mild occasional discomfort.

Finally, a married senior illustrated a loving acceptance of his wife's intellectual excellence. An incident exemplifies their relationship and his identification with her. Once, very depressed by a low grade on a test, he returned home to find her radiant over an A she had just received. He reported that his pleasure at her triumph and her happiness relieved his depression.

The proportion of intellectually insecure men was not any higher among the sons of the less-educated fathers than among the sons of college graduates. Religious affiliation affected the rate of insecure men in only one respect. The proportion of Jewish males among those so troubled was only 13 percent though they constituted 31 percent of the sample. The Protestant and Catholic students had a similar proportion of troubled men. The adjusted Jewish seniors included all the varieties of adjustment just described, but of the three cases in which the intellectual companionship was highly valued in an equalitarian relationship, two were Jewish and one Protestant.

DO WOMEN STILL PLAY DOWN THEIR INTELLECTUAL ABILITY ON DATES?

Can we explain, at least in part, the adjustment of the majority of interviewed seniors in intellectual relationships with women by the readiness of women to play down their abilities? That such behavior has occurred is attested by several studies (Komarovsky, 1946; Wallin, 1950; Horner, 1972).

When confronted with a projective story about a girl "playing dumb" on dates, three or four seniors considered such behavior understandable and even praiseworthy. "Her intentions were good, she wanted to make the guy feel important," remarked one student. Another said: "He should feel honored. She didn't want to scare him off by appearing too smart."

But the great majority expressed indignation over such "dishonest," "condescending," "infuriating" behavior. To be sure, their indignation does not necessarily tell us anything about the realities of the situation and the extent to which dissimulation, supportive of the male ego, continues to be practiced. At least one engaged woman in describing her social circle maintained that women deliberately, or simply habitually, continued to play the feminine role in mixed social groups, irrespective of their abilities. The women asked questions, made comments, whereas the men acknowledged, criticized, praised, or dismissed these feminine contributions, all the while addressing their important intellectual pronouncements to the other men in the group. Both sexes, she claimed, might if asked directly, profess equalitarian ideals and even cherish the fiction that they adhere to them. A male senior who found male classmates more stimulating than co-eds, added an insightful observation. "I confess," he said, "that I tend to associate a brilliant point with a guy even if a girl makes an identical point. I think it is because women make their points in the form of questions and in a tentative, feminine way whereas a fellow is likely to state his opinion more forcefully."

A few scattered studies of women show that the playing down of intellectual abilities on dates is less prevalent than it was in the 1940s. A questionnaire was filled out by seventy women in two coeducational sociology classes in 1970–71 in an eastern college, duplicating the study done at Stanford in 1950. Granting that the different campuses of the two studies make the comparison inconclusive, the findings are consistent with the author's informal observation that dissimulation in question is somewhat less pronounced than it used to be. Table 2.2 presents the results.

Table 2.2.   Readiness of Women to Play Down Intellectual Abilities (In Percentages)

			Advanced
1. When on dates how often have you pretended to be intellectually inferior to the man?	Wallin* 1950 (N = 163)	Sociology Class 1970** (N = 33)	Sociology Class 1971** (N = 55)
Very often, often, or several times	32	21	15
Once or twice	26	36	30
Never	42	43	55
2. In general, do you have any hesitation about revealing your equality or superiority to men in intellectual competence?	Wallin* 1950 (N = 163)	Sociology Class 1970** (N = 33)	Advanced Sociology Class 1971** (N = 55)
Have considerable or some hesitation	35	21	13
Very little hesitation	39	33	32
None at all	26	46	55

*Paul Wallin, (1950).
**Mirra Komarovsky, unpublished studies. The 1970 class was a course on the family, and the 1971 class probably recruited a relatively high proportion of feminists.

On the other hand, there is no denying that this muting of competence still occasionally takes place. This means that the possession of a quality valued in the college community is, understandably, an asset to the male in relation to women, whereas it may still be a liability for an exceptionally able woman.

A replication of Komarovsky's (1946) and Wallin's (1950) studies in Iowa State University in 1970 and 1972 was reported in an unpublished paper by Dwight G. Dean, et al. (1973). The findings challenge the earlier studies in two significant respects. The responses of Iowa State female students were nearly identical with Wallin's 1950 sample. The small study in an eastern college, cited on page 55, suggested that the female tendency to play down intellectual abilities on dates has declined since 1950. Regional differences may have accounted for this divergence. Our 1971 class possibly recruited a disproportionate number of feminists. A more interesting departure of the Iowa State study consisted in the finding that males also pretended inferiority on dates, if less frequently than did females. Future research should explore the motives for such a pretense on the part of each sex. Possibly, men simulate inferiority when they perceive that their dates are so inferior that intellectual prowess would be wasted on them or when intellectual discussion is deemed inappropriate on a given occasion or in a given milieu. Women, on the other hand, play dumber than their dates in conformity with the norm of male superiority and in the hope of thereby pleasing the men. Should, however, contrary to these assumptions, the motives for muting one's ability on dates prove to be identical for the sexes, the original thesis would be put in question both for the present time and for the 1940s. [6]

In returning to the adjusted majority who deny any problems of intellectual insecurity, let us grant that the women's deliberate or unconscious supportiveness may still play some role in male self-assurance. But another influence may be at work. The importance of male intellectual superiority may be giving way to an expectation of companionship between equals.

6. Matina S. Horner's well-known (1972) studies bear upon intellectual relationships between the sexes. Horner infers from her data that able women fear achievement and success because these are felt to be unfeminine. This achievement-related conflict is said to inhibit female performance and level of aspirations. David Tresemer and Joseph Pleck (1974) caution against a view of a generalized fear of success on the part of women. They distinguish between the nature of the task and the style of adatpation to the environment. Insofar as intellectual and professional achievements become more acceptable for women, the feminine "fear of success" should diminish. See evidence of such decline in studies of Adeline Levine and Janice Crumrine (1973) and Janet T. Spence (1974). Conceivably the differences between Horner's and these later studies reflect differences in methods.

As long as the expectation of male superiority persists, anything near equality on the part of the women carries the threatening message to the men: "I am not the intellectually *superior* male I am expected to be." But when the ideal of intellectual companionship between equals replaces the expectation of male superiority, the pressure upon the man eases and changes. Now he needs only to reassure himself that he is not inferior to his date, rather than that he is markedly superior to her. Given a generally similar intellectual level, comparative evaluations are blurred by different interests, by complementary strengths and weaknesses, and occasionally by rationalizations ("she studies harder").[7]

The hypothesis that the emerging ideal of intellectual companionship serves as a buffer against male strain could not be tested in the absence of some index of intellectual ability. We attempted to study the relationship between stereotypical beliefs and strain. To the extent that men uphold stereotypes of masculine and feminine personalities, these stereotypes might mold their normative expectations. Failure to live up to masculine norms, consequently, might lead to strain.

The relationship between beliefs as to psychological sex differences and degree of strain proved complex. Of the twenty-seven men who disagreed with the proposition that the "reasoning ability of men is greater than that of women," five reported intellectual insecurity vis-à-vis women, and of the thirty-four men who believed in masculine superiority or were "uncertain," nine experienced strain. Most troubled were the twelve men who were "uncertain," four of them admitted insecurity. But interviews belied the simple relation between expressed beliefs and experience. For example, one subject who believed males had superior

7. The postulated relationship between the male's intellectual ability, the norm of male intellectual superiority, and the presence (or absence) of male sense of insecurity may be presented in the following schema.

RELATIVE INTELLECTUAL ABILITIES OF MALE AND FEMALE	Norms	
	MALE SUPREMACY	INTELLECTUAL COMPANIONSHIP OF EQUALS
Male intellectually superior to his date	No strain	Possible dissatisfaction with female (20 percent of our sample expressed this dissatisfaction)
Male generally equal	Strain	No strain
Male markedly inferior	Serious Strain	Strain

reasoning ability, having experienced insecurity in encounters with bright women, clung all the more tenaciously to traditional ideology. The clinical psychologist described him, solely on the evidence of psychological tests, as "unreflective in accepting conventional values, with a high need for dominance, higher, perhaps, than is justified by his resources."

Other traditional and intellectually insecure men were shaken in their beliefs in male intellectual superiority by encounters with bright women. Four such men were "uncertain" as to sex differences in reasoning ability. One man, for instance, described his technique of "putting down" (by clowning) his intelligent date, whenever she made perceptive observations. This degree of insight may have forced him to question "male supremacy," in contrast to the traditional but unreflective man described above.

The link between belief and experience may be modified by other factors than psychological insight. Some men gave a liberal answer as a matter of principle. Only one of the nine black seniors agreed with the proposition that the men's reasoning ability was superior to that of women—perhaps rejecting all such group comparisons in intelligence. A liberal answer was, in other cases, given by men, so secure on the score of intellectual competence that they could afford to be hospitable to new ideas. The link between beliefs and adjustment in such instances existed but the direction of the causal relation was the reverse of the one we posited. As long as the traditional ideal of male superiority still exists, the surcease afforded by newer ideals of equality might be available to secure men who need it least, men who in fact embody traditional masculine qualities.

We shall return to these issues in the discussion of emotional and power relationships with women.

The psychological profiles of intellectually insecure men were contrasted with the scores of adjusted men on the California Psychological Inventory and the Adjective Check List. On the Adjective Check List the differences in scores between the intellectually insecure and the adjusted majority were marked on three traits. The intellectually insecure were high on Self-Abasement (61.5 percent of the scores at the mean or above, as compared with only 44.2 percent of the adjusted men), high on Counseling Readiness (with respective percentages 61.5 for the insecure and 39.5 for the adjusted). On Aggression, the intellectually insecure were lower than the adjusted men (38.5 percent of the former and 67.4 percent of the latter scoring at the mean or above).

On the California Psychological Inventory the intellectually insecure students were lower in Dominance (54.5 percent of the insecure but 73.9 percent of the adjusted men had mean scores or above) and lower on Femininity with percentages for each group identical with those on Dominance. Low scorers on Femininity are described in the CPI. manual as being "active, robust, restless, masculine . . . impatient with delay and reflection."

The intellectually insecure men did not differ from the adjusted men on the psychological tests as sharply as did the troubled and adjusted students in sexual and power relationships with women and in degree of occupational commitment, to be discussed in the following chapters. Neither did the intellectually insecure men have an excess of unhappy paternal or maternal relationships. Nevertheless, perhaps both as cause and as result of humiliating experiences, the intellectually insecure men were less reflective, dominant, and self-satisfied than the men who were adjusted in their intellectual relationships with women.

3

SEX IN THE
LIFE OF
COLLEGE MALES

We shall presently describe the variations in the sexual experiences of college students—the virgins, those playing the field, affairs with no likelihood of permanence, and those certain to eventuate in marriage. But one phrase expresses the ideal, as well as the longing of the great majority of these young men. The morally approved and fervently desired goal is to "establish a meaningful, authentic relationship with a girl," with sexual, emotional, and intellectual rapport.

THE DOMINANT ETHIC AND SOME ALTERNATIVE NORMS

Only 7 percent of the seniors upheld the ideal of premarital chastity—for themselves, they were quick to add, disclaiming any censure of men who choose to live by other standards. But if premarital chastity is discarded as a value by all but a handful, so is promiscuity. Some disdain for promiscuity on the part of the majority is unmistakable, even if expressed in blandly tolerant words of "immaturity," and "hang up." Not only promiscuity but even casual dating with a great variety of partners appears to be regarded by many as a necessary evil in one's search for "the meaningful relationship." A visitor from Willard Waller's (1938) college scene of the 1930s would be struck by the near scorn of the majority for the game of flirtation for its own sake. The adventure, freshness, sense of discovery in a new encounter appear to be expendable values when pitted against the lure of a secure relationship. Far from being "aim-inhibited," as Waller had described dating, several seniors indicated that "anyone you date is a possible candidate for marriage." Moreover, some students felt insecure in new relationships or felt that the first formal dates were bound to be expensive. [1]

The dominant ethic was described at its clearest by a twenty-year-old student who, at the time of the interview, had a steady sexual partner.

"Casual dating is a drag," he explained, "It is boring, expensive, and inconvenient. On first dates the conversation is bound to be banal and superficial. How many times can I enjoy telling my life history and what my brother does for a living? How attached can one get seeing a girl once in two weeks and how open can one be with a stranger? In such superficial relationships the girl will be likely to date other men; that means that arranging dates will require a lot of advance planning."

As to sex, he has to be fond of a girl before going to bed with her. He had actually refused to take advantage of several opportunities because he felt nothing for the girl as a person. Admittedly, this spontaneous comment implied that there was something noteworthy about turning an opportunity down on such sentimental grounds. On the one occasion when this student did sleep with a girl without being sure he really liked her, he felt "fantastically guilty" afterwards. As to the girl's attitude, "I will not sleep with a girl if I am not sure that she also wants it," he said, "the only time I might try to talk a girl into going to bed with me is when I feel that she is deterred solely by social inhibitions."

Such distaste for sex as conquest of a resisting female was expressed by half a dozen men. A slender, short, boyish-looking senior, who has already had five sexual partners, remarked: "I do not want to be an imposing male. I don't like to proceed when it is

1. Though we have no earlier studies of male undergraduates on the same campus, one research finding may be suggestive of the trend away from dating many persons simultaneously. Bell and Chaskes (1970: 83) report that in comparison with female undergraduates in 1958, those in 1968 on the same campus dated just as frequently but dated fewer different individuals. In 1958 the mean number of different individuals ever dated by the coeds was fifty-three whereas by 1968 this number had declined to twenty-five.

'no, no, no,' and then finally overcome this resistance. It happened to me once and I didn't like it afterwards. With my first girl friend it came very naturally. We just took off our clothes and had sex."

This spontaneously expressed denial of any pleasure in sexual conquest was relatively infrequent. Whatever the psychological sources of this attitude—timidity or a narcissistic need to be sexually aroused by the partner's desire or love—there was an unmistakable normative element in this rejection of the role of the "imposing male" who "invades the woman."

The dominant ideal is confirmed by a troubled young man whose problem was precisely his inability to attain it. When asked about sources of guilt, he responded:

"I feel guilty because of my lack of involvement with women. I have had several completely cold affairs. In my sophomore year I met this chick. She was new in the city and all that. I made love to her in her apartment and finally lost my virginity. I started having a little affair with her, but she was chubby and older than I was. Kept trying to mold me into something. She was rich too, made me feel like a kept man, and I didn't like that. I started dating other chicks. The general pattern of my affairs in short. The next girl I slept with was twenty-six years old. I asked her to clean up after a party, and wham. Then I broke up with her. I slept with a lot of girls. But I feel I ought to be doing something else than just sleeping around.

"After all, getting a woman is no problem. I want to elevate the relationship from lusting to also liking. I've found very few women who want just sex. I seem to attract women who are very lonely and I have to lie to them about my feelings. I lie even to myself. I have come to a point when I feel that unless I am to have a real relationship with a woman, I am wasting my time."

Another man, worried about his promiscuity, wrote:

"The things which promise fulfillment to me seem to be embodied in a female. I tend to be quite a flirt. I am always on the lookout for a certain smile and scan every face for a certain warm glow—on the street, at an airport, on the beach, in the subway, everywhere. I am aware of women. But sexual promiscuity begins to be very empty. One comes away with assorted shames, worries about possible repercussions, and insomnia. Sleeping around is, after all, a kind of lackluster mutual masturbation."

The tribute to the ideal love relationship is also seen in the somewhat wistful words of another man for whom reality fell short of perfection. "I never said, 'I love you' to Emily," he remarked of his girl friend, "nor she to me. We might have said casually, 'of course, I love you.' "

In comparison with all but one of the previous studies of American college males, these seniors were the most permissive in attitudes, since 93 percent approved premarital coitus in "meaningful relationships." This phrase appears to be similar to Ira L. Reiss's "permissiveness with affection." We elicited these attitudes in the course of the interview and, possibly, the results are not strictly comparable with several previous studies using scales or questionnaires. Moreover, there is no indication that the other student samples were limited to seniors, as was ours, and permissiveness increases with age (Reiss, 1967: 125–26). Of the male students cited by Reiss (1967: 29) only 36.9 percent agreed that "full sexual relations are acceptable for the male before marriage when he feels strong affection for his partner." Harold T. Christensen and Christina F. Gregg (1970) found that 55 percent of male students in their midwestern and only 38 percent in their intermountain (Mormon) sample approved of premarital coitus. The formulation of their question and the measure of approval clearly implied permissiveness "with affection." College females are generally reported to be less permissive than college males (Eleanore B. Luckey and Gilbert D. Nass, 1969; Christensen and Gregg, 1970; Reiss, 1971: 174–77; Alfred M. Mirande and Elizabeth L. Hammer, 1974[2]).

To the best of our knowledge only one study raises the possibility of a higher level of permissiveness among American undergraduates than that characterizing our seniors. Daniel Yankelovich (1974) asked his college student sample to respond to the proposition "casual premarital sexual relations are morally wrong." In 1969, 66 percent and in 1973, 88 percent refused to condemn such relations.

While 93 percent of seniors in our study expressed approval of a meaningful sexual relationship, this ideal could not be always realized in practice. The gulf between one's highest aspirations and reality exists also for the young, notwithstanding their impatience

2. For example, Mirande and Hammer (1974) found in a study of attitudes in 1971–72 that the proportion of college females accepting coitus "when strong affection is felt for the partner" was 45.8 percent of Virginia and 41.9 percent of North Dakota undergraduates. Luckey and Nass (1969) sampled unmarried university students in twenty-one American colleges and universities. When asked about the type of relationship viewed as appropriate for considering coitus, 65 percent of women (ages 21–23) and only 38 percent of men in this age group specified "only if married or officially engaged." Conversely, 35 percent of women and 62 percent of men held relatively permissive attitudes.

with the hypocrisies of their elders. In search for the meaningful relationship, many engaged in short-lived or even single sexual encounters. The compromises with the ideal that life exacted gave rise to an "operative" code which came closer to regulating sexual behavior. "Casual" sex may be disparaged in the ideal code, but the very definition was occasionally such as to permit sexual relations upon early acquaintance. One student, for example, who had intercourse with a young woman after only two dates, indignantly denied that that was casual sex. "We liked each other and expected to continue dating. I was thinking seriously about her." "Sex is casual," he continued, "when the man has no interest in the girl apart from sex." According to this view, to qualify as "noncasual," sexual relationships need not necessarily be expressive of existing affection; it suffices that the possibility of such attachment is not ruled out at the outset. Sexual relations after only a brief acquaintance were not uncommon among the sexually experienced respondents.

So much for the dominant ethic and some compromises.

Though explicitly endorsed only by a small minority, the traditional double standard ("guys can sleep around, girls should not") with its correlate of "bad" and "nice" girls is still alive, as is the game of sexual conquest, played in part for the prestige frequent scoring brought among male friends. At least one young man was known to place a mark on the wall of his dormitory room for every new conquest.

Such unabashed defense of the double standard was relatively rare. The great majority conceded in principle the fairness of a single standard of sexual morality for men and women. But, as we shall show in a later section of this chapter, the operative norms sanctioned female polygamous escapades more severely than those of the males.

We did not inquire systematically about contacts with prostitutes, but the impression conveyed by the interviews was that such contacts were extremely rare. "People our age," explained one senior, "don't go for it. The nearest thing is some rumor, and it may be just a rumor, that a fraternity house might hire a prostitute for a Christmas party." "No, that wouldn't appeal to me," said another man, "you may as well work in the gym, getting nervous release from exercise." Again, a virgin, mortified by his timidity, was asked whether he had ever considered going to a prostitute, and he explained that such an act would constitute the final proof of his inadequacy. In all the interviews we encountered only one case of a contact with a prostitute, by one respondent and his friends on a trip to Paris.

The main patterns with regard to sexual behavior at the time of the interview may be summarized as follows. Out of every ten seniors, three were still virgins. Of the seven sexually experienced students, one was married, one was formally engaged, and two were having sexual relations with their current steadies. The remaining three were playing the field; generally having broken up with one steady partner, they were in search of another. In the total sample (including the virgins) with the modal age of twenty-one, 50 percent had had intercourse with three or more different partners; some with ten or more. Of the sexually experienced students, 22 percent had had one sexual partner; 70 percent had three or more.

Luckey and Nass (1969) found that 24.3 percent of their American college males had one sexual partner; 57.8 had three or more.

Christensen and Gregg (1970) report that in 1968 the percentages of male students with premarital coital experience, were 37 percent in the intermountain (Mormon) sample and 50 percent in the midwestern sample. These rates are below the 74 percent of sexually experienced students in our 1969–1970 eastern Ivy League college sample. One explanation of the wide difference may be the older age of our students. There is no indication that the Christensen and Gregg samples were limited to seniors. Incidentally, the rates of premarital coitus among the male undergraduates studied by Christensen and Gregg remained virtually unchanged between 1958 and 1969. On the other hand, the female rates rose sharply during that decade.

The relationship between attitude and behavior is a problem of wide concern in many areas, apart from sexual experience. In our sample, the attitudes towards premarital coitus were more permissive than actual experience, since 93 percent approved of premarital sex and only 74 percent were sexually experienced. Reiss (1967: 112) also found that of those Iowa college students who expressed permissive attitudes towards premarital coitus, only 64 percent had actually experienced it. Christensen and Gregg (1970) addressed themselves explicitly to the relationship of behavior to attitudes. In the restrictive moral climate of 1958 (and, especially, in their Mormon sample) students tended to be more permissive in practice than in attitudes towards premarital coitus; that is, a certain number violated their standards. But during the decade between 1958 and 1968, male attitudes have been liberalized more rapidly than their behavior. This reversal in the direction of value-behavior discrepancy appears plausible. When attitudes towards premarital sex are very restrictive, the strong sexual drive would lead a certain proportion to deviate from the ideal norm. On the other hand, the rapid liberalization of attitudes towards premarital coitus need not invariably cause behavior to coincide with the new permissiveness. Some men have internalized the prohibitions acquired early in life, even if intellectually they uphold newer norms. Moreover, whatever one's ideals and desires, opportunities for their satisfaction are not always available.

So much for studies of the sexual behavior of college students in the 1970s. One 1974 report shows a new trend: an increase in incidence of premarital coitus among male and female adolescents. Vener and Stewart (1974) resurveyed in 1973 a school system in Michigan originally studied in 1970. Their sample consisted of white school children, aged thirteen (or less) to seventeen (or more). The results show a significant increase in coitus for fourteen- and fifteen-year-old males and females between 1970 and 1973. In 1973, by the age of seventeen, 34 percent of boys and 35 percent of girls had experienced coitus. Sex differences in the incidence of premarital coitus have declined over the three-year period. In 1973, although the sexual involvement of boys was higher than that of girls at the younger ages, by the age of seventeen, the reported incidence of coitus was, as seen above, nearly identical. (See also Zelnick and Kantner, 1972.)

Of the sexually experienced seniors, 35 percent were married, formally engaged, or committed to marry their current sexual partners. Over 20 percent were living with women but without any commitment for the future. The largest single group, 42 percent of the experienced men, was playing the field, generally having had in the past at least one affair of some duration as well as briefer sexual encounters.

The following pages do not purport to present a comprehensive review of premarital sex. Here, as elsewhere in the book, the emphasis is on strains, their sources and consequences.

The strains of premarital sex may derive, first of all, from the moral censure still attached to it in society. Even among the youth, emotional emancipation from traditional morality may not be complete. Moreover, the youth culture is not completely isolated from the adult community and we shall examine both the conflicts and the modes of adaptation in the relationships between the young and their more conservative elders. The moral censure of premarital sex is not the only possible source of strain. Some problems appear to be endemic in this sexual trial-and-error pattern. Admittedly, one can conceive of institutional and personality changes which in time might minimize even these intrinsic stresses. But it is useful, nonetheless, to distinguish between difficulties which today stem from the censure of premarital sex per se and those deriving from other features of premarital sex.

MORAL CENSURE OF PREMARITAL SEX
AS A SOURCE OF GUILT

Feelings of guilt, whatever their causes, were tapped at various points of the interview, most directly through the question on the self-disclosure schedule: "What kinds of things make you feel guilty?" Guilt was expressed also in response to direct questions about strains in relationships to women and in descriptions of love affairs. Although we did not systematically inquire into the incidence of guilt feelings over the loss of virginity, our impression is that shame over virginity was much more prevalent among these students than guilt over premarital intercourse. The testimony of the virgins tends to support this conclusion. Three respondents, and only three, stopped having sexual relations after only one or two episodes in the past, but only one of the three—a young man, converted to Catholicism and intending to become a priest—attributed his subsequent chastity to moral scruples. The second man, also a Catholic, had a devout Catholic steady, who having had intercourse with him once, refused to do it again prior to their marriage. He resented her attitude, was tormented by temptations to join his buddies in sexual adventures but was deterred, as he put it, "fifty percent by shyness and fifty percent by loyalty to my girl." The third senior, having had two sexual experiences in prep school, was "uncomfortable at the thought of sex." "His "shrink," he explained, attributed this attitude to his "tendency to over-rationalize everything."

Another senior, a nonpracticing Catholic, who lived with his sexual partner, had this to say on the problem of guilt: "It is not a major problem most of the time, it is like a mosquito." This came in response to the question as to whether his girl's parents knew of their relationship: "They must suspect," he said, "and when I think about it in philosophical terms, I wonder. If we really believed in what we are doing, wouldn't we be forthright and tell her parents? It gets convoluted. Do I conceal the truth to avoid hurting her parents or do I still have a feeling of guilt? But though there may be some discomfort to realize that the majority plays by other rules it is also enjoyable to flaunt those rules."

Prudential considerations appear as important as the moral uneasiness in the reactions of another student who shared an apartment with his girl friend during the summer of his junior year. He felt that it was not right to be living together without being married. Though most of his friends "were after any girl they could get," a few disapproved of premarital sex. In the back of his mind, he admitted, was also the fear that his unconventional behavior might adversely affect his future political career. His girl friend, incidentally, also had some moral misgivings about the relationship. Since several of his friends lived in the building, she did not want to be seen walking around with men's shirts and no wedding ring on the way to the laundry, but at the same time, "she felt bad to have me do the wash."

What some respondents referred to as "residual" guilt over premarital sex may be exemplified by a newly married senior. Prior to his marriage, he and his girl friend used to feel "very sinister" registering at a hotel as "Mr. and Mrs." On an out-of-town visit shortly after their marriage, they stopped at a hotel. The young husband caught himself flashing his wedding ring in front of the clerk.

Conceivably, a more thorough exploration might have uncovered additional instances of guilt. Though the following illustration is provided by the fiancée of one of our respondents (this woman volunteered to be interviewed after a chance meeting with the author), it nevertheless shows how unexpectedly such guilt may surface in a casual remark, despite all previous denials to the contrary.

This young woman, a senior, had had, prior to meeting her fiancé, a two-year affair which had left her "hard and bitter" ("my boy friend more or less threw me out of the apartment for another girl"). She and our respondent had heard about one another from mutual friends. On their third date they had a long "passionate 'make-out' session," but he did not pursue it further. "Usually after such a session men are ready to strip your clothes off," she explained. "I was surprised myself that I held back. I considered him very attractive and he conducted himself very well. Perhaps I didn't want him to think that I was too easy." The sexual relationship was consummated on the next date and the couple began living together, alternating between their two dorms.

Neither in her actual behavior nor in any expressed attitudes was there any hint of moral uneasiness about premarital sex. But an incident revealed her true feelings. On a visit home, her fourteen-year-old sister, who had the habit of looking through her pocketbook for cosmetics, found some birth control pills. "Are you using the pill?" she asked her older sister. "There was a minute of hushed silence, but I told her the truth," reported our informant. "It was unfortunate. I wish I could be a perfect eldest sister, but I can't measure up." And at another point of the interview she again expressed her moral ambivalence: "*Unfortunately* [emphasis ours], there is no disapproval at all from my peer group in the dorms about premarital sex."

We conclude that premarital intercourse per se did not engender in the majority guilt feelings of any intensity, if at all. Christensen and Gregg (1970) found that in their most conservative intermountain (Mormon) culture only 7.1 percent of male college students in 1968 acknowledged feelings of guilt or remorse following their first experience of coitus. In the same year in the midwestern, and more permissive, sample the percentage admitting guilt was 6.6 percent. Female students reported somewhat higher proportions of guilt and remorse following the first premarital coitus, 9.1 and 11.1 percent, respectively, in the two regions.

Other sources of guilt, for example, over exploitation of the sexual partner or over unfaithfulness will be considered later in this chapter. Moreover, the next section dealing with parental attitudes toward premarital sex, will also occasionally refer to guilt feelings over violating parental norms.

MORAL CENSURE OF PREMARITAL SEX AS A SOURCE OF STRAIN IN RELATION TO PARENTS AND THE COMMUNITY

In only four or five of the sixty-two families have parents sanctioned, or even openly discussed, the sexual activities of their unmarried sons. A twenty-one-year-old Catholic son of a blue-collar worker had a steady girl friend in high school. She was also Catholic, one of eight children of a family residing close to his own. The girl's family treated him like a son. Despite their youth, the young man reminisced, he and the girl felt mature and devoted to one another. They talked of marriage but broke up when he went away to college. At the time, he confessed, they were very worried about what their parents thought, with him coming home at 4 A.M. Then, one day, his mother said to him: "Be careful, don't get her pregnant"; and her mother similarly cautioned her about possible pregnancy. Nothing else was said, but the young couple "felt a whole lot better after that."

In another case, an immature twenty-year-old only son of a Jewish white-collar employee was still emotionally dependent upon his parents. His mother insisted on knowing every detail of his life. "She even asked me," the son told the interviewer laughingly, "whether I was having sex relations with my girl friend. So I told her! But this didn't stop her. She still has to know everything I do." At one time, having felt that he was slow in developing dating skills, he asked his father about the latter's adolescent experiences, including the age at which his father had his first woman.

Another youth, a black senior and a son of professional parents, was sufficiently free from parental control to bring his current girl friend home to share his room over weekends, despite the protestations of his mother. Her own attitude towards premarital sex was not, apparently, the issue at stake—she was mainly concerned about the neighbors' gossip.

Finally, an engaged senior started living with his fiancée in his freshman year, though the couple had had a period of separation in the intervening years. The young man thought that his parents must have guessed that his girl friend was living with him because he wanted to leave the dorms and move into an apartment of his own. By the beginning of the senior year, it became an open thing—his parents would drive him and his fiancée back to his apartment at night after dinner. All their friends knew that they lived together. Perhaps the only residual form of concealment was their agreement that he would be the one to answer late-hour phone calls.

So much for the rare cases of open discussion of sexual behavior between the son and his parents. In a couple of cases parents so strongly condemned premarital sex that they would not settle for avoidance of the issue. "I have to let on," said a son of a conservative Protestant family, "that I am still a virgin and have to pretend that my girl friend doesn't stay with me Saturday nights. It's sort of a nuisance."

By far the dominant pattern was evasion; an unbroken silence, a complete avoidance of the subject of sex. The parents might or might not have known the truth—they did not ask. Neither were the sons eager for a confrontation (though, as we shall see, some wished to precipitate open rebellion) and they joined in the taboo. When the young lovers shared living quarters mere avoidance of any reference to sex did not suffice. Some deliberate deception was required to avert if not the suspicion, at least the outright exposure of the truth.

The avoidance of the subject of sex was well documented in the self-administered schedule on self-disclosure. The schedule contained the statement: "the facts of my present sex life, including knowledge of how I get sexual gratification; with whom I have relations, if anybody." The rating scale of disclosure ranged from "0," "if you never talked about this aspect of yourself to the person," to "3," "if you confided *fully* about this aspect of yourself." The respondent was instructed to place an X in case he lied or misrepresented himself to a given person on this aspect of his life.

Of the eighty-six ratings on this question of sex disclosure to mother or father supplied by the sexually experienced men (exclusive of those married) 70 percent were either "0" or X.[3]

3.   *Self-Disclosure Ratings on "Facts of My*
              Present Sex Life"
       (N = 43: virgins and married excluded)

Mother	.43
Father	.37
Brother	.79
Sister	.52
Closest male friend	1.40
Closest female friend	2.00

The reign of silence concerning so vital a part of life is bound to create some estrangement between parents and their sons, but for a considerable proportion of these young men this avoidance provided a tolerable adaptation. This was particularly the case when the sons surmised that, verbal pieties notwithstanding, parents expect that "boys will be boys" and merely ask that their children do not openly confront them with such moral inconsistencies. One Catholic student recalled with cynical amusement the moral lecture delivered by his father when he was ready to leave for college. As this college-educated father was explaining "the facts of life" his son "had a hard time listening with a straight face." But the apex came when, having finished his sermon, the father added: "Remember, if you do, be sure to take precautions." "My parents *never wanted* to know. I believe they preferred it that way," remarked a student. Another senior was living with his girl friend in his off-campus apartment. It was agreed that she would never answer the phone in case the call was from his widowed father. Once his father took him to the theater and on the way back invited himself up for a drink. Since the girl was in the apartment, the young man offered some excuse. "But, he is no fool," the boy mused, "he must know."

The dominant mode of adaptation to differences in the sexual codes of the young and their parents is for both parties to respect appearances and to agree to maintain certain fictions. For example, even when the parents strongly suspected that their son had intercourse with his girl friend, they would not countenance allowing the couple to share a room on a visit to the parental home.

But avoidance and pretense do not work in all cases. Some young men, a minority in the sample, knew that their parents would strongly disapprove and, at the same time, needed parental approval and were disturbed by the necessity to lie. Put in other words, not all the sons could accept a remark made by a senior to his girl friend: "In the year 1970, you should either be able to tell your parents that you are living with me or deceive them without guilt." A number of our male respondents could neither confide in their parents nor lie to them with an untroubled conscience. A son of foreign-born parents, deeply respectful of his father, concealed from his family the fact that he and his fiancée lived together, alternating between his and her rooms in their respective dormitories.

The interviewer asked the young woman: "Do his parents know that you are living together?" "Oh, heavens! No! Wow!" exclaimed the girl. "We talked about it and I asked him 'What would happen if your parents found out?' " "Their respect for you," he said, "would go down like to zero—and for me too!" "His parents," she continued, "can't find out, God forbid, I never answer the phone in his room." That his father's approval mattered deeply was evidenced by the son's jubilation after the first visit of the girl to his parental home: "He likes you, he likes you, he likes you!" he kept repeating on their way home. He proposed marriage a month after their first intercourse.

Whether the strain of secretly violating the parental code precipitated the decision to marry was not as certain in this case as it was in two or three others. This was, incidentally, one of the relatively exceptional cases in which premarital sex was more acceptable to the girl's sophisticated parents than to the bridegroom's "old world" family.

A religious son of a devout fundamentalist church members explicitly linked his decision to marry at the end of his junior year (instead of waiting until his graduation) to his unhappiness over the deception of his parents. He started dating his future wife in high school. They began having intercourse in his sophomore year in college and "it bothered me a lot to think how upset my parents would be if they knew."

Concealment of the affair from parents, whether this does or does not trouble the son, breaks down completely as a mode of avoiding conflict when the need to defy parents is precisely the motive for the affair, as exemplified in the following case.

A nineteen-year-old senior referred to his unsatisfactory family relationships as the major strain in his life. In the spring of his junior year he had a steady girl friend who was his first sexual partner. When the end of the college year was approaching, she said that she might take an apartment and remain in the city for the summer instead of returning to her home town. "Great!" he exclaimed. As they debated various arrangements they decided that he might as well move in with her and "give the relationship a chance to grow." He didn't enjoy living at home and the inconvenience of staying over at her apartment two or three times a week were other factors in their decision. "Besides," he added, "I just wanted a little adventure."

Before moving in with the girl he announced his intention to his parents. "I told them I would listen to what they had to say, they could voice their opinions, but that my mind was made up." Later, his twenty-two-year-old brother present at the discussion, admonished him, "You

just don't tell certain things to your parents," but our respondent remarked, "I was going to rebel."

His parents were very upset. They couldn't understand his plan, expressed opposition to the girl, who was of a different religion, and voiced
the fear that he would be forced to marry her.

The ambivalence on the part of the son became apparent when he
added, "I was pleased that they raised objections to the particular girl rather
than to the plan itself. This may have lessened any anxiety that I myself had
felt at the time." Clearly, the young man wanted both to defy his parents
and to receive their absolution.

The respondent did move in with the girl and within three weeks they
discovered that she was pregnant. (We shall return to this case in the
section on "Risks of Pregnancy," pp. 86–87.)

Confirming our findings, Eleanor D. Macklin (1974), in a study
of cohabitation at Cornell University cites parents as the most
important source of major problems acknowledged by the students.
She states: "One third indicated that their parents definitely did not
know about cohabitation at the time, and nearly 80 percent had
tried at some point to conceal the relationship from their parents."
Consistent with our evidence of the double standard, the author
adds: "Female students were much more likely to have this problem than males" (p. 57).

MODUS VIVENDI

The concealment of the affair from parents required special care
when the couple shared living quarters. A successful deception
frequently demanded the cooperation of friends. The length to
which the couples occasionally went to keep the joint residence
secret from parents (especially from the parents of the girl) tells
something about the strength of parental ties. [4] The following cases
will serve as illustrations.

One couple lived together in the young man's apartment. The woman kept
a dormitory room and would return to it to do her hair, to change clothes,
or occasionally to study. Her parents, residing in another city, were kept in

4. Eleanor D. Macklin (1974) in her study of Cornell University defined cohabitation as "having shared a bedroom and/or bed with someone of the opposite sex
(to whom one was not married) for four or more nights a week for three or more
consecutive months." More than three-fourths of the cohabitants officially maintained two separate residences (p. 57).

ignorance of the affair with the help of her girl friends in the dorm who would let her know when she received any phone calls from home. Now and then she would have to invent some excuse for not returning the call sooner. Once her parents called when she and her boy friend went on a visit to another city. Her roommate phoned long-distance to inform her of her mother's call and she called her mother from a pay phone in that city and explained that she had just returned from the library and found the mother's phone message.

The guilt experienced by the girl over the concealment of the affair from her parents generated the pressure for marriage in the case that follows.

This affair began in the sophomore year of our male respondent. The two used to spend weekends in his dorm room. He recalled a "beautiful experience" when the two ran all the way from a neighborhood movie because they wanted to make love and knew they had only an hour left until curfew.

Eventually they decided to live together. But even though the girl's parents resided in another city, she insisted that they take two apartments within a block of one another. They sublet one apartment to a friend who agreed to cover for the girl. They installed two telephones with the same number with the phone ringing only in their own apartment. When the girl's parents visited the city, she would rush to the other apartment and put up her favorite posters so that her mother would not become suspicious. "I thought that was humorous," said the youth, "but she would get very upset. She could not take this deceit. She cried. So I finally decided that I am hurting the woman I love. I had been against marriage in principle. But things were happening at the time to change my attitude. My radical role models were getting married. Perhaps, I thought, it is not after all a violation of real principles. So finally I said to her, 'Okay, let's get married, but none of this bullshit. No wedding ceremony.' "

The girl's parents were the victors in the conflict over the wedding: it was a big catered affair. "But we got even," the boy summed up, "at the engagement party my friends smoked marijuana, and the parents didn't know, they just thought it was queer that the same cigarette was passed around. At the wedding we all smoked hashish."

The active assistance of friends in concealing the affair from parents reveals the acceptance of premarital sex on the part of the peer group. The respondents frequently indicated such support; for example, staying out of a room while the roommate entertained a girl.

A fiancée of one respondent described their living arrangement. This was the couple who became engaged four weeks after their first intercourse. The young woman stayed in the respondent's dorm room with all the men on the floor aware of the arrangement. But since her own dorm room was much larger, he moved into her dorm. At first she was uneasy, since she was the only senior on the floor and didn't know the girls well. But he soon became an accepted member of the floor community, defrosting the icebox and performing other chores.

Moral censure is not the sole source of strain. The seniors experienced other conflicts. Only a few of them would eventually marry their first sweethearts. The majority would have several sexual partners who would have had prior sexual experiences. Without assessing the general toll exacted by this trial-and-error pattern of mate selection, this section will examine the "intrinsic" problems of multiple sexual affairs in our society. These problems might be expected to include anxiety over sexual performance with an experienced woman, jealousy of the former lover of one's girl friend, risks of pregnancy, guilt over unfaithfulness, trauma over termination of the affair, and the insecurity of arrangements that lack the instituonalized protection of marriage.

All these problems do exist. Sixty-five percent of the seniors reported some stress (including a few poignant and shattering experiences) over one or more of the problems listed above. But the stress was not universal nor as severe as a traditional moralist might have anticipated with the increase in sexual permissiveness. Even when allowance is made for the possible lack of candor and for the repression of pain endured and inflicted, the majority of the sexually experienced seniors did cope somehow with both the past and the precariousness of the present. We are referring to the immediate effects leaving open the possibility of other long-range consequences of their experiences for personality and social relationships. The dark prophecy of traditional moralists failed to take account of the new values, fictions, and rationalizations which the permissive sexual code brings in its wake.

But to say that the majority appeared to cope reasonably well does not gainsay the existence of strains or the further fact that the coping mechanisms themselves exact a price. For one thing, they often entail some compromise precisely with the honesty, spontaneity, and openness that the young value so highly in personal relationships. The majority, it must be repeated, was searching for a meaningful relationship, i.e., for a sexual partner who would provide companionship, emotional security, and psychological intimacy. Their ideal was not the playboy world of body-centered sex, nor some utopian community with group marriage and the censure of possessiveness. But the search for this difficult ideal was pursued in an individualistic milieu with few secure guidelines and few protective and sheltering institutions to help the young avoid or adjust to failure. We shall see that for the shy, the self-doubting, and the unstable, the environment was particularly harsh.

ANXIETY OVER SEXUAL PERFORMANCE
WITH EXPERIENCED PARTNERS

The traditional expectation is that the male will be sexually the more experienced partner and will perform in the role of a teacher rather than a learner, in sure command of the relationship. But with the sexual emancipation of women the young man may be exposed to a more experienced partner who can appraise his performance and rate him in comparison to her former lovers.

Robert R. Bell and Jay B. Chaskes (1970), in comparing the premarital sexual experience of female undergraduates in 1958 and 1968 concluded that there had been an increase in the proportion of women who experienced coitus while dating or going steady. Engagement, they report, had become a less important precondition for coitus in 1968. Keith E. Davis (1971) reviewing a number of studies of sexual behavior on college campuses concludes that "college women . . . are having more sexual experience, earlier, and probably with more partners than was true of the pre-1960 students" (1971: 142). Harold T. Christensen and Christina F. Gregg (1970) conclude their findings on attitudes with the statement that females moved towards permissiveness more than did males during the decade between 1958–1968, resulting in a greater convergence of attitudes on the part of men and women.

Ira Reiss (1972: 166), summarizing recent studies, states that by the age of twenty, about 40 percent of college girls are nonvirginal. Kenneth L. Cannon and Richard Long (1971) note regional variations in the incidence of premarital coitus. "The proportion of females participating in some areas is greater than the proportion of male participants in others," they remark.

Finally, Luckey and Nass (1969) stated that the mean age of first coital experience of American college students was 17.9 for males and 18.7 for females. In their American sample, 58.2 percent of males and 43.2 percent of females have experienced coitus.

We conclude that, although male students generally exceed the females in the incidence of premarital coitus, the chances have increased for the male to encounter a female with equal or greater sexual experience.

In order to ascertain the extent of anxiety, if any, felt by the seniors over sexual performance with experienced women, we culled from preliminary interviews with male undergraduates the three following excerpts and used them as quasi-projective tests.

"Making love to someone more experienced frightens the hell out of me. . . . I want to marry a virgin not because she's pure but because she's less experienced than I (if she's more experienced, then she should pretend not to be)."

A student said he'd feel funny, less masculine, making love to a more experienced girl.

One interviewed student reported that he made a pass at a girl and she appeared to be very shy. But as they went on he realized that she actually was quite experienced. He was indignant at her deception and her pretense of femininity.

Unlike the virgins whose anxiety was increased by the rumors of the sexual emancipation of women, relatively few of the sexually experienced seniors resonated the emotions expressed in the above excerpts. Among the few was an undergraduate who had felt that he and a new girl friend had "really hit it off." However, knowing that she had had a lot of experience, he felt so inhibited that he lay next to her in bed for a long time before he could muster the courage to make love to her.

A senior with traditional attitudes towards sex roles, described his first sexual affair in his sophomore year. He was in love with a co-ed and after four or five months of dating they had intercourse. Although she assured him that he was her first lover he did not believe her. "She knew exactly what she was doing," he said, "and it bothered me that I was so new at it and couldn't take command." This affair ended in heartache because he eventually discovered that his girl had all along been involved with a guy in Vietnam. Deeply hurt, he "stayed by [himself] except for a couple of casual dates" during his junior year. He hoped to marry a virgin because he would be greatly disturbed to know that a wife of his had had prior relations with other men.

Still another youth confided that he was especially insecure about his first physical approach in any new relationship. "I have to be sure it is expected, I don't want to appear foolish," he explained. While admitting anxiety in all sexual relationships, he described one particularly trying situation. A former lover of one of his girl friends was "a Yogi of the sexual act, holding muscular control for hours. Apparently this is exceptionally satisfying to women." His girl's account of the exceptional prowess of his predecessor exacerbated his anxiety.

"A shy, inexperienced girl is safer for a man," remarked another senior. But although "it scares" him to sleep with someone who is more experienced than he, he does it nevertheless, when confronted with such a situation.

"The male is vulnerable," reflected one senior, "if a pass he makes is more innocent than serious he may feel that he must prove himself. His manhood is challenged and this causes strain. There is such a big deal made of sex, especially during adolescence. The male must be the fantastic lover, a sexual animal. In my case, a girl once made an advance and my reaction was: 'What do I do now?' Society offers no excuse for an inexperienced male."

Several men made a distinction between casual sexual encounters and meaningful relationships; greater experience of the woman would not matter in the former case but would in the latter.

But these reactions were exceptional. If relatively few seniors appear troubled by the sexual expertise of women it may be because at their stage of life their experience more than matched that of their women friends. Nevertheless, as the men reminisced about their past, additional evidence came to light. Five or six men confessed that they had lied to their first sexual partners, exaggerating their past exploits. For example, a fiancée of one of our respondents, also a senior, reported in an interview with us that shortly after their first meeting they had discussed their sexual pasts. "I spoke first," she said, "and I had had sex for two and a half years. He said, 'only a year and a half for me.' " But when they became engaged, some three months after their first meeting, he told her the truth. "It was so hard," she continued, "that that was the nearest he ever came to crying in my presence. 'Oh, God,' he said, 'I lied to you, I had had sex for only six months before I met you.' I guess he didn't want to seem like a babe in the woods."

In another case, a sophomore did not tell his first partner, an experienced college girl of his own age, that she was the first girl with whom he had slept. They used to laugh about inexperienced guys and he was pleased to have had enough self-confidence to carry off the deception. He dated this girl mainly for his sexual needs and the deception did not trouble him. But similar deception aroused feelings of guilt in other men. One junior, savoring his girl's perception of him as a playboy, could not bring himself to tell her that their liaison was his first experience with intercourse. Eventually he confessed the truth. The motivation for lying in another case was the embarrassment of still being a virgin in his sophomore year as well as the desire to reassure his nervous virgin partner. This couple eventually became engaged and the young man confessed his lie.

In the foregoing illustrations the failure to live up to the norm of masculine superiority in sexual experience led to lying and pretense. This solution aroused enough guilt in relationships which grew in intimacy that the men eventually confessed the truth.

But the superior experience of the girl friend did not always engender humiliation or embarrassment. In the case to be described, the rewards of sexual intercourse with a beautiful girl, together with her manner of handling herself, more than made up for whatever awkwardness this youth had experienced at the beginning of the affair. This senior reminisced about the summer of his freshman year when he was eighteen years old and the girl (whom he eventually married) was a few months older. Because he liked to talk frankly about intimate concerns he had told her early in their six-months' acquaintanceship that he was still a virgin. She confessed that she had had two sexual episodes with two different men in her senior year in high school and, when they had met, was breaking off a year-old affair with a third man who turned out to be "impotent, with premature ejaculations." At first our respondent admitted he was "bumbling a bit." Nevertheless, the knowledge of her prior experience did not disturb him. "She didn't show it," he explained, "she just lay there but I could see she enjoyed it. Anyway, I wasn't bumbling for long. I read manuals and talked to friends, especially one guy who was like a freak. This guy knew Kinsey by heart and knew all there was to know about sex and contraception, having had a girl friend since the age of fifteen."

Although he claimed that his girl's past experience presented no problem, he worried a lot when she failed to achieve an orgasm. He knew when she did because "she would moan and groan and I could feel it in her whole body." He blamed himself for being too quick and too clumsy. There was a period, after they moved into the same apartment, when his wife could not use the pill. "Using a prophylactic made me almost impotent—it goes down at once and I take a long time to get excited again. Often, I would come rather quickly at night and the morning was hers."

The senior males who volunteered the preceding accounts of love making with experienced women had all implicitly accepted the norm of masculine superiority in sexual experience.

However, six respondents revealed the emergence of a new and more equalitarian set of expectations. "Having intercourse with a virgin means that you are the one who is teaching her and that is nice," remarked one senior, "but you can have a much more fluid experience with the other kind. It is a lot more fun. If she is more experienced, you can learn something. She can bring new ideas. After all, we are sharing something. I don't mind in the slightest learning from a girl." This young man was referring not merely to casual sex but particularly to emotionally significant affairs.

To sum up, either because they rejected the norm that the male must be the more experienced partner (as only a few did) or because the majority lived up to it, anxiety over sexually experienced partners did not appear to be widespread. Of the fifty (virgins and nonvirgins) for whom this information was available, only nine said that they would want to marry a virgin ("I would be flattered to be the first," was the way one of the nine put it). Had prior sexual experience of women constituted a threat, preference for virgins would have been more prevalent. The great majority would not demand virginity in their future mates though they would reject "promiscuous" girls. Among them a few volunteered the information that they would have given a different answer in their freshman year when they did wish to be the first lovers of the women they married. His fiancée, remarked one of these men: "Sometimes says that she wishes she were a virgin when we met because the first time is very important." As for him: "you'd like to be the first, but it is just pride, why let the idea fester. You've got to consider it from her point of view; she wasn't your first either." Finally, some men, in answering the question about virginity of the sexual partner, made a distinction between playing around and a serious commitment. The man who "would be flattered to be the first" lover of his future wife admitted that in casual sex encounters he prefers experienced women: "the idea of a virgin scares the hell out of me."

So far we have focused upon male anxiety aroused specifically by confronting a sexually experienced partner. As to general anxiety over potency and sexual performance, the interviews contain several illustrations of such anxiety. For example, one senior, in response to a question about three major strains of the masculine role, said: "There is a kind of anxiousness, I guess, yeah, like women don't have the fear of impotency but as a kid you have a fear, well not a fear but a worry about the future." But, by and large, the sexually experienced seniors do not leave the impression of serious and widespread concern. Clearly, the men felt a responsibility to fulfill their mates sexually. The sexual response of the woman has become the measure of masculine virility. The wish to afford pleasure has become fused with self-centered need for self-validation. The capacity for multiple orgasms in women, and other findings of Masters and Johnson were frequently cited —occasionally with envy, at other times with anxiety. "She thought she was a one-orgasm girl," said one senior, "I would have liked to change that. I don't know, maybe she said that just to tease me." Four or five experienced seniors, in response to the question about current strains, did include "satisfying a girl." One felt that he "comes too soon" though he quickly assured us that his girl friend had no such complaint against him. Another senior explained that satisfying his girl was especially difficult after he reached a climax. Although he always achieved satisfaction for himself, he knew that on occasion his girl remained unsatisfied, at which times he felt that he had let her down. Another senior wished he were more potent and did not require over an hour to be aroused again; he wished he could do it again in fifteen minutes.

Even allowing for the underreporting of such problems, the interviews with the sexually experienced senior did not convey the impression of widespread anxiety on this score. The virgins, as we shall see, present another picture.

JEALOUSY OF FORMER LOVERS OF THE MATE

Jealousy of former lovers of their sexual partners presented a manifestly disturbing problem for only three of our respondents. In each of these three cases the respondents knew the men and circumstances made encounters unavoidable.

The relative absence of reported jealousy appears to be due to two major mechanisms of avoidance: an effort at suppression and a taboo on the discussion of the past; a taboo, imposed, we have the impression, with greater persistence by men than by women. As one senior put it: "I tell girls quickly enough that I don't want to know any details [of their former loves]."

The suppression of jealousy is motivated not merely by the wish to avoid pain but by normative considerations. Jealousy is condemned as possessiveness and a survival of the orthodox double standard of morality. A young man, who has had several sexual partners, was having an affair at the time of the interview with a woman whom he had met some three months earlier. He knew that she had had at least three other lovers before she met him. The first two he had never met, "but I am not sure about the third," he remarked. "I think I know him but I don't want to ask her. It worries me that he had my girl. *It is very petty of me*" (emphasis ours).

"Momentarily, when I am alone," remarked another youth, "a thought might pass, 'how was she with others?' But I don't ask her. If I did, perhaps there would be an adverse comparison and the whole thing would be a hang up. As it is, as long as she digs me and has no complaints, I am satisfied."

The same effort to put the past out of his mind is reflected in another comment: "I sometimes wonder, is she comparing me with others? But I rationalize it, she wouldn't remember details, she'd just know whether it was good or bad. After all, she's not the first girl I have ever liked, and I love her now."

The following case reveals both a reserve with regard to the woman's prior sexual experiences and, perhaps, some traces of the double standard. An affair, begun in the freshman year of the respondent, eventuated in a formal engagement in his senior year. But there were two breaks in the relationship, the first at the young man's instigation, the second initiated by the girl. Having reunited after the second parting, our respodnent told her that he had had intercourse with another girl during the separation. He "surmised" that she also had a brief affair with the boy she dated during that period. But he did not ask her, neither did she volunteer the information.

The pattern of discreet avoidance of the girl's past affairs is illustrated finally by the censure of those who violated it. A senior reported that the former lover of his fiancée, having met the engaged couple at a social gathering, made a tactless reference to their past in the hearing of several friends. Our respondent wanted to punch the man but he and the other friends just walked away in embarrassment.

Another report also illustrates the existence of the code. One of our respondents was engaged to a girl who had had a very unhappy prior love affair. A married friend of this respondent had not been as fortunate—*his* wife kept bragging about the sexual prowess of her former lover. "You have it easy," the married man remarked enviously. "Finally," reported our informant, "my friend came home one day and shut his wife up for good by informing her that her former lover was a fag."

Another mode of coping with jealousy was suggested by the frequency with which the man described the former loves of their current mates as "self-destructive," and "unhappy." This may have been an accurate portrayal of affairs which obviously failed to endure. Nevertheless, there was something suspicious about the frequency of such portrayals. If this was the way women presented their past, it was a version readily embraced by the men.

The clampdown on the discussion of the past was occasionally placed by the girl. One senior at first wondered how much of his active past sex life (he had had some twelve affairs) was he honor bound to disclose to his current steady. She solved the problem by stopping him firmly: "I don't want to know."

That the silence about past affairs was a means of muting jealousy was indirectly confirmed by the exceptions to the rule. In one turbulent, on-again-off-again affair, each asked the other, while making love: "Where did you learn this trick?" But under the guise of joking, those remarks expressed jealousy and, perhaps, even self-torment.

In another case, the young man had nothing to lose from his girl friend's full disclosure. He first met his future wife when he was a seventeen-year-old freshman. She was two years older and soon started to confide in him the details of her unhappy affair with a senior. She was so dissatisfied with her lover, and our respondent so confident that he could win her love and thus triumph over the older rival, that the girl's confidence only served to bring the two closer together. After they had their first intercourse, the girl broke with her former lover. During the summer of his freshman year, the respondent went to Europe where he had a brief sexual escapade. He described it in his letter to his future wife and upon his return she wanted to know all the details. "I guess she may have expected such a European adventure," he added, explaining that the matter did not create any jealousy in her.

We conclude that the main mode of coping with jealousy is to avoid discussion about past affairs, though the very effort of "not letting such thoughts fester" (in the words of one senior) does bespeak some suppression of pain.

ANXIETY OVER PREGNANCY

Despite the universal use of some form of birth control by the forty-six sexually active seniors or their women friends, there were three pregnancies and nine cases of false alarms. Two of the pregnant girls had abortions and the third gave birth to an illegitimate child. [5]

Whether deeply involved with the woman or not, the men as a rule did not take the news of a possible pregnancy lightly. It aroused strong feelings, occasionally panic.

One student began having sex relations with a young woman in the summer following his freshman year. In the fall of the sophomore year: "We had a scare," he confessed, "which lasted fifteen days and aroused a tremendous sense of guilt in me. We talked for hours about this threat of pregnancy. I didn't want to get married, but I told her I would do anything she wanted, including marrying her. Marriage, abortion, have the child, anything. I kept on saying, 'it has to be your decision.' "

But while he tried to reason with her, all she did was to cry and repeat: "I don't know what to do." They celebrated by going out for

5. The liberalized New York State abortion law went into effect July, 1970.

dinner when they learned that it was a false alarm. This crisis estranged them because it revealed to him that she was a much weaker person than he had imagined her to be.

Another student, a Catholic, in love with his first sexual partner, also a Catholic, had been the one to use birth control because she felt reluctant to assume this responsibility. Confronted with the possibility that his mate was pregnant, he spent two weeks of utter misery. He wasn't ready for marriage, he stayed awake nights, turning over various solutions including marriage, giving the child up for adoption, or an abortion. He would try to busy himself in books but couldn't concentrate and a word on a page such as "abortive" would suddenly jump out at him. At first his roommate was in the same boat but the latter's girl friend got her period and he was left alone in his misery. Unable to sleep at night, he couldn't attend classes in the daytime.

When the relief finally came and it turned out to be a false alarm, they found that, surprisingly, the whole experience had drawn them closer together. They hoped to get married as soon as it was feasible.

With only three cases of actual pregnancy we are in no position to ascertain the degree of pressure upon young men, in general, to marry their impregnated partners. None of these three cases ended in marriage but there were a few others, who like the two men just described, at least considered marriage, however reluctantly, as one of the possible courses of action.

In the total group (including actual pregnancies and false alarms) the couples estranged by the experience were equal in number to the couples drawn closer together by it. One couple, despite the fact that the alarm proved groundless, decided as a result of the crisis to move their intended wedding date forward.

The men were generally prepared to assume the costs of abortion. In one case, the girl got what her boyfriend termed a "zippy needle" abortion. If that hadn't worked, he remarked, he would have had to go into debt for a couple of years paying for the regular operation.

A black student reported that the guys would help a friend in such an emergency if he did not have the money to defray the cost.

Though deviant in our sample, one respondent reported a dutch treat abortion. The man in this case was the defiant youth who informed his parents that he was moving for the summer into the apartment of his girl friend (see p. 73).

After four weeks of their joint residence, a doctor confirmed that the young woman was pregnant. The young man reported to us that, of course, he felt anxious, but there was also some excitement in doing something for the first time. They never even considered marriage or having the baby. An abortion was a foregone conclusion. Since the abortion was done in another city and was expensive, they decided to split the cost. She didn't have her share and he laid out some $200 for her, a sum which she still owed him at the time of the interview. This relationship was terminated by him at the end of the summer. He felt that she should have returned her debt. He was tempted to forfeit the money in order to make the final break with the girl but she phoned from time to time to say that she would pay him eventually.

He was the one who used contraceptives. "Had she ever accused you of being careless?" probed the interviewer. "No," he answered, "if she had, I would have said that it was up to her to use the pill." Had he ever considered, continued the interviewer, assuming the full cost of abortion? "Why should I," he queried in turn, "what kind of statement would that have made?" He brushed aside the suggestion that since this woman had actually undergone the abortion, the psychic costs of the experience were not identical for the two. The young woman in the case apparently shared his moral definition of his obligation, or lack of it, expecting no special chivalry on the part of the male, and an abortion in the case of pregnancy.[6]

Whereas this case was normatively deviant, another couple, parents of an illegitimate child, appear psychologically deviant.

The troubled youth, an upper-class college dropout, returned for his senior year at the age of twenty-three and flunked out in the middle of the year. He had shared an apartment with a young woman whom he described as "mentally unbalanced and suicidal." She became pregnant but he did not want to marry her. It was he, however, who insisted upon her having the child, having known a girl who was badly hurt by an abortion. He paid for the home where his girl friend spent the last period of her pregnancy and he visited her daily. The child was placed for adoption at once, without the mother having seen the infant. He was shocked to realize that she hated the unborn baby and the idea of having a child. He, on the other hand, was deeply moved to see his own child and could not shake the experience. The affair continued on and off because the woman

6. This case is suggestive of a type of ostensibly "liberated" relationship that may well work to the disadvantage of the woman.

pursued him to another city. She even sat one time outside his window begging him to take her back. He was trying, so far unsuccessfully, to break up this relationship.

THE DOUBLE AND THE SINGLE STANDARDS

A twenty-year-old senior who proclaimed unabashedly that "guys can sleep around, girls shouldn't" belonged to a small minority who upheld the traditional double standard of morality. His case will exemplify some problems of maintaining it in the contemporary youth culture.

This youth belonged to a fraternity in his freshman and sophomore years. The girls who came to weekend parties at the fraternity were "low class and incredibly loose. They were a joke. You could take them to your room. A girl might spend Friday night with one guy and Saturday with another." But he had little money and no way of meeting other girls.

He generally liked to bring nice girls home because his parents were hospitable and interested and the girls enjoyed such visits. But the girls who came to fraternity parties were not the kind you could take home to Mother.

At the end of the sophomore year, he started seriously dating a girl he had known in high school. He didn't try to get her to come to his room. "She was the only girl I thought of as a possible wife. I wouldn't want to sleep with her unless we were married." At the time of the interview he still expressed a preference for marrying a virgin but he was beginning to wonder whether any upbringing a girl received could be strong enough to withstand current pressures.

His nice girl friend resented his "sleeping around with lots of girls." Nevertheless, they saw one another frequently and he was about to get pinned to her when a party of friends invited him to go away for a weekend of fun, in a cabin in the woods with some girls and a lot of drinking. He had a great time but his girl friend found out and broke up with him over that weekend.

Asked about changes he would have liked to make in this girl, the young man responded that she was "too backward in necking. Her mother programmed her that way and that was good, but, still and all, if it's always to be *me* kissing *her*, well really, forget it!"

The girl who was "programmed," as he put it, for the chastity that he desired in his future wife, turned out not to be sufficiently responsive to satisfy his physical needs. Moreover, the double standard is becoming increasingly unacceptable to the "nice" girls, as this student discovered to his sorrow. Finally, although his expectations that "guys will sleep around" would seem to require girls who make themselves available, his chagrin at the "incredibly loose" girls who came to the fraternity house bespoke his dissatisfaction with such partners.

One member of a Catholic fraternity upheld the double standard by agreeing with "nice" girls to pet to a climax without having intercourse. However when he told some fraternity brothers about it, they made fun of him, and even wrote a poem about it.

Another supporter of the double standard was a black senior, the son of a Protestant college-educated father. This youth was seriously considering eventual marriage to his current girl friend and sexual partner. He expressed the double standard in the following words: "It is a mark on the guy if his girl is seen going out with another guy. But it is a mark on *him* if he doesn't step out. Unless, that is, there are immediate plans for marriage. The guys would say, 'He is locked up.' Suppose a bunch of guys plan to go to the store for sandwiches. They will tease you: 'I guess you have to get your permission slip from Mary.' After curfew at [the woman's college] the guys will help you to sneak off and expect you to go with them to some party with girls. If the guy doesn't go along, the assumption is that he is weak and tied to her apron strings. They'll tease, 'When's the wedding date?' "

Still another senior revealed his sentiments when, in illustrating unfeminine behavior he described a girl who "thinks she owns her steady." It is natural, he thought, for a guy to be jealous of the girl, if he goes steady with her, but the girl shouldn't be possessive.

Such outright defense of the double standard was rare. The majority endorsed the single standard, in theory, conceding that equity and logic demanded it. But their sentiments did not always harmonize with the ideal principles. This conflict between head and heart is revealed in three departures from the single standard. These departures are: the expectation of fidelity on the part of the woman but tolerance of occasional infidelity in the male partner; greater censure of promiscuity or dissociation of sex from affection in women than in men; and censure of sexual initiative on the part of women (in the early stages of a relationship).

With the exception of a few strict adherents to the single standard (see pp. 97–98), the men, unfaithful to their steady partners, viewed their own transgressions as morally imperfect but to be expected in males. However, they demanded fidelity from their girl friends. In the words of one senior: "I think it is all right for me to go out occasionally with other girls but I couldn't accept it if my girl friend dated others. Perhaps it is inconsistent but I just couldn't resolve it. Maybe it is sexual jealousy."

Another senior, who entered college at the age of fifteen and was gratified by the sexual conquests he had made despite his youth (he lied to girls about his age), was having a steady sexual relationship with a young woman who was attending a college at some distance from his own campus. She warned him that unfaithfulness on his part would terminate their relationship, but he has been able to conceal from her various episodes with other girls. He would be deeply hurt were she unfaithful to him, but felt that he could trust her ("she is not the type to play around"). He characterized his double standard as "illogical." "Why should a girl be more restricted than a guy? " he asked. "If I were in my room and a girl walked in, provided she was not too unattractive, I would sleep with her at the drop of a hat. Why should I, then, expect a girl to behave differently? It is inconsistent."

But this intellectual rejection of the double standard has not evoked in this man any troublesome feelings of guilt. Nor has his behavior created external complication, perhaps because geographical separation helped to keep his girl friend ignorant of his derelictions.

The intellectual adherence to the single standard was qualified in still another respect. In the words of one respondent: "If I had to argue with somebody, I'd say that a girl has a right to sleep around with anybody she likes and as much as she wants to, but I wouldn't want to go out with a promiscuous girl." The disassociation between sex and affection was countenanced in a man but disapproved of in a woman. As one student put it: "A girl can have an affair or two before marriage, but these affairs should have meaning for her; a guy can just satisfy his sex drives." Some respondents were resentful of women who were ready to have intercourse "right off the bat" even when they themselves were the beneficiaries. One student met a girl in the park and described their brief affair:

The young woman was in the process of getting a divorce. They had sex relations on the second night after their meeting. She was a hippie type and she introduced him to pot and hashish. He did not approve of her going to bed with him so soon after their first meeting. He soon realized the meaningless of a purely physical relationship. He wants sex only when a relationship has had a chance to grow into a more meaningful one.

The same respondent met some "band girls—a very hard type of chick." He explained: "If there are five boys in the band, the girls can sleep with a different one every night." Now that he has met this kind he knows whom to avoid.

Another student met a European twenty-year-old student at a college mixer and she came to his room in that very first night. Their affair lasted fourteen weeks and he was the one to terminate it. He resented that "she was doing it backwards, first sex, then love; she enjoyed it but then she wanted to get emotionally involved. She counted on sex to help develop a relationship. I felt it was an entrapment—'hook him and then tell him.'" Perhaps she counted on habit. As for him, he now says, "select, don't settle."

A few men were troubled by their intellectual acceptance but emotional rejection of the single standard. In the words of one senior: "I have to talk to myself, I have to say, 'don't be stupid, be rational.' I know that I am not evil because I've had several affairs. I don't think I am promiscuous."

The last feature of the single standard which was emotionally repellent was sexual initiative taken by women in early stages of relationships, as is illustrated in an excerpt from a case history.

A politically radical student, separated from his wife, expounded his views: "If a woman is so uptight about sex that there is no sex unless one is ready for a permanent commitment, well, I have no respect for such an attitude. Sure I want a girl to be sexually liberated, to be ready to sleep with me, perhaps even on the first or second night."

But the liberation of women may not, apparently, include a "forwardness" on their part. He described an occasion when he was showing a stranger, a beautiful, twenty-one-year-old co-ed from an Ivy League college, the quarters of some student activity, including the room where persons who worked late could stay over night. "Oh great," exclaimed the girl, "then we can ball here tonight." "She was beautiful, I was flattered and I had a big grin. Sexually it was wonderful, but two hours later I didn't feel too good about it and I'll not see her again. I don't know why. Maybe I was taken aback by her forwardness, maybe I looked down upon her."

That the repellant feature of this encounter with the beautiful woman may have indeed been her "forwardness" is suggested by another experience of the same senior.

He joined in a demonstration in support of draft resisters at which some co-ed bands were to perform. On the way to the city where the demonstration was to take place, he stayed overnight with fellow demonstrators from other communities. He reported: "We had to sleep over in one house in one room, twenty-five people, two double beds, but the rest in sleeping bags. Some talked all night. I was near an attractive girl on the floor. I knew I wouldn't be able to sleep. She also moved about a lot. It was dark. I went to the bathroom and came back and laid down closer to her. She moved to me. We made love for an hour. It was dark. Someone walked over us as we were making love. She cried out at the moment of orgasm. We then got dressed and took a walk to get to know each other. She was a nice person, not radical, she just came to hear the band perform. She was at some community college. After the walk we made love again. In the morning we said good-bye. I prefer this to a date and the whole seduction pretense. Dinner, theater, 'no, no, no,' when all along, from the first, your idea is to seduce."

The episode just described apparently evoked tender memories. This second girl also made herself available—with even fewer preliminaries than the first. But this time he took the initiative. His positive reaction to spontaneous sex when initiated by himself contrasts with the offense he took to the "forwardness" (the respondent's expression) of the first girl, and lends support to the conclusion that this student embraced a double standard.

The persistence of some aspects of the double standard of sexual morality is confirmed by other studies done in the late 1960s on college campuses. Gilbert R. Kaatz and Keith E. Davis (1970) found that while there was little evidence of the double standard when the scale referred to women in general, the results differed when the woman in question was a sister or a potential spouse. The authors conclude: ". . . as the person about whom the standard is expressed becomes more meaningful to the respondent, the greater is the double standard" (p. 394).[7]

GUILT OVER EXPLOITATION OF WOMEN

We concluded in an earlier section that premarital intercourse per se did not cause intense guilt feelings, if any. Guilt over the

---

7. For other studies bearing upon the decline but, nonetheless, some survival of the double standard, see bibliography cited by these writers, 1970:398–99.

"exploitation" of the sexual partner is another story. Although meaningful relationships were deemed preferable, "purely physical ones" were also accepted. The ethical problem arose when the two partners held different expectations. Some men felt absolved of moral responsibility as long as they did not feign love or make false promises to obtain sexual ends. In the words of one senior: "I tell a girl in advance, because we have sex, it does not mean I want to get married. I don't want a girl to entertain false hopes." Others, with a more sensitive conscience, felt troubled even when they made clear at the outset the limited nature of their emotional involvement. Some felt uncertain as to the responsibility they assumed by sleeping with a girl.

Theoretically, either sex may be at the losing end in such encounters. Insofar as women accept the single standard, perhaps an increasing number of them are prepared to enter a sexual liaison for its physical rewards and limited companionship with no expectation of a deep emotional involvement. Indeed, it is noteworthy that the complaint, traditionally considered typically feminine: "You don't love me, all you want is sex," was voiced by a handful of men. One youth commented sadly: "She said that sex was a way to express her love, but I felt that all it meant to her was having someone to sleep with." Another student confessed that whereas he sometimes used women sexually, "not as persons," he himself bitterly resented when he suspected that a woman treated him in a similar fashion. A third youth asked a girl whom he knew to be a virgin, whether she would have intercourse with him. She acquiesced because, as he surmised, she felt it was time she found out what it was all about and that any man would have been acceptable. He felt used by her and unhappy over the experience.

A few men, on the other hand, disavowed any resentment about being used sexually by a woman. One senior felt relieved to learn, when his own interest was primarily physical, that his partner's involvement was also limited. A couple of men attested that they would be flattered if a woman sought them out for sexual ends—"It's a compliment to be appreciated for sexual prowess, but it would be an insult if she found nothing else to admire."

All in all, however, such complaints about women were rare. A much higher proportion of men perceived women as the victims of sexual exploitation and expressed various degrees of guilt over their own conduct.

"Lots of girls," said one student, "still regard sex as a statement of intent and I had plenty of one-nighters that were not that." He "felt badly and sort of guilty about it." Another senior, now engaged, remarked: "Sex can be just an ego thing for the man, of no benefit to the girl. I remember an instance when I was out for sex and she was out for sex, but she wanted something else too. It's very unnerving to know that you've hurt someone. I know several girls who have been hurt by men—one is becoming an alcoholic." This youth, prior to his engagement, felt deeply the conflict between his aggressive sexuality, on the one hand, and chivalry and decency towards women, on the other.

A similar theme dominates another youth's story of his loss of virginity in his freshman year. Like other inexperienced males, he had envied those "who scored often and performed well." Consequently, his first six-week affair with a girl served as a tremendous release for him. The deep guilt he felt was for the hurt he had inflicted upon her.

The young woman in question was a bright, but unsosphisticated freshman, new to the metropolis, and daughter of a conservative family. He was her first date on the campus. Soon after they met he invited her for coffee to his room and they necked. Then came the experiment of dorms exchange and she, together with a few other students of the women's college, moved into his dorm. He asked her whether she wanted to have intercourse with him. He didn't pressure her at all, repeating that the decision was hers to make. She said: "that sure will be a complete break with my family and background," but she agreed. Then his roommate left and she brought her books and things into his room and for a couple of weeks they lived together. When his roommate returned, she moved back to her dorm.

She cried after the first time, but seemed happy throughout the six weeks. She said she loved him but never asked whether he was in love with her, nor did he ever profess love.

The break came during the Easter vacation when he went home despite her wish that they spend it together on the campus. "By this time, I felt that I was not sufficiently involved with her to continue the relationship," he said. "I felt guilty and uptight about living with a virgin [sic] and the guilt turned to a kind of repugnance. What's more, it bothered me that I would have to lie to my parents about having to study during the vacation. I did go home and that reawakened and reinforced the parental image of me. Upon return I just stopped calling her and was very standoffish when we did chance to meet."

Several people in his dorm knew of his six-week affair with the girl. He was especially distressed later upon learning from a fellow he knew that this girl became very cold. This fellow took her out and said that "she kept reading a French book while he was playing with her on his bed."

"Sometimes I see life at this university," summed up this student, "as a battle against becoming callous and hard. I hope to retain my willingness to be vulnerable." He, in turn, was deeply hurt in a subsequent affair when he allowed himself to fall in love with a woman who had warned him at the outset that she was involved with a man who lived in another city.

The guilt of this youth was caused by his perception, no doubt accurate, that, whatever gratification the affair afforded the girl, it did not match his glorious triumph in overcoming his own "virginity hang up." Moreover, he soon realized that she was not the kind of girl he could love whereas she professed her love for him.

Several other seniors, in describing women, attributed a woman's tendency to "play it cool," to a painful previous love affair.

Another illustration of masculine guilt is provided by a senior who is now "playing the field." He expressed equal anxiety about both his readiness to "take advantage of girls at every opportunity, which isn't the right thing to do," and his relative lack of success at this game. He feared that his "lean and hungry look" makes his motives all too transparent to every date. His first affair, now terminated, was with a girl who had had prior sexual experience. He recounted an incident which continued to cause him guilt and regret. This girl was so terrified of pregnancy that she always wanted to know the brand of condoms he used and to inspect them in order to make sure she was safe. He once played a rather cruel joke, by withdrawing and gasping to create the impression that something had gone wrong. To make matters worse, her period was a week or so late and even he became frightened although he knew (and told her) that it was only a joke.

Certain social factors increase the likelihood of guilt or at least of some conflict over sex relations. A few of our respondents were members of male cliques with values strongly reminiscent of the lower-class male values that have been revealed in other studies. These cliques prized male solidarity, virility, dominance, sexual "scoring," and a "cool" attitude toward women. Sentimental attachment to women threatened the solidarity of the group and pressure was exerted against excessive loyalty to the girl short of a formal engagement.

Marginal members of a clique, or simply members who became seriously involved with a woman, often experienced a status-set conflict between values limited to the position of a clique member and those of a lover. Popularity and prestige within the clique required actions which violated obligations towards the girl friend. For example, one fraternity member, who had had a two-year affair with his steady, described Friday night socials at the fraternity: "You try to pick up a girl. I go through the motions to please the guys. If I didn't, they would say that I am on a string to my girl friend. The guys might say, 'Let's go and find some girls.' I go along, but I feel pretty bad going to see my girl after such parties."

A more pervasive status-set conflict revolved around the question of privacy. One senior was very explicit: "With all the talk about free sex on this campus, if you don't have any experience the guys feel that there is something wrong with you. So naturally if something happens, you immediately tell the guys about it. It builds you up but it isn't a nice thing to do." Once he told his friends about a very attractive girl whom he brought to his room and felt very guilty about the disclosure.

One respondent's mode of coping with the surveillance of male associates was to assume an ambiguous manner which suggested victories without claiming them outright, even occasionally saying, "Well, I messed it up this time." The vagueness hints at conquests and "still, no one could say, 'you said it.'"

Another adaptation to the potential conflict was to vary disclosure to male friends with the kind of relationship. "Certain girls are taken to the room in order to make a big score. If you don't like the girl or if she did not mean anything to you, you might give a lot of details. The more serious you are with the girl, the quieter you become."

This latter mode of avoiding conflict worked best when women could be clearly classified at the outset. But as the distinction between "bad" and "nice" girls weakens, problems arise. At the early stages of the relationship, the young man may talk all too freely about her. But should he eventually become serious, in the words of one senior: "It becomes embarrassing to realize that all the guys knew what went on between you and it's hard to protect the girl and that is a very unhappy situation."

INFIDELITY, GUILT, AND JEALOUSY IN ONGOING AFFAIRS

For the overwhelming majority the ideal norm demanded exclusivity and fidelity on the part of both sexes towards their partners. The operative morality was, as usual, less stringent. In every type of relationship, including formal engagement, some men were occasionally unfaithful. The exact extent of female infidelity is unknown to us since it would have come to our attention only if discovered by our respondents. Even when the admission of infidelity, "I sneaked out on her," was made with hardly a trace of guilt, the expressions used and the concealment bespoke the violation of the ideal norm.

Among couples who had relations over an extended period of time, there were only three or four who reluctantly granted each other the freedom to have other sexual partners while continuing the relationship. But this freedom exercised generally during periods of relative estrangement since these were on-again-off-again affairs. Moreover, in every one of these open relationships, the freedom was wrested by the less involved partner (male or female) and accepted by the other as the price of continuing or renewing the relationship. Put in other words, the more involved mate carried on an unsuccessful struggle for fidelity on the part of the other.

A case in point is a senior who lost his virginity in his freshman year in an affair with a freshman co-ed who had had some prior lovers. Their own relationship lasted, with two intervening separations, until the fall of their senior year. They shared an apartment that preceding summer and this experience strained the relationship to its final breaking point.

She was a pretty girl who wanted to get married and have children but, much as he liked having her around, he knew that she lacked the intellectual and social qualities he wanted in a wife. The young woman knew that she couldn't count on him. During their separations he had several other sexual experiences and she once returned to a former lover. These facts came out in the course of their quarrels.

Still another departure from the norm of exclusivity stemmed neither from unresisted temptations, concealed from the mate, nor from the struggle for power and the high bargaining position of the less involved partner. Some of the psychological roots of permissive attitudes emerged in the analysis of the senior who complained (see page 62) about his "completely cold affairs." Though he was fonder of the girl with whom he shared an apartment at the time of the interview than he had ever been before, he was not sure he loved her. He had been unfaithful to her, diagnosing his infidelities as "pseudo-accomplishments," triggered by some failure in another area of life.

This young man assured the interviewer that he would like his girl friend to have an affair and had told her as much. "It would be a good and broadening experience, since I was her first and only lover—not that I might not be terribly jealous." He felt that unless she had such an affair, ten years later, as a suburban housewife, she would regret her lack of experience. Better now, he figured, than ten years later when he would be more deeply attached to her. He denied that he wished such broadening experience for her in order to insure his own freedom. His motivation may have been an erotic one, as suggested by the experience he had in high school when he took a girl friend away from his closest buddy. He "felt guilty and yet it was very nice to share the girl with him."

From a sociological point of view, a significant element is the emerging attitude that to have only one lover in one's life is to be denied adequate sexual experience. A recently married young man, whose sexually experienced wife was his first and only sexual partner, professed deep love for her and happiness in his marriage. But they have apparently discussed in the course of their year-old marriage, the possibility that he might be unfaithful to her in the future, "perhaps on a trip away from home," he explained. He cited his wife's understanding attitude and her request that he not conceal anything from her.

In all, only two youths proclaimed so radical an ideal as an enduring but open relationship in which each partner enjoyed the freedom to engage occasionally in other affairs.

To turn from the operative norms to the actual behavior, male infidelity was somewhat less frequent in the committed relationships. Among those engaged and those contemplating eventual marriage to their current steadies, the proportion of unfaithful (one or more times) was 33 percent, whereas the comparable percentage among steady and uncommitted men was 63 percent. One black student, about to announce his engagement to the girl who had been his steady sexual partner since his sophomore year, still found himself attracted to other girls. His escapades were once or twice discovered by his girl friend and it took her a couple of months to get over each. He remarked that he "feels a lot more guilty about the other girls because I know I'll marry Agnes (his steady) and will not leave her high and dry."

In order to avoid hurting his occasional girl friends, he followed two rules: He didn't "stick around with any one girl for any length of time," and he did not date seniors—"They get hurt the most." He explained the younger girls can afford to waste time. No, he replied to our questioning, he never told a girl that he was about to become engaged: "That would be counter-productive. I would rather have her think that I had liked her and lost interest, than that she was a plaything from the beginning."

But not all men could so structure their polygamous drives as to avoid either guilt or hurt. The following case will portray the difficulties of a youth with simultaneous relationships.

This twenty-one-year-old black student was the only sone of college-educated parents. He was poised and articulate during the interview, indeed exuding so much warm optimism, that the interviewer felt compelled to remind him that the object of the study was to discover real experiences, more than ideal hopes.

Jim lost his virginity at age twelve and since then had many lovers, "perhaps thirteen or more." His attitude towards sex is conveyed in the following excerpt from his interview. "I think," he said, "that many men feel that if they thrill a girl in bed, then she will love them. But I think it is the other way around. I've slept often enough with women to know that the actual physical act is not exciting unless it's with somebody that you have a feeling for. For me, therefore, it's love that initiates the enjoyment of sex, not the other way around."

Jim prided himself on remaining good friends with former girl friends.

"There were times, he admitted, "when things got very juggled. Like when I made love to two of my girl friends on the same day. I felt bad. My dream was to have all three of us living together and loving each other but, of course, I knew that was only a dream. The young woman (one black, a high school lover of old standing, the other, white) suspected the truth. The white woman, he was told by mutual friends, spent many evenings crying because she knew he was with her rival. That made him very unhappy. The stormy affair with the young white woman included a separation during the summer when she, in turn, was unfaithful to him. When they were subsequently reunited, she told him of her summer experiences and, though he played it cool, he felt angry and determined to hurt her. He began a campaign to win her love with the intention of dropping her ultimately as a revenge. But instead he fell in love with her all over again and they had an idyllic spring together before she left the country for a year abroad.

While she was away he met another young woman, sweet and vulnerable, whom he thought he might marry. He had been faithful to her for a year. Unfortunately the past caught up with him. The white woman came back from abroad. Though she understood from his letters of his new involvement, she agreed to spend two days in his apartment. "All I really wanted," Jim explained, "was for us to part as friends and to make her realize that I really still loved her. For me the vehicle for that was to make love," but she refused to sleep with him. While she was still in his room, he received an urgent call from the roommate of his current "true love," the girl he thought he might marry. This girl, knowing of the return of his old flame, took a lot of aspirins and kept drinking until her roommate felt concerned and called him. He left in the middle of the night to calm his sweetheart and returned hime at 4 A.M. At the time of the interview, but for the disturbing visit of the white girl, he felt loyal and committed to his quiet and vulnerable current steady.

This youth, so overflowing with love in his various open relationships, was not free of jealousy or of guilt for the pain inflicted upon his women friends.

Another advocate of open relationships, a radical white youth whose wedding is described on page 75, came to rue his ideology after marriage. Throughout his relationship with his future conventional wife he tried passionately to convert her to radical political and sexual ideology. "Remember," he reiterated, "you do not *belong* to me, you are a human being in your own right." When he discovered her first unfaithfulness with a coworker of his it was her turn to recite his credo: "You don't own me." This marriage ended in divorce.

AFFAIRS AND THE QUESTION OF MARRIAGE

Granted the acceptance of premarital sex, certain questions nevertheless do arise when we turn to men who have had a steady sexual relationship of some duration without any commitment for the future. Does the sense of impermanence or an explicit concern about marriage create strains?

The eleven steady-but-uncommitted couples presented several patterns. In one case, both suspected that their relationship would probably not survive the woman's intended transfer to another college for her senior year. Neither apparently was so deeply involved as to be pained by the prospect. "Of human bondage" was the theme of another relationship in which the girl had been repeatedly unfaithful and the young man could neither compel fidelity nor give her up. In four out of the ten couples the bone of contention was the male's occasional infidelity. Several men conveyed the impression that their steady girl friends would be willing to marry them, were they to propose. In none of these cases was marriage seriously discussed.

The uncertainty about the future of the relationship can create an area of reserve even among couples who pride themselves upon honesty and openness, as is illustrated by the following couple.

A twenty-three-year-old senior, a nonpracticing Catholic (son of a Catholic father and a Protestant mother), who spent two years in the Peace Corps and returned to finish college, was having an affair with a graduate student. He is troubled because he doesn't know what he wants to do after graduation. Marriage seems remote and is never discussed with his girl friend. He said: "It would be completely incongruous to talk about it—like *Alice in Wonderland* kind of talk. You cannot discuss marriage without facing the issue of getting married or breaking up. We don't want either and therefore we don't discuss it. I can't even take care of myself, how can I tell anyone 'don't worry, rely on me?' We don't know whether this bohemian life style is a positive goal. It functions for me and for her. But I am not so committed to it as to believe that it is the only valid way to live. I am not philosophically opposed to marriage. I may get married someday."

At another point in the interview, this young man confessed that he experienced a "nagging uneasiness." "Not that we are personally incompatible," he said, "but maybe the relationship is a dead-end one. Is it good for me, is it good for her? When she or I crave reassurance (and both of us do from time to time) we cannot ask for it explicitly. Only bitterness would come from a frank discussion. I cannot offer her security and it would be heartless to be honest and say: 'Who knows what tomorrow will bring?' " In response to our question, he replied that he would certainly hesitate to declare to his girl that he loved her. The two are more likely to exchange pleasantries in the light spirit of a Doris Day movie.

It is generally assumed that such anxiety about the future is experienced more intensely by women than by men. Some three or four seniors did indicate that pressures from their girl friends for an early marriage caused the termination of the affair. One of them, a black senior, was both upwardly mobile and firmly opposed to a wage-earning wife. Understandably, he intended to delay marriage. For a few others, engulfed in emotional problems, marriage appeared remote. Another black student remarked: "Girls in the second half of their senior year get uptight and begin pushing: 'We've been going out for two years—let's make it formal.' After a couple of years a break up is a difficult extrication. I watched some couples move away and then get back. Maybe it's 'I don't want to hurt,' or 'I realize how much I miss.' " He concluded: "If you find someone with whom you hit it off, why not marry?"

This last phrase expressed the sentiments of the majority. Of the committed men, only a couple voiced some misgivings. One confessed a conflict between his "mature, monogamous" self and his self-image as a playboy. Seduction of a girl was very tempting, even as he recognized how morally reprehensible it was to use another human being for "ego gratification."

The favorable attitude towards early marriage was attributed by the respondents partly to economic factors—the still abundant, in 1969–70, supply of fellowships, grants, and loans for graduate study. A good job market for women was an additional economic asset for those who could accept dependence upon a wage-earning wife.

The fact that marriage no longer necessarily required having children or implied stodgy respectability was also mentioned as an incentive to marry. As one recently married senior put it: "I am contemptuous and scornful of the old idea that the day after marriage you are supposed to take out insurance, buy a plot in the cemetery, and wear a business suit. I still wear dungarees, I haven't cut my hair, we have plans to travel with knapsacks all over Europe, we are not 'settling down.' "

Economic exigencies not only did not prohibit an early marriage, they occasionally dictated it. Once the relationship was serious, with exclusive dating and mutual concessions required by close association, to remain single was often more expensive and a joint residence for unmarried couples sometimes entailed intolerable deceptions. Two establishments were more costly. Many men sounded the same note: Once the man is sure of the girl, why wait with marriage?

A heavy schedule of study did not offset but, on the contrary, intensified the desire for marriage. A science major with three theoretical courses and twenty-five hours of laboratory work a week was exasperated: "If I don't go out, I go crazy, but if I do, I can't get my work done." He heard that married students did better academically and wondered whether marriage would not be a solution for his problems.

The men gave voice to another motive for an early marriage: loneliness and the desire to hold on to a satisfactory relationship once it was established. "Were I to remain on the east coast, in this city," remarked one senior, "I might wait with marriage. But suppose I were accepted for graduate study at some far away place, say Minnesota. I wouldn't want to go out there alone. It is in the middle of nowhere. I might get married out of necessity." Another senior explained: "If for some reason a relationship with a girl breaks up, the guy is lonely and he is searching, and it may take months before he can find someone he is able to talk to and be understood. That is why, if one finds such a person, one wants to be sure of her, to chain the girl down, so to speak."

These were the words of a black student, popular with women, but a similar note was struck by a twenty-one-year-old white senior. Asked to list his four major strains, he began with "the problem of finding the right marriage mate. Once you've found her, you feel more secure, but it is a great strain to know that you still have to go on looking for the right kind of marriage partner."

Acceptable as an early marriage was in principle, only three seniors were married and one other was separated from his wife and playing the field again. Seven men were formally engaged and five others were committed to marry their current sexual partners. What distinguished these committed men from the majority?

THE YOUNG MARRIEDS, THE ENGAGED, AND THE COMMITTED

In only one case could the decision to marry be attributed to a single precipitating factor. The others, married or committed, were under a variety of converging influences. In this one case (see pages 75, 100 for other references) the youth agreed to marry his sexual partner because she could neither tell her conventional parents about their sexual relationship nor deceive them without extreme guilt. "So I finally decided," the man explained, "that I am hurting this woman I'm in love with. The most important thing is our mutual relationship." The fact that a number of his radical friends got married about the same time weakened his ideological objection to the institution of marriage.

In two other cases, the man's guilt was an element precipitating the formal commitment. Both youths were closely bound to their conservative fathers. They admittedly suffered because they had to deceive their fathers. That such guilt was a factor in formal engagements and marriage in only two out of sixteen cases (and even in these only over deception of parents) testified to the acceptance of premarital sex on the part of the majority.

Parent-child relationships can play a complex role in an early choice of a mate, both directly and as mediated by the personality of the son.

An escape from a stormy, ambivalent relationship with parents, and especially with the mother, appeared to be a decisive factor in the marriages of two juniors. One of these youths felt that his parents exacted his submission by their unnecessarily miserly financial handouts. He was plagued by his economic dependence. The capacity of his parents, especially of his mother, to enrage him and cause him pain symptomized other disturbing elements in the familial situation. In his freshman year in college he fell in love and found in his girl and her warm and supportive parents a haven from his own family. His parents-in-law were both more gracious and better able to help the young couple financially. The marriage took place in his junior year and at the time of the interview, one year later, he could cite no costs, only benefits, of his early marriage. His parents still had the power to cause him occasional pain but the escape from economic dependence upon them was cited by him as one of many advantages of marriage.

Ambivalence towards his mother was a factor precipitating the marriage of another junior. This young man described his parents as selfish and preoccupied with marital battles. His older brother enjoyed a more favored status with their mother. In his freshman year he fell in love with a girl who was a year older than he and their intention was to get married after his graduation. But his mother's vociferous opposition to his girl friend and the growing tension between his parents and hers precipitated the decision to marry in his junior year. This young man cited his in-laws' and his bride's opinion that, despite his strained relationship with his mother, he was dominated by her. His ambivalence was revealed when, presumably because of the difficulty of finding an apartment, he brought his bride to his parents' home, knowing full well the antipathy between his bride and his mother. This joint residence was terminated by a bitter quarrel and the young couple's sudden departure.

The direct influence of familial relationships upon early commitment was not always of the type just described. In a third case, the bridegroom referred to his great pleasure in proving to his parents that he was able to win an acceptable marriage partner. Much as he yearned for parental approval there is no denying that the need to similarly reassure himself served as another impetus to marriage. All through high school, and until he met his future wife, this youth had grave doubts about his attractiveness to women.

For the sample as a whole, the quality of father-son relationships was not associated with an early choice of mate. The distribution of highly satisfactory, tense, and average relationships for the sixteen married, engaged, and committed students was similar to that of the sample as a whole. But these early choosers had a higher proportion of tense relationships with their mothers and fewer highly positive ones. Out of sixteen committed seniors only 19 percent enjoyed satisfactory relationships with their mothers as contrasted with 37 percent in the total sample. (See Table 3.1.)

Table 3.1.   Early Choice of Mate and Parental Relationships

	Percent of Specified Relationships			
	Relationship to Father		*Relationship to Mother*	
PARENTAL	COMMITTED	SAMPLE	COMMITTED	SAMPLE
RELATIONSHIPS	N = 16	N = 62	N = 16	N = 62
Highly satisfactory	24	26	19	37
Average	38	31	43	37
Highly unsatisfactory and ambivalent	38	43	38	26
Total	100	100	100	100

The interviews were completed in 1970. We have noted the openness of the seniors to the idea of an early marriage, citing the remark of one not untypical youth: "If you find someone with whom you hit it off, why not marry?"

The age at first marriage is so sensitive to various conditions that behavior and attitudes shift relatively quickly. A recent trend towards later marriages has been recorded for the country as a whole. A repeat study of our campus in 1976 would, no doubt, present different expectations as to the preferred age of marriage. The change in behavior is clear enough.

The median age at first marriage began to rise from 22.8 for men and 20.5 for women in 1966 to 23.1 for men and 20.9 for women in 1971 (Robert K. Kelley, 1974: 297). Put another way, Paul C. Glick (1975: 17) shows that in 1974 as many as 40 percent of women between 20 and 24 years of age were single, whereas the corresponding figure for 1960 was only 28 percent.

The college we studied does not collect data on the proportion of alumni of given years who are married. But the coordinate women's college on the same campus issued striking figures of the trend towards later marriages of its alumnae. Of the women graduates in the spring of 1970, 27 percent were married by January, 1971; of the class of 1971, 20 percent by the following January; and of the class of 1972, only 16.2 percent were married by January, 1973.

The trend towards later marriages among college graduates may be explained by a number of influences. The growing acceptance of cohabitation without marriage removes the guilt or the external pressure to marry. Economic conditions have worsened with the decrease in government aid for graduate study and with the likely decrease in financial assistance from the parental families. The Women's Movement may have increased professional aspirations of women at the expense of an early marriage. Among the alumnae of the women's college on the campus of our study the proportion of women who were pursuing graduate study one year after graduation ranged from the low 37.4 percent for the class of 1971 to 54 percent for the class of 1973.

Glick (1975: 17) points to another demographic factor, the baby boom after World War II, which, for the country as a whole, may have contributed to the delay in marriage. Since young women marry men who are on the average two or three years older, the female products of the baby boom outnumber their prospective mates.

4

SEX IN THE LIFE
OF COLLEGE MALES:
The Virgins

Seniors, who were virgins at the time of the interview, constituted 26 percent of the sample. Among the nonvirgins were three men who had had only a single sexual episode in the past. One of these three converted to Catholicism and intended to become a priest; the second was in therapy and attested to discomfort "at the thought of sex"; and the third could not persuade his Catholic steady girl friend to have intercourse again unless they got married.

Only a few virgins, and 7 percent of the total sample of seniors, invoked the ideal of premarital chastity and attributed their abstinence to moral or religious principles.[1] Theirs was the problem of upholding a moral position judged to be old-fashioned by their peers. But three out of every four virgins made no reference to moral scruples in explaining their chaste life. For the majority of the virgins their chastity was a more or less disturbing personal problem; in their words, an "accident" or a "hang up." As we shall show in the conclusion, it does not appear far-fetched to consider chastity in the perspective of deviance.

1. Daniel Yankelovich (1974) found that only 34 percent of college youth in their 1969 sample held that "casual premarital sexual relations are morally wrong."

THE VIRGINS AND THEIR SELF-FEELING

A few of the virgins appeared untroubled by their lack of sexual experience but they were the exception rather than the rule. One such composed senior admitted that "some men might feel pressured to participate in the so-called sexual revolution, if only to prove to themselves that they can." As for himself, he was seeking a deep relationship that would lead to an early marriage. A much more typical attitude, however, was expresssed by another virgin who stated that premarital intercourse between affectionate partners should be a part of every man's experience, adding, "I am not proud of my virginity. We are getting into my hang ups here." As still another man put it: "The question of sex is really a very serious problem for a sensitive person. It's bad because when a guy gets to college he is going to feel inadequate as a man if he doesn't have a certain amount of experience. He is going to be different from other guys and they all make such a to-do about it." Again, another virgin remarked with a touch of envy: "I know some couples living together who are reasonably happy. The guys tell me that this is really the best way—they are even able to study better. I feel frustrated and tense because I don't have a girl. Since the atmosphere and the girls are very permissive, it makes me even more tense!"

Even the few men who professed a belief in the ideal of premarital chastity were not free of conflict. Contemporary values were sufficiently influential to rob the believers of a sense of moral superiority. While they condemned casual sex and promiscuity, even the believers in chastity condoned (for others, not for themselves) premarital sex within a loving relationship. At the very least they exhibited the detachment shown by the young man who, having explained that he expected to remain chaste until marriage, added, wryly, "good old Protestant ethic." Even when prevalent attitudes did not shake the respondent's moral certitude, they nevertheless created some anxiety about the possibly deleterious effects of virginity upon personality and future marriage. A twenty-one-year-old Protestant, with strong religious principles about chastity, explained that he tried to cope with his strong sexual drive by means of physical exercise and, particularly, by "escaping into work." But he worried quite a bit about the future: "What is going to happen some day when I am married? Will the pattern of escape be so rigidly set that I will not be able to do things right any more?"

A senior, who had recently become engaged, described his long period of chastity with its "agonizing moral and intellectual reflections, guilt, fear, and the painful indecision." "Many girls," he remarked, "are more sexually liberated than Jewish middle-class males." Indeed he had had greater reservations about premarital sex with his fiancée than she had.

In comparison with nonvirgins, the virgins were characterized by low self-esteem and self-confidence. This is the unmistakeable evidence of the psychological tests to be presented in a forthcoming section. But if psychological traits played a part in the lack of sexual experience, the interviews show the process to be circular. The failure to live up to role expectations with respect to sexual experience in turn undermined their self-esteem.

RELATIONSHIPS WITH WOMEN

One of the striking facts about the virgins was the relative meagerness of their social contacts. Not only did they abstain from sexual intercourse, half of them either did not date at all or did so very infrequently. Some basic difficulty in social relationships may have manifested itself in the sexual sphere as well. But the process is cumulative: the failure to live up to role expectations in the matter of sex leads to a withdrawal from dating. Several men were quite explicit on this score. "It would be difficult," said one senior, "to be friendly with a girl without making advances and I am afraid I'd be clumsy and not know what to do." Another young man who had dated only three or four times during his four college years confessed that he did not know what girls expected on dates. He gathered from the talk of the fellows that a girl would feel insulted if he did not make a pass. He was not ready to sleep with a girl, but neither did he want to hurt a girl's feelings by his inhibitions. Balswick and Anderson (1969) found that, in a pick-up situation, male students perceived females as expecting males to be more aggressive than they really were. Another senior who did date occasionally confided his worries: "Suppose I meet a nice girl and after two or three dates she'd expect me to make love to her. I'll have to explain my views all over again. I have this anxiety in meeting new girls. I guess I am peculiar."

Again, another virgin felt that women had on occasion given him a "guarded invitation," whereas his own preference was "to go slow."

Complete avoidance of dating, as a way of coping with the threat that sexual relations posed, presents an interesting problem in deviance. These youths withdrew from the sexual role which their milieu regarded as the very touchstone of masculinity. For a very few men, as illustrated by the two following cases, this proved a more or less viable mode of existence. In presenting these cases we shall search for conditions that made such deviance tolerable.

AVOIDANCE OF DATING AS A SUCCESSFUL
MODE OF ESCAPING STRAIN

Among the exceptional virgins who appeared to be relatively untroubled by their lack of sexual experience was Ed, a twenty-one-year-old Protestant, from a small midwestern town, whose father, a high school graduate, was active in local church affairs.

Ed continued to attend church regularly throughout his college years in the East although he has begun to question religious dogma and church organization. "Are you a religious person?" asked the interviewer. Ed answered: "In action I am religious, but I am not sure how deep my commitment to religion really is." Ed intends to go to graduate school and get a doctorate in a physical science, leading to a career in research. He occasionally wonders whether such a long range commitment may not be too narrowing. He considered also other possibilities. He heard of a law school which paid a student's way through law school for a career in patent law.

Ed expects to remain chaste until he marries. If he felt strongly enough about a girl to contemplate sex relations: "I would want to marry her," he said. But marriage is not a realistic possibility for at least four years or more, until he can support a wife. He would not be comfortable having his wife support him in graduate school. Lack of time is even more of a hindrance to an early marriage than lack of money. Graduate study will be so time consuming that it would not be fair to a wife. All of his siblings married young but he is the only one who has gone to college with professional ambitions.

Ed denied being disturbed by his lack of sexual experience. He was asked to comment upon an excerpt from an interview with another respondent who claimed that a college man who has not had some sexual experience is made to feel inadequate by his fellows. Ed dissented from this view. A virgin need not feel inadequate as a man and "sex isn't the only thing that is discussed." He conceded that he might have been subjected to pressures to date were he attending some state university in the Midwest, but "around here people are willing to let others do their own thing." The only person who is surprised that he is not dating is his mother, all the more because all of his siblings married young.

Ed's serenity, apparent or real, is attained at least in part, by considerable isolation from all social contacts.

He was on the debating team in high school and occasionally, but infrequently, dated a girl member of the team. He did not date at all in his freshman year at college and only three or four times in his sophomore year. During his junior year he had trouble with a science course and that kept him too busy for dating. Moreover, he explained, he doesn't want to get involved at this point in his life; since he isn't looking for a wife, he doesn't see much point in dating.

Ed does not have close male friends. He asked for a single room in his freshman year and has continued living alone in the dorms. His relationships with fellow students are "casual," "his favorite adjective," commented the interviewer. Most of his friends do not have a steady and date only casually. Now and then he goes to a movie with a fellow student who lives in the single room next to his.

The most telling signs of his isolation are his low self-disclosure scores: 31 to "closest male friend," compared to 80.2 for the sample as a whole; the comparable scores for "closest female friend" are respectively 11 and 97.8. His disclosure score to parents is similar to the group average, but his disclosure score to siblings is below average. He cited the age difference between him, the youngest child, and geographical separation to account for his low disclosure score to siblings. He described most of his family relationships as "neutral" with the exception of two: with his mother —"somewhat close and intimate"; and with one older sister— "somewhat strained."

Ed expends much of his energy on his studies. His academic average is B+ with which he is not wholly satisfied. He has some artistic hobbies.

Ed appears to have created for himself a way of life that may be described as emotionally muted or "casual." Having come from a homogeneous small town in the Midwest, he denied that the encounter with heterogeneous values was in any way disturbing: if other "people feel differently," it doesn't disturb him. "Everybody is entitled to live as he wishes." Nevertheless he appears to have some need to minimize differences in values and behavior, assuring the interviewer that mass media exaggerate the sexual revolution.

The few indications that the controlled, emotionally bland façade is not without some cracks come from the Adjective Check List. Ed's "ideal man" would be more "excitable" and "imaginative," have wider interests, be more active and less "pessimistic" about the possibility of solving major social problems than he is. If he were more excitable, he explained, he wouldn't be so inclined to "just let things slide" and would be moved to do something about urban social conditions.

Ed was exceptional both in the extent of his isolation from women (and, indeed, from men) and his apparent adjustment to it, though a deeper psychological inquiry might have uncovered psychic costs hidden from us. The only similar case was Jason, an Orthodox Jewish senior of twenty, who, despite differences in their cultural backgrounds, shared many traits with Ed. We shall describe Jason and then summarize the lesson implied in these cases.

Jason, an only child of a demanding widowed mother, has the support of his cultural milieu, e.g., his mother and the neighborhood synagogue, for his style of life. Though he assured the interviewer that he had no religious scruples about premarital sex he hoped that he personally would experience it only with the kind of girl he would be ready to marry. Jason spends every weekend at his family home, partly out of choice, his sense of obligation to his widowed mother, and his inability to travel on Saturday. His two best male friends from high school are also virgins, and according to his report there is very little talk about sex when they meet. His attachment to the neighborhood institutions and to his home, both directly reinforce the traditional ideology and, by removing him physically from the college for long weekends, serve to blunt the possible impact of more permissive codes of the college.

In checking traits of his "ideal man," Jason omitted "sexy," "masculine," and "aggressive." Just as in the case of Ed, his self-description was quite favorable. It contained adjectives such as "artistic" and "sensitive." On the negative side, he recognizes his "immaturity" and feels that an early marriage is not likely in view of his career plans. His comments concerning the few girls whom he has dated were shallow, both in his descriptions of their personalities and his assessment of their reactions to him. This may reflect his infrequent and superficial contacts as well as his immaturity. His ideal girl, in addition to being intelligent and honest, must be emotionally outgoing "to compensate for my reserve. That should level things out nicely between us."

Music and physical exercise are his preferred outlets in periods of tension. He has dated a few times but prefers large and informal parties.

Both Ed and Jason maintained their self-respect by isolating themselves from the majority of their fellow students with more permissive sexual views and behavior. Jason had the added advantage of his weekends in the parental home and neighborhood. Ed volunteered the observation that he felt freer from surveillance and possible ridicule of fellow students in a large cosmopolitan university than he might have felt in a midwestern state college.

Ed and Jason drew support from religious traditionalism concerning sex roles. Finally, both had strong achievement drives. If, as is frequently alleged, masculinity in our society is validated by sexual and by work performance, Ed and Jason, withdrawing from sexual relationships, invested much of their psychic energy in their roles as students and future workers. They had long-range and ambitious career plans. Both came from uneducated families in which their aspirations were exceptional and they sought self-respect from academic achievement.

The relative adjustment of Ed and Jason to the nearly complete avoidance of dating was the exception rather than the rule. Andrew, a twenty-one-year-old senior who has had only four or five dates in his entire life, was more typical of the virgins we interviewed. Andrew's inhibitions in relation to women stemmed from complex psychic problems. We shall presently describe other troubled virgins, who for all their anxieties, do not appear as psychically impaired.

Andrew was a Protestant whose father died when he was only two years old and whose mother remarried and then divorced. His vulnerabilities as a male may be inferred from the qualities he attributed to his "ideal man" and missing from his self-description. These adjectives included: "ambitious," "calm," "capable," "confident," "courageous," "determined," "energetic," "forceful," "independent," "resourceful," "sociable," "self-confident," "stable," "strong." He was dissatisfied not only with his lack of ascendancy traits but his difficulty in expressing, or even feeling, affection.

Andrew described his strong sexual desires. He started masturbating as a child before he "even knew what it was all about." He had necrophilic fantasies when masturbating. As a schoolboy he romanticized girls. Back in the fourth grade he had a crush on a little girl and brought her presents. As he entered adolescence, everything went wrong. At present, he is still interested in girls but he is afraid that he may be turned down and humiliated if he asks a girl for a date. Moreover, he is not ready to go beyond kissing but he understands that girls nowadays expect more. He is also afraid that were he to make love to a girl with whom he did not have strong emotional ties, those troublesome sexual fantasies would creep in and he would treat the girl as an object rather than a person.

Andrew had suffered a serious depression in his junior year and psychiatric treatment since that time has helped to alleviate his problems.

The psychological profile of Andrew, written by a clinical psychologist solely on the basis of psychological tests follows:

This is the profile of a seriously disturbed man. His anxieties are close to the surface although he is unable to deal with them constructively or insightfully. His impulses are strong and uncontrolled, he avoids reflection, tends to be irritable, changeable, and restless. He rejects both academic and social involvement, but he is not self-satisfied about it. Rather he is self-punishing and complaining. He may project what are essentially his own conflicts onto circumstances and be vocally critical. He looks for support from others in a submissive, dependent way and tries to be patient and agreeable. However he feels moved by forces beyond his control and may be unable to supress his anger or his desire to show off. In addition, he may be quite hostile and hurtful to others, this thinly covered by a veil of nurturance. All in all, he is still a little boy, grandiose in his fantasied ability to either hurt or help others; unable to check his impulses to show off, demand attention, unable to read another's point of view or reaction, unable to make sense of the world and his place in it and, finally, feeling very small.

Despite Andrew's problems with women and his conservative political outlook, he was sympathetic to women's occupational aspirations. Having criticized women who used bad language and looked untidy, he went on to present liberal attitudes towards feminism. He did not express any negative stereotypes of women's personality traits. He felt that circumstances might dictate the priority in the timing of a wife's graduate training over her husband's and remarked: "Girls, unless they are really stupid, will not get satisfaction out of just keeping house for the rest of their lives."

The three virgins described so far avoided dating as a mode of coping with their deviant attitudes towards sex. Another method of coping with sexual inhibitions (moral or psychological) was through selective dating.

SELECTIVE DATING AS A MODE OF ESCAPING STRAIN

The virgins who did date more or less frequently had to cope in a different way with the conflict between role expectations, their own moral scruples, and personal inclinations. One mode of adaptation was to select, deliberately or unconsciously, girls whose conservative sex standards promised safety. The availability of such dating partners made this a workable adjustment for several men. Occasionally, however, in avoiding girls who were too experienced, some men found their dates not responsive enough. A twenty-one-year-old virgin who explained that he "will probably not have intercourse before marriage" (though he does not condemn others who do) had dated girls who were equally inexperienced. "In fact," he added, "they have been too repressed. They were scared of any contact, even of kissing." He hoped to meet some girls who were "less repressed." His male friends were "all in the same boat," they were also virgins and they, too, complained about dates who were too repressed.

How to strike just the right balance with regard to sexual responsiveness was not the only problem in selective dating. Some men could not avail themselves of this adaptation for other reasons. Sexual standards are not unrelated to attitudes in other spheres of life. The men who were, or wished to be in other respects than sex, part of the liberal, radical, or secular subcultures, could not solve their problem by associating with conventional girls.

A twenty-one-year-old Catholic man, who had attended parochial primary and secondary schools, illustrates this situation. Upon coming to college he "wished, more than anything else to establish a meaningful relationship with a woman." He was strongly attracted to "earthy, free, unconventional girls who can talk about important issues and hold their own in argument." But he was afraid to approach such girls. Intellectually, he remarked, he did not consider premarital sex a sin but having been brought up as a Catholic he was not able to escape his emotional inhibitions.

In his junior year he fell in love and eventually became engaged to a Catholic girl who was attending a conservative Catholic college. He broke the engagement in the middle of his senior year, having recognized the unbridgeable differences between them. His fiancée was in every respect a conventional girl, whereas he was a rebel. At first, as they attended Sunday mass together and she saw him wearing a tie, and generally looking very proper, she assumed that his rebellion was but a passing phase. She urged him to cut his long hair, fit in with the system "and cease sympathizing with the radicals." These demands finally convinced him of their incompatibility. He described, incidentally, his sexual strain during their engagement, which his fiancée never fully understood. "A woman likes to be cuddled and she doesn't realize how little it takes to turn a man on." They petted but never had intercourse. He felt very foolish having to tell her in the middle of love-making, "now let's just calm down for a bit."

Another virgin, a twenty-one-year-old Jew, also could not avoid strain through selective dating because his conservative sexual attitudes did not harmonize with his general style of life. He shared an off-campus apartment with a roommate and the roommate's girl friend. His affluent parents were mystified by him. "Are you on drugs?" his mother asked. "Why are you so peculiar if you are not on drugs?" "I have long hair," he remarked, "and long hair, drugs, and loose living are supposed to go together. I am not on drugs and I don't live loosely. Why, then, my family worries, don't I want to fit into society?" If his family found his behavior inconsistent, so did his unconventional friends. His friends knew that he was a virgin and occasionally a friend might say: "Man, you are silly. Let go. You are a college senior, you ought to get together with a chick." But he did not feel ready: "That kind of thing ties you down, encumbers you. When I get straightened out so that I don't have to be by myself for such long periods, then it will be different."

This young man has two women friends. One is three years older than he, sexually experienced, who shares his interest in music and in good conversation. "She isn't pressing," he explained. "She digs it the way it is. She wouldn't want me to make any moves until I am comfortable." The other girl whom he sees frequently is a virgin.

In accordance with the conventions of his peer group, his apartment is open to friends who sometimes stay overnight. The younger of his two women friends, who attends an out-of-town college, has stayed overnight in his room on a few occasions. "It's real weird," he observed, "I say to myself, 'man you should get with it,' but in the morning I am relieved that I stayed cool. Once you've acted you can't retrieve it." He is the youth, referred to on p. 6, who after one such overnight visit, phoned the girl at 2 A.M. to apologize for not having made love to her. She reassured him by saying that she would have been upset had he done so. All the same, on a subsequent trip they took together to visit some mutual friends, she hinted that she had changed her mind and would be more receptive in the future.

The sexual reserve of this virgin presented an especially acute problem because he was a member of a peer group that sanctioned overnight visits by out-of-town women friends in his room, as well as joint trips to visit friends or to attend music festivals. In such circumstances his sexual inhibitions became all too apparent.

DATING AND STRAINS

Neither complete avoidance of women nor the careful selection of "safe" dates was the dominant pattern of the virgins. The majority did not give up dating despite the conflicts it presented. John will illustrate the problems of a virgin who had gone further in establishing some relationships with women than any of the virgins described previously.

John gave ample evidence of what he desired and what threatened him in women. The discrepancies between his egalitarian ideals as applied to women and his preferences recurred throughout the interview. "Very great need," he responded to the schedule dealing with the need for feminist reforms. "Women have been discriminated against. A woman who is capable should get the job she deserves." But he personally would discourage his wife from working. Housework, boring as it is, need not occupy the whole day; his mother found interesting and satisfying hobbies and he would wish the same life for his wife. Again: "Any major, including the sciences, is suitable for a girl and I admire girls who are intelligent in any field," he remarked; but when it came to personal preferences he preferred to date women who major in the arts "because then there will be no danger of competition. I tend to be competitive . . . a girl I once knew was literally a genius. I felt she was dominating the relationship and we split up." Dependence upon a wage-earning wife through graduate school is all right for other people. As for himself: "It would upset me to be supported by a woman. I wouldn't get married until I was established."

During the first three years of college John dated Carole, a girl he had known since high school. They kept breaking up (generally at Carole's initiative) and reuniting until the final break at the end of his junior year. After Carole, he had had a few casual dates. He resented Carole's independence and self-sufficiency. "My problem is," he explained, "that I try to maintain control. I feel things should revolve around the man. I want to make myself dominant but I am afraid I won't be. Carole could be warm and dependent in a nice sort of way. But, then, sometimes I felt that she forgot all about me. Once she came to a party with one of my best friends. It was very depressing. I had the desire to possess her to the exclusion of everybody and everything else but I wound up being dependent upon her."

The most galling evidence of Carole's independence was that she had an apartment of her own whereas he continued to live with his parents. His mild but chronic illness and its financial cost provided some excuse for his living at home but he confessed that he basically agreed with Carole's accusation that he was immature, too dependent upon his parents and afraid to move out and cope with the real world of paying bills, signing leases, and the like.

John engaged in heavy necking with Carole and once "had an opportunity to go all the way with her but did not." His parents were in the next room and besides, "You are getting into my hang ups here." He added: "Though I wanted [intercourse] I was afraid of not being proficient at it."

John's root anxiety stemmed from his expectation that "the man should dominate a relationship" and his perception of himself as weak, submissive, and undeserving. His "ideal man" on the Adjective Check List contained the following traits, missing from his self-description: aggressive, adventurous, dominant, energetic, enthusiastic, self-confident, and resourceful. He was seemingly unaware of the contradiction between the strongly feminist values he voiced and his preferences. Only a few close male friends knew that he was a virgin—generally, he said, he tried to give the impression that he was sexually experienced.

RELATIONSHIPS WITH MALE FRIENDS

The inhibitions which curtailed dating on the part of the virgins need not have affected their social life with male friends. They could, after all, conceal their virginity from fellow students. And, indeed, all reported some male friendships. But, even with regard to the latter, the virgins were more reserved than the sample as a whole. Their average self-disclosure score to male friends was 72.8 as compared to 80.2 for the total sample. The causation is no doubt circular. Basic difficulties in all intimate relationships may have been at work. But the lack of sexual experience, a deviant pattern for the group, must have had a dampening effect on social contacts with male friends. A twenty-year-old senior, a virgin, cited an incident in his freshman year, the sting of which had not diminished with the years. Some fellow students "razzed him" about his sexual inexperience. The pressure to claim sexual experience was generally acknowledged. "I know quite a few guys to whom nothing has happened," a student said, "but they said that it had." Even women exerted such pressure, according to one senior, who heard a girl express worry about her brother because he was still a virgin at twenty-two.

The greater sophistication of the majority inhibited the virgins even in their initial approaches to women. "The co-ed class is not a good source of contacts with girls; my techniques would be too visible to the audience of men," explained one student. Although we have no systematic evidence regarding the extent of selective association among men, the virgins, especially those who dated infrequently, repeatedly described their male friends as ". . . in the same blessed state," "we are all in the same boat," "they don't date either."

Selective association with men whose sexual experience was also limited served to reassure and protect from invidious comparisons but it may have had a less beneficial consequence of reinforcing fears and giving rise to a defensive mythology. The virgins exchanged purported incidents of women's sarcasm at college mixers or on dates: "That girl really cut him down," "girls act as if they are doing you a favor when they dance with you." "It angers me," said another senior, "that a girl will give you just one dance to make it or break it and will promptly thank you and walk off without giving you even a chance to get an exchange going. It angers me that girls can be so callous in disregarding the guy's feelings."

Not all virgins or sexually inexperienced men limited their close friendships to like-minded men. One senior shared an apartment with four other football players, all from the same home community. "We are much closer than most families," said John. "If someone said something against any one of us, we'd do anything to defend him." John had intercourse once with his Catholic high school steady but she felt too guilty about premarital sex to continue sex relations. All the roommates led active sex lives and urged our respondent to follow up an encounter with a girl at their parties or in a bar, but he never did.

This youth preserved his much treasured membership in this clique by sometimes playing the "oddball" and other times concealing his hostility towards their sexual and political attitudes. He was a "marginal" man in this very conservative clique. But while he occasionally expressed his liberal views, he did so in a way that would not antagonize them. "What are you, a nigger lover?" his roommates would say. "You don't really believe it, you are saying it just to argue." He would often shrug off their reactionary remarks for fear of losing their friendship. "You are really going out of your way to be odd," the roommates would remark. In sum, this young man preserved his place in this clique by playing the role of a stubborn but unthreatening oddball, at the cost of some guardedness in peer relationships.

WHO ARE THE VIRGINS?

The preceding pages discussed some consequences of virginity for the self-esteem and the social relationships of the virgins. To turn from the consequences to the causes of virginity: Who are the seniors who remain chaste despite the prevailing trend toward sexual permissiveness?

There were no virgins among the nine black students, raising the percent of virgins among the whites to 30 percent. Reiss (1967: 36) found black males to be more permissive than the whites in attitudes towards sexual behavior and this difference remained when the comparison was controlled for class. In our sample, among the white males, differences in religious affiliation ranged from 37 percent of virgins among the Jews to 31 percent among the Protestants and 25 percent among the Catholics. There is a suggestion that if the Jews were more chaste in fact, they were somewhat more liberal in ideology. Were this confirmed by a larger sample, it would provide another illustration of the disjunction that often exists between verbally expressed attitudes and actual behavior.

Father's education did not affect the proportion of virgins; the ratio of upwardly mobile sons among the virgins was nearly identical with their proportion in our total sample. Reiss (1967: 66) questions Kinsey's position that the lower classes are more sexually active than the middle or upper classes. But Reiss's data pertains to attitudinal permissiveness, not to behavior. Reiss concludes that the relationship between social class and permissive attitudes varies with the level of conservatism (or, conversely, liberality) in nonsexual spheres. More specifically, in the conservative groups, the lower classes had more permissive attitudes towards sex, whereas among liberal adults and students alike, the higher third of the class pyramid was more permissive than the lower third. Our data did not permit a similar test.

Five or six of the sixty-two seniors expressed some anxiety over possible homosexual tendencies or reported some homosexual experience. But none of the few men who admitted serious homosexual anxieties were among the sixteen virgins in the sample. This does not mean that all of the virgins were necessarily free of homosexual tendencies because the interviews did not systematically investigate homosexuality. However, those whose homosexual anxieties or experience became known to us had all had some heterosexual experience.

In contrast to social factors which, in our sample, failed to distinguish conclusively virgins from nonvirgins, psychological tests show striking differences. On the Gough Adjective Check List, the virgins show a very unfavorable self-image as compared with the sexually experienced men. Table 4.1 summarizes the results for seven traits pertaining to the degree of self-satisfaction. The virgins are consistently more anxious, self-critical, lacking in self-confidence and dominance than the nonvirgins. They are worried about themselves, as seen in scores for Counseling Readiness. Sixty-two percent of the virgins but only 40 percent of the nonvirgins scored 50 or above (the high scorers are worried about themselves). On Abasement ("high scorers see themselves as weak and undeserving") 85 percent of the virgins but only 35 percent of the sexually experienced students scored 50 or above.

The California Psychological Inventory revealed consistent results, portraying the virgins as less dominant and less self-accepting (see Table 4.2).

Table 4.1. Comparison of Virgins and Nonvirgins on Some Traits of the ACL

| | Percent of specified group falling below the standard mean score of 50 or scoring 50 and above | | | |
| | Virgins (N = 13) | | Nonvirgins (N = 45) | |
	BELOW 50	50 & ABOVE	BELOW 50	50 & ABOVE
Favorable Adjectives	77	23	51	49
Self-Confidence	77	23	34	66
Dominance	77	23	37	63
Abasement[1]	15	85	65	35
Unfavorable Adjectives	31	69	51	49
Defensiveness[2]	62	38	44	56
Counseling Readiness[3]	38	62	60	40
Exhibition[4]	69	31	44	56

1. "High scores see themselves as weak and undeserving."
2. "The lower scoring person tends to be anxious . . . self-critical."
3. "High scorer is worried about himself."
4. "Low scorers lack self-confidence."

Table 4.2. Comparison of Virgins and Nonvirgins
on the CPI

| | Percent of specified group falling below the standard mean score of 50 or scoring 50 and above | | | |
| | Virgins (N = 15) | | Nonvirgins (N = 41) | |
	BELOW 50	50 & ABOVE	BELOW 50	50 & ABOVE
Dominance	53	47	22	78
Capacity for Status	47	53	22	78
Sociability	73	27	29	71
Social Presence	27	73	12	88
Self-acceptance	47	53	2	98
Well-Being	80	20	63	37
Responsibility	27	73	56	43
Socialization	60	40	61	39
Self-Control	33	67	73	27
Tolerance	47	53	39	61
Good Impression	53	47	37	63
Communality	73	27	56	43
Achievement via Conformity	53	47	46	54
Achievement via Independence	0	100	10	90
Intellectual Efficiency	33	67	32	68
Psychological Mindedness	13	87	17	83
Flexibility	0	100	15	85
Femininity	27	73	32	68

The lack of self-confidence and the generally unfavorable self-image of the virgins, so clearly documented in the psychological tests, must have been both the consequence of deviance in their peer society, and also the cause of it. Support for the personality as an independent variable in the lack of sexual experience comes from the study of family relationships of the virgins. They tended to be less favorable than of the nonvirgins. To the extent that the family is "the cradle of personality," we may assume that certain of the psychological traits revealed in the tests predated their attitudes towards sexual behavior.

The self-assessment of family relationships consisted in checking one of five possible answers for each dyadic relationship: "very tense and strained," "somewhat tense and strained," "neutral," "somewhat close and intimate," "very close and intimate." Table 4.3 combines the first and the last two answers into "unfavorable" and "favorable" categories respectively.

The only pair relationship that does not differentiate virgins and nonvirgins is the one to the mother. For each group the mother is the closest parent and the percentages of unfavorable, neutral, and favorable relationships are nearly identical. In other relationships, the virgins reported more strain than the nonvirgins. Especially striking are the differences in the relationships with the father: only 42 percent of the virgins checked "favorable" as contrasted with 62 percent of the nonvirgins. The contrast does not end there. Exactly 50 percent of the virgins checked "neutral" as descriptive of their ties with the father as against only 16 percent of the nonvirgins; "neutral" was frequently a label for detached and uninvolved fathers. On the other hand, 22 percent of the nonvirgins reported "strained" feelings between themselves and their fathers, with only

Table 4.3. Family Relationships of Virgins and Nonvirgins

	Percent in Each Category	
	Virgins	*Nonvirgins*
Relationship	*N = 16*	*N = 46*
Mother and Father		
Unfavorable	33	31
Neutral	17	6
Favorable	50	63
Mother and Me		
Unfavorable	8	11
Neutral	15	10
Favorable	77	79
Father and Me		
Unfavorable	8	22
Neutral	50	16
Favorable	42	62
Brother (or Brothers) and Me		
Unfavorable	27	25
Neutral	27	22
Favorable	46	53
Sister (or Sisters) and Me		
Unfavorable	25	5
Neutral	25	15
Favorable	50	79

8 percent of the virgins falling into this category.

As to siblings, the virgins and the nonvirgins did not differ significantly in their attitudes towards their brothers. But the virgins reported more strain and less closeness than nonvirgins when they described their sisters. Nearly 80 percent of relationships with sisters on the part of nonvirgins were favorable as contrasted with only 50 percent for the virgins. The latter also reported more strain in relation to sisters.

Much of the psychoanalytical as well as popular literature emphasizes mother-son relationships in accounting for the sexual problems of males. Contrary to that emphasis, unsatisfactory relationships with fathers proved the most significant factor differentiating the students who were virgins in their senior year at college, from the majority who had had sexual intercourse. The psychological tests portrayed the virgins as low in self-esteem. This suggests that unsatisfactory paternal relationships may have been related to the virginity of the sons through the intervening variable of low self-esteem. That the boys' level of self-esteem is related to the supportiveness of father-son relationships has been confirmed in previous research (see Kohn, 1969, 126; and Rosenberg, 1965).[2]

Though as a group the virgins were characterized by a relatively unfavorable self-image, they varied from the severely disturbed to those who functioned adequately in other roles. Moreover, whatever deeper fears or psychological problems accounted for the avoidance of sexual relations in some cases, other seniors were affected more by social factors. These were men, who for a variety of external circumstances, dated infrequently in high school. The climate of sexual permissiveness to which they were suddenly exposed in college proved inhibiting. By the sexual standards of their new milieu they were retarded, and the moderate sexual play appropriate to high school adolescents was deemed immature. Particularly threatening were the rumors of the sexual expertise and expectations of women. Having omitted the earlier stage, they felt the expected standards of performance to be unattainable.

The relationship between self-esteem and sexual attitudes and behavior were studied by John R. Stratton and Stephen P. Spitzer (1967) and Daniel Perlman (1974). The earlier of the two studies is not strictly comparable to ours because the authors investigated

2. See also, A. B. Heilbrun (1962) who found that maladjusted college males were significantly less identified with their fathers than were the adjusted males.

attitudes towards sex in relation to self-esteem whereas this chapter tests the relationship between sexual *behavior* and self-evaluation. The 1967 study reports that in the conservative culture, people who are traditional rather than permissive in their attitudes towards premarital sex tend to evaluate themselves positively. The authors hypothesized that such individuals have internalized the dominant norms. By contrast, people with permissive sexual attitudes will tend to have an unfavorable self-image because they perceive their deviation from dominant norms.

Perlman's study (1974) comes closer to the present inquiry because it includes measures of sexual conduct in addition to measures of attitudinal permissiveness. In accord with our findings, in a liberal subculture, Perlman found that students who engaged in premarital intercourse reported higher self-esteem than those who did not. Perlman's interpretation, however, still follows Stratton and Spitzer. He suggests that conformity in attitudes or behavior to internalized norms (whether conservative or permissive) tends to lead to higher self-evaluation, whereas deviance lowers self-esteem. He further notes that self-esteem is more closely related to normative behavior than to normative attitudes.

In contrast to these earlier studies, we stress the circular nature of the relationship between self-esteem and sexual behavior in the permissive subculture of our sample.

CONCLUSION

Only five years ago, Ira L. Reiss (1970) published an article entitled "Premarital Sex as Deviant Behavior: An Application of Current Approaches to Deviance." The author argued that though premarital sex was heretofore not included in the standard texts on deviance, it qualified as such, because 77 percent of a national sample (those twenty-one years and older), considered premarital sex as a violation of a major code (Reiss, 1967). The author recognized the generational differences in norms since only 42 percent of his student sample condemned premarital sex.

For the seniors in our study virginity, and not premarital sex, constituted the deviant condition. It might appear tempting to follow Reiss in applying current theories, such as "labeling," "anomie," and "social and cultural support" to virginity as deviance. But the relevance of these approaches is likely to be limited. Deviant acts are not all of a kind. Existing theories were developed to interpret the kind of transgressions of laws or of major social norms that are defined as social problems. A senior, who is still a virgin in the liberal subculture of our campus, has failed to live up to his own and his peers' ideal of masculinity. This relative failure to attain the norms of a given age-sex role may damage his self-esteem or lower his status among his peers. But, as conveyed by the phrase, "poverty is not a crime," this is not the kind of deviance that provokes moral outrage.

Moreover, virginity is easy to conceal. Thus, the labeling theory is of limited interpretative value in this area. Since virgins do not need to reveal their state, the derivative "secondary deviance," (Lemert, 1951), produced by social reaction to the primary deviance, is likewise, not likely to be elaborated. Lemert's concept of primary deviance[3] might possibly apply to a shared mythology about women which was manifested by male virgins exchanging stories of women's sarcasm and cruelty.

The theory of anomie would likewise appear to be inapplicable to the case of the virgins. Possibly one might see in the unwilling virgins signs of retreatism, insofar as some despaired of conforming to the sexual standards of their peer group. This would require the further assumption that religious, traditional, sheltered or unsatisfactory family backgrounds hindered some students from acquiring appropriate skills to attain the socially sanctioned goals.

Whatever the influence of social factors upon the incidence of virginity among college male seniors, within our small sample the social factors included in the analysis failed to distinguish the virgins from the nonvirgins as conclusively as did the psychological tests. The lack of self-confidence and the generally unfavorable self-image of the virgins was shown to be both the effect and the cause of their behavior. The relatively high proportion of unfavorable family relationships among the virgins does not rule out social determinants but suggests that these operated indirectly by shaping distinctively the personalities of virgins and nonvirgins.

---

3. "The deviations remain primary deviations . . . as long as they are rationalized or otherwise dealt with as functions of a socially acceptable role" (1951: 76, cited in Reiss, 1970: 79).

5

POWER AND
EMOTIONAL
RELATIONSHIPS
WITH WOMEN

The traditional masculine role calls for the male to be superior to the female in aggressiveness, self-assurance, decisiveness, independence, and stability in the face of stress. Such attributes contribute to power and leadership in interpersonal relationships. Whatever the genetic sources of sex differences, children are still socialized in our society so as to maximize ascendancy traits in boys and mute them in girls.[1] Moreover, certain masculine privileges remove decisions from any contest and cede advantages automatically to the male. For example, the majority of young women in our study granted priority to their mates' careers and, in case of conflict, were prepared to scale down their own occupational aspirations.

Neither the genetic endowment, however, nor the socialization

1. Eleanor E. Maccoby and Carol N. Jacklin (1974: 287–95) report surprisingly little differentiation in parental treatment of sons and daughters. The authors themselves call attention to the paucity of data concerning working-class families and fathers as informers. Moreover, parents are not the sole agents of socialization and, until evidence to the contrary is forthcoming, it would appear safe to assume that the combined effect of socialization is to minimize the ascendancy traits in women as compared with men.

of men ensures that all men in fact possess the expected characteristics, nor have they always possessed them in the past. Certain new
conditions may be expected to exacerbate male strains because
women today present new challenges to male undergraduates, as
was illustrated in the analysis of intellectual relationships. Moreover, as equalitarian values become more common, male privileges may be less readily taken for granted. They may no longer be
conceded as a matter of tradition to a man who is not strong enough
to earn them. The male who has internalized the norm of dominance is increasingly called upon to attain it by virtue of personal
attributes and over increasingly strong female associates. "Things
should revolve about the man," a mild, insecure youth remarked
wistfully, but his independent girl friend was far from taking this
imperative for granted. The senior who maintained that a man
should be "a lot more worldly wise than his date" might encounter
similar problems.

Some may challenge this hypothesis of the beleagured male by
claiming that genetic qualities, as well as the traditional socialization of the sexes, still ensure male assertiveness and female docility,
thus reducing the likelihood of any pervasive power problem for
males. Another hypothesis is that the new egalitarian values may
have already become so prevalent as to free men of the need to
present a dominant posture.

Our first task was to discover whether the seniors actually experienced any strain because they found it difficult to live up to the
traditional expectation of superior psychological strength in relation to women.

THE FAILURE TO LIVE UP TO THE IDEAL OF
MASCULINE STRENGTH: THE EXTENT
AND VARIETIES OF STRAIN

The evidence for this strain comes from the description of actual
relationships with women. Only the nondaters were classified on
the basis of attitudes expressed towards women in general, as well as
towards themselves, particularly as they attempted to explain their
lack of female friends. This section deals solely with the male role
vis-à-vis women friends. The respondents who felt that they lacked

assertiveness in other statuses, but expressed satisfaction with their relationships with women, were not included in the "troubled" group.

Men, for whom relative strength vis-à-vis women constituted a more or less serious problem, were generally classified on the basis of their own admission of inadequacy. Some, however, were included because they reported their mates' grievances. For example, in answer to our standard question about changes that the closest girl friend might wish to make in him, one senior said: "She likes to be dominated. She would want me to be more decisive. When I become pushy she does yield. I prefer a more equal relationship in which neither party has to hassle."

Several men claimed that women themselves, rather than men, stood in the way of more equalitarian relations between the sexes because: "Women want to be dominated, they want to be told what to do." These youths were included among the troubled men when, apart from their general criticism of women's demands or of traditional values, they expressed dissatisfaction with their own lack of assertiveness.

So much for the basis of our classification. The central finding is that the inability to present a strong, self-assured "masculine" image constituted a prevalent problem among these men. What is more, the pressure from their female friends intensified their feeling of inadequacy. When the men were asked to list changes their women friends would wish to make in them, "more decisive," "more dominant," and the like, appeared more frequently than the reverse, e.g., "less bossy." The men perceived, probably accurately, that, at this particular stage of life, women wanted of their men more support, self-assurance, independence, and responsibility than the men were able to provide. This is not to deny that women also wanted in men certain "feminine" traits, such as more sensitivity and emotional expressiveness.

Of the fifty-six men whom we were able to classify with confidence, twenty-five men or 45 percent had experienced strain in this sphere varrying from severe to mild.[2] Conversely, thirty-one men, or 55 percent of the group, were judged to be adjusted on this score.

2. See p. 154 for further evidence of the strain, derived from the comparison of the seniors' responses on the Gough Adjective Check Lists for "my ideal man" and "my real self." The self-concepts fell short of the ideal with regard to the assertiveness cluster of traits.

It would be a mistake to assume that the thirty-one adjusted men were all strong, assertive, and confident. Some were but other types were also included among the adjusted. Of the thirty-one adjusted men, only six were clearly stronger than their current girl friends, fiancées, or wives. They were able to live up to the norm of masculine dominance, shared also by their mates. Two or three couples were adjusted in equalitarian relationships. Four men found strong and supportive women, who neither challenged them nor stirred feelings of shame or over-dependency. A few men, who did express feelings of inadequacy, found still weaker girl friends at the cost of some, but not serious, sacrifice of other needs. Fourteen men playing the field (and a few nondaters) were deemed adjusted because our indirect and direct probing uncovered no anxiety about any lack of assertiveness.

Of the twenty-five seniors, troubled by their lack of masculine assertiveness, fifteen were acutely distressed and ten only moderately so. The major cause of strain was a conflict between the norm that "men should come on strong" and a self-perceived lack of psychological strength. This type of conflict will be amply illustrated in the following cases. But seniors expressed other varieties of problems in relation to power. Some youths denounced the traditional ideal of machismo. Thus, a twenty-one-year-old senior remarked: "One thing that bothers me is the way they always picture men as having to be dominant and strong. That puts a lot of strain on a man."

This was a son of college-educated parents who said, in the course of the interview, that he would much prefer to "share things, and you cannot dominate and share at the same time. Unfortunately too many girls are willing to be a man's shadow. Girls like a hard exterior in a man. You see it on the campus: there are guys who practically do not listen to a girl when she talks to them and the girl eats it up." As for him, he does not consider lack of consideration of the girl's wishes as strength. His own mother is an exceptionally able woman but she has to "sidle up to my father and sort of ask permission to do things." He described himself as similar to his mother rather than to his father in temperament. He has had three affairs and when one of his past girl friends became pregnant they decided on an abortion. He is dealing in marijuana. While he expressed satisfaction with his sexual adequacy he felt insecure about his ability to "keep up the girl's interest in a viable relationship." Among the adjectives he listed in describing his "real self" were "spineless" and "submissive."

Current criticism of the ideal of machismo may have alleviated the plight of this man, lacking in masculine strength, but it has not solved his problem.

Men, such as the one described above, were caught between pressures from women (their role partners) for greater assertiveness, on the one hand, and their own psychological constitution or their equalitarian ideals, on the other.

Another group of the troubled men confessed that their frustrated yearning for dominance was compounded by feelings of guilt.

"Despite my egalitarian proclamations," wrote one youth, "tugging at my psychic strings is the thought that I am really most comfortable in a situation where my fragile sense of security is not threatened by a woman, where I can maintain a comfortable dominance. Thus my basic insecurity conflicts with my liberated conscience, making me feel like a double-talking hypocrite."

Unlike the majority of the troubled men, this youth faced the double problem of frustration and guilt. His slight, unathletic build and his psychological insecurity, made it difficult for him to be the "top man" in interpersonal relationships. He was exasperated by his inability to score with popular campus women. At the same time, as a member of a "hip" clique, he intellectually despised the very male chauvinism he yearned to be able to embody.

Men torn by conflicting psychic needs suffer from psychological ambivalence, those subject to antithetical social norms or pressures illustrate, what has been termed, "sociological ambivalence."[3] Examples of both kinds of ambivalence abound in case histories. One senior admired women who, like his mother, were willing to stand up for their opinions and did not let anyone take advantage of them. "Nobody can pull the wool over her eyes," he exclaimed admiringly.

But the same senior who respected strong women also believed in masculine dominance. He expressed his distaste for competitive women and refused to date a girl who performed better than he in a class they both attended. How then to find an admirable, independent woman who would not turn into a competitive and dominating one?

3. See Robert K. Merton and E. Barber (1963).

Another ambivalent senior was a very shy youth who felt "tongue-tied on dates." He was attracted to lively, articulate women who put him at ease by "filling in the silences." He was so worried about pleasing others and so watchful for cues that he himself could not define a relationship. But this was also a competitive man who sought refuge from competition in a loving relationship with a woman. His problem was to find a woman who was gregarious and self-assured enough to "fill in the silences" but who, at the same time, would not threaten or overpower him.

Andrew, another "ambivalent" man, was the son of Protestant high school graduates. He was a strong man with conservative political views.

Andrew liked to consider himself a pillar of strength and in one relationship with a girl, enjoyed the fact that she sought his advice. Perhaps his ideal of masculinity made it difficult for him to express his own feelings openly. At least he reported the grievance of one of his girl friends who accused him of not being affectionate and demonstrative enough. He conceded these limitations. He disliked women "who dominate men" and who are "too preoccupied with academics to make themselves attractive."

So far Andrew's attitudes are consistent. But there is another side to his personality and values. Typical feminine helplessness repels him nearly as much as feminine dominance. He admires independent, quick-witted girls who can manage by themselves. His wife will have to be "highly intelligent," and able to handle household and other responsibilities efficiently. The unhappy girl who had at first attracted him by her very need of him, proved disappointing in the long run. No woman, he felt, should be so overdependent, so lacking in personal ambition. Not that he would want a working wife: "I want her to get my supper on the table."

Just as the choice of a supportive woman carried the risk of a dominant wife, so Andrew's fantasy of a bright, independent woman raised the question whether such a woman would be likely to play the submissive role he expects of his wife.

The men who felt inadequate on the score of assertiveness coped with their inadequacy in various ways. The following cases will illustrate their problems more fully and will attempt to explain why coping mechanisms, available to some, could not help others, equally lacking in assertiveness. Of the fifteen acutely distressed youths, nine were virgins, though virgins constituted only 26 percent of the total sample. As the chapter on the virgins shows, in comparison with the sexually experienced seniors, they were characterized by a weak and unfavorable self-image. It is not surprising therefore that the following case, describing avoidance of women as a defense against the sense of powerlessness, should be relevant also to the problems of the virgins.

AVOIDANCE OF WOMEN AS A DEFENSE AGAINST STRAIN

Complete avoidance of dating was an extreme reaction to the sense of inadequacy in masculine strength. Apart from its intrinsic costs, it subjected the nondaters to the criticism of the peer group. The size of the college and its values affected the intensity of the peer group pressure. Several nondaters compared their present college favorably with high schools and other colleges. They claimed that the anonymity and individualism of this campus provided a degree of surcease from the mockery to which they had been subjected elsewhere. All the same, they felt deviant.

Both of the following cases illustrate avoidance of women as a defense against strain, but they vary. Edward was completely immobilized—having hardly dated in high school or in college. His case illustrates vividly the lack of congruence between an internalized ideal of masculine dominance, on the one hand, and a weak personality on the other. An inability to assert himself, coupled with a need to please others, appears to accentuate Ed's fear of any social involvement.

In contrast to Ed, John is psychologically stronger and his problem has a manifest social component. He had a conventional Catholic upbringing and came to the metropolitan campus from a small town. The transition was disturbing to his cautious but yet somewhat open personality. He can neither "go home again" nor does he feel confident enough to cope with the kind of women on this urban campus who both attract and threaten him.

Ed is twenty-one years old, Jewish, and a son of college-educated parents. He is a virgin. He never dated in high school and his feeling about this was reflected in an episode in his senior year in high school. The teacher in a health course asked a fellow student if he had ever dated. "I felt very, very relieved," said Ed, "that he hadn't picked on me." He added: "Whenever people talk of dates, I just leave the conversation. I felt awful not having spoken to a girl the entire freshman year" (in college).

At times he worried, Ed admitted, whether he might be a homosexual but he realized that all his fantasies were about girls. In fact he felt that physically he was adequate and even attractive to girls.

His main handicap, in his opinion, was his quietness. On the three or four dates he had during the four years of college, his mind invariably blanked out and he couldn't think of anything to say. He has never dated the same girl twice. He described a date, arranged for him, with a sister of a male friend. "I wasn't nasty to her," he explained, "or unfriendly. I just didn't say anything. When I thought I was drunk enough at a party that night I finally danced with her. When I dropped her at her dorm I said goodnight and walked away."

Interviewer: "Were you afraid she would reject you?" "I rejected myself," Ed answered. "I hadn't done anything to deserve to make advances to her or to even consider a future date. I didn't call her up for a second date because I was afraid the same exact thing would happen again. It would be difficult to be friendly without making sex advances to a girl, and I'm afraid of making advances, I'd be clumsy at it and not know what to do." He had never been to a prostitute and had never really considered it because he felt that he would "mess it up." In his junior year his roommate offered to set him up with a college girl for fifty dollars but he "chickened out at the last minute."

Ed's timidity with women coexisted with quite traditional views about feminine roles. He felt that engineering and sciences should remain masculine fields. He had not liked working one summer for a woman supervisor. "I guess I don't want to accept women in a superior position. I felt very out of place. I guess I would have preferred instructing women."

The portrait of his ideal woman confirmed his traditional outlook. She should possess three qualities: "Sympathy, in the sense of listening and trying to understand my ideas. A sense of modesty, of quiet, not pushing her ideas onto me. A willingness to give up many of the things she wants in favor of the things I want, like the place she wants to live."

Contrasting with these requirements are the traits desired in a male friend: "He has to be willing to stick to his ideas rather than agreeing all the time. He has to be willing to argue with me."

Reflecting no doubt his own experience and fears, though not his ideals, Ed checked "disagree somewhat" with the statement that "men are more aggressive than women."

Apart from his feeling of inadequacy, Ed described another barrier to forming relationships with women. He feared the loss of freedom that this would entail. He explained: "If I went out with a girl I'd have to change my behavior. When I'm alone, I can do what I want to do. With a girl I would always have to accommodate myself. When I call a girl up I may not want to take her out tomorrow or the next day. I don't want to get involved. If I do go out with a girl, I'd like to have a close relationship with her, but at the moment I'd lose too much with such a relationship; I'd lose my independence; I'd have to conform to what I thought the girl expected of me, to what is expected on dates. I'd have to go to proper restaurants, and so forth."

Ed's interview throws light also upon his problems in all his major statuses, as citizen, son, and student.

Ed explained that his timidity extended to other situations beyond dating. During a political upheaval on his campus he did not take a stand: "It was unmanly—I actually signed two contradictory petitions because of social pressure." He cited other illustrations of his lack of assertiveness. He was at first rejected by the college he now attends. He was truly happy because he felt he did not deserve and did not want to go to an Ivy League college. But his school and his parents were so elated when he was finally accepted that he refrained from telling them of his real preference to attend another college. The second incident dated back to his childhood days. He lost a fight at camp at the age of eleven and he kept this humiliating secret from his parents for a long time. When he finally told them they reprimanded him for not hitting back.

Ed admired his father and yearned for his approval. His father was the stronger of the two parents. Though dominant, his father had difficulty in expressing his feelings, apart from being sarcastic and cynical (more so with Ed's rebellious younger brother and other members of the family than with Ed). His father's main limitation was that "he had as much trouble talking to me as I had talking with him. We were never close. I could not share my problems with him." His mother's main defect was a tendency to push and nag with regard to school work, school applications, and social life.

In college Ed was performing adequately but below his aspirations. He complained during one interview that, having just spent four hours in the library, he hardly remembered the contents of the book he had been reading, and certainly had no creative or original ideas about it. He felt he wasn't "psyched up" enough to go to graduate school and might teach science in high school, instead of pursuing his original plan of working for a Ph.D.

We conclude with Ed's psychological profile drawn by the clinical psychologist on the basis of the psychological tests.

This is a constricted, repressed young man. He feels "out of things," unable to enjoy himself, preoccupied with worries and pessimistic about his future. He is doubtful about his worth, doesn't assert himself but looks for guidance from others. He prefers to avoid new situations. He is not uninterested in others. He is very concerned about their reactions to him and is always on the alert about what others want. This constant alertness about the expectations of his associates dampens his vitality and leaves him dissatisfied. He is as unhappy about his future prospects as about his current status. He is skeptical about rewards of achievement and even more unsure about his ability to do well. Despite his conscientious nature he finds himself disorganized under pressure. His failure to perform intellectually may be due to a passive anger at being required to perform but he is probably unaware of the forces that keep him from meeting requirements in areas of his own interest and choosing.

In the next case, the avoidance of women is neither so extreme nor so clearly related to idiosyncratic psychological factors. Problems of upward mobility and marginality experienced by John had consequences for his attitudes toward women.

John started dating Mary when both were juniors in high school. She remained at home and went to work as a salesperson whereas he went away to an Ivy League metropolitan college. Their families are friendly and assume that the young couple will eventually get married. Everybody is all for it, John explained, and he is the only one who is not sure and feels edgy. An incident at Mary's home is typical. He was having dinner with her family and mentioned that he liked pretty much any kind of food. "You are going to be easy to feed," Mary laughed, but he was irritated: "Oh, wait a minute," he said. Not that Mary herself pushes him into marriage.

John and Mary had sex relations only once. She thinks it is a sin and is afraid she'll get pregnant. He, on the other hand, resents her attitude. He wishes she weren't so tied to her mother: "She is twenty-one and is paying her rent."

Mary does not go out with anyone else. Neither does he, but in his case it is not for lack of desire to do so. He often has fantasies about girls in his classes and wishes he had the courage to take a girl out. "Back home," he explained, "I'd know how to act. But the city co-eds are more sophisticated and they know how to play the game." As for him: "I'd feel funny going to a night club or I might not know how to make advances or might not be able to bring myself to do it."

His experience in the urban university caused some disenchantment with Mary. "She doesn't use her mind. She says stupid and inane things. I can't talk to her about what I am reading. 'I wish I were smart,' she tells me. This makes me mad. I tell her, 'You are not stupid. All you need to do is just read this book.' But she doesn't."

John is more open with Mary than he is with anyone else but even with her he must be guarded not to let her know how much he yearns to go out with other girls. His roommates are always urging him to phone girls he meets at parties they attend together. He observed that, when he does meet a girl he likes at a party, he suddenly feels tired and goes home to sleep. He himself attributes his failure to follow up such encounters with girls 50 percent to guilt (fear of being disloyal to Mary) and 50 percent to insecurity, the fear of saying something naive or not knowing how to act.

The contrast between John's self-assured posture with his hometown girl, Mary, and his insecurity with the urban co-eds validates our emphasis on social factors but there are also psychological sources of his difficulties. The clinical psychologist summarized his test scores in the following paragraph: "This man describes himself as a he-man kind of guy. He feels fairly confident of his intellectual abilities and his independence. Closer personal relationships are more difficult for him, however. He feels awkward, inhibited, and under-confident and is seen by others as cautious, aloof, and distant. His independent spirit does not pervade his interpersonal relationships about which he feels some concern."

The foregoing cases described men for whom the prospect of initiating a relationship with any woman (or the kind they desired) was so threatening as to cause avoidance of women. A different reaction to a lack of self-confidence is described on pp. 97–98. This promiscuous man, as he himself so perceptively diagnosed, used his "completely cold" sexual affairs to assuage feelings of worthlessness and frustrated dependency. He was not as sexually potent as he would have wished to be, but neither was he as terrified of women as was Ed. His insecurity, sexual and general, was one source of his promiscuity.

The man who felt deficient in masculine strength exhibited two other reactions which occasionally resulted in tolerable adjustments. They searched, and sometimes found, a strong and supportive woman, or, quite the reverse, one still weaker than they perceived themselves to be. We shall describe these patterns and attempt to discover why some and not others succeeded in their search. One general observation pertains to both the men who searched for support and the others who looked for exceptionally docile women. The more specialized the psychic needs, or the more deviant, the larger the pool of eligible mates must be to provide the probability of a complementary choice. Conversely, if personal or situational factors limit access to eligible women, the chances of fulfilling such specialized requirements are reduced. Obviously the men who dreaded the very act of asking for a date were severely handicapped. But for the rest, a somewhat greater self-assurance, a higher rank on the scale of courtship desirability, resulted in a greater chance of success.

Among the structural features of the social environment affecting the pool of eligible dates, the ratio of males to females may be a dominant factor, either raising or lowering the bargaining power of each sex. Opportunities for relatively informal contacts with women is another factor. Even a timid youth may muster up the courage to invite a co-ed in his class for a cup of coffee, whereas a more formal dating system puts greater demands upon self-assurance in initial contacts. A large and impersonal campus may shield a timid youth from surveillance of his strategy with women or conceal his failures from his peers.

The interplay of psychological and social variables will be illustrated in the following cases of men who were (and were not) adjusted in relationships with stronger and supportive women.

Steve, whose case is presented next, felt deficient in masculine strength but if his stronger and supportive girl friend occasionally troubled him, the relationship was satisfactory enough for Steve to contemplate marriage to her "in three or four years."

THE SEARCH FOR A STRONGER AND
SUPPORTIVE MATE

Steve (a Catholic youth, age twenty, whose parents had less than twelve years of schooling) described his "ideal man" as "aggressive," "dominant," "masculine." None of these adjectives were included in his self-description. He felt that the expectation of male dominance was a great burden for men. He was clearly attracted by the strength of his high school steady, also Catholic, who had continued to be his sexual partner through college.

Steve's parents were "very strict and overprotective. Home was more like army barracks, with lots of rules." His mother was a dominating woman and the family boss. His girl friend's parents were, on the other hand, "easy-going and warm."

Steve admired his girl friend's "intelligence, efficiency, and independence". "I admired her for being more independent in high school than I was," he readily admitted. "She was always a better student. She is very lucky on exams; she can take them very well." He appreciated, also, the fact that she did not pressure him, especially about marriage. He had no intention of marrying before he completed his professional school.

As to his dissatisfactions with her, "Sometimes she is not as sensitive as I'd like her to be. When I look for a little sympathy and go to her I don't get it. Her mother is very efficient on her job but she is different at home. I can always play her off when I need sympathy—she falls all over me. Oh, no my girl doesn't mind. She knows I am putting on an act for her mother. She herself has a lot of traits both from her mother and her father—she can be very efficient and very easy-going at the same time."

His girl friend's major dissatisfaction with him, Steve said, was that he let her make too many decisions. "Once in a while she would like me to take more initiative. She might also want me to be more ambitious."

In describing the early stages of their relationship, Steve said: "Much as I disliked my mother's ways, I tended to be domineering and lay down the rules and regulations with my girl friend, the way my mother did with me. I was very possessive. But my girl helped me. She helped me recognize and admire her independence."

Steve's dissatisfactions were mild and he was on the whole successful in his search for a supportive mate. Charles, in the case that follows, also found in Sally what he searched for—an athletic, independent, and strong woman. She fulfilled some of his emotional needs but he was still dissatisfied with himself. He felt that he fell far short of his ideal of physical and moral courage, independence, and perhaps even dominance over women. He judged Sally's criticisms of him to be wholly justified because both share the same image of masculinity. The role young women play in the socialization of their mates into the adult masculine role is, again, apparent.

Charles is a twenty-one-year-old son of Catholic, college-educated parents. He is having an affair with a Catholic girl and they intend to get married "in a couple of years."

He was asked to describe his ideal woman and interrupted his narrative to exclaim: "I am really describing Sally." She has the courage and independence which he feels he lacks.

His self-portrait is unflattering. "Courageous," "forceful," "strong," "masculine" were adjectives checked for his "ideal man," but were missing from the self-description.

One of his major dissatisfactions is his continued residence with his parents and his financial dependence upon them. His father is "over-

dominant" and the stronger of the two parents. Both parents are conservative, he disagrees with them violently and their relationships are very
strained. "I kind of imagine," he admitted ruefully, "that I am not very
courageous. I should say to myself, 'if I don't get along with my parents, I
must leave home and support myself through college,' but it is not that
simple. Most of the time I try to smooth things over at home but when I do
lash out they think me ungrateful."

The conciliatory posture at home is the one he takes in all his relationships. "I don't pick fights. I would rather concede and forget it. I just wash
over it rather than really take a stand. If something is unjust, I'd rather just
sit back and bemoan it than go out and try to change it. I take the easy way.
I just copped out in several campus political crises because I was afraid to
have my skull smashed." Among his fears is the fear of solitude: "I don't
like to be alone even in the house at night. I just get uneasy."

Sally, Charles reported, felt that he was too dependent upon his family,
that he should have moved out and tried to support himself. "She wishes,"
he said, "that I would get involved in social causes, misfits, also peace and
poverty marches. She is very much into that sort of thing." At one point of
the interview he alluded to another of his problems with Sally: "When you
really want to please the woman, it's hard to always be the dominant one. I
am aware of Sally as an equal and it's a very thin line that has to be drawn."

Charles did find a strong, independent woman but she put
demands upon him that he could not quite meet. The foregoing
excerpts illustrate Sally's demand for more independence and for
political participation on his part. But the pressures he exerted were
even more complicated. She was also a feminist and tried to
convert him to her point of view. Some of the seniors appeared to
reach out for the feminist ideology out of their own sense of
dependence. But Charles came from a conservative background
and could not conceal from himself his failure to conform to his
ideal of masculine strength. "Trying to smooth things over," which
in a woman might be viewed as approved "expressive" behavior,
Charles regarded as a contemptible weakness in himself. But
neither could he quite please Sally on the score of feminist ideology. Even when he accepted the logic of the argument, his
feelings were traditional. The resulting guilt is manifested in the
words which recurred as he expressed his views on feminine roles:
"I know I shouldn't feel that way, but I do."

Charles was too committed to the ideal of masculine dominance
to be able to accept without conflict his psychic need for a strong
woman. One of the many factors that make it easier for some men

to satisfy such a psychic wish is the availability in their social milieu of the cultural alternative of a "doting" wife. One senior felt free to declare that he was looking for a doting wife who would relieve him from all the bothersome details of the daily routine and, who, by her admiration and support, would motivate and reward him for high achievement in his career. This youth never lived away from home and was very dependent upon his parents, especially his mother, for advice and praise. The picture he drew of his ideal wife was modeled upon his mother. He stopped dating one girl because he was annoyed by her need for reassurance and emotional support. Characteristically, he approved of the girl in a projective test story who played dumb on the grounds that she was trying "to build her date up."

The unabashed fashion in which this youth acknowledged his need of a doting and supportive woman contrasted with the apologetic confession of another senior: "I am sorry to admit it, but I am a leaner and I need a lot of emotional support from a woman." What for this second senior was a violation of an ideal of masculinity clearly had no such connotations for the first, equally dependent, man.

Another "leaner," this time one who had no insight into his emotional needs, was a son of Jewish college-educated parents. He entered college at the early age of fifteen.

This youth enjoyed satisfying relationships with the strong women in his family, his professional mother and his older sister. He expressed pride in being able to "score" with girls in the face of competition from older suitors. "He blusters his way to masculinity," observed the interviewer and the respondent's own view was quite similar. "I dominate a girl at first," this senior explained, describing himself as "boastful" and "obnoxious." But he soon finds such dominance unfulfilling. He was disappointed in his current girl friend because she turned out not to be strong enough and was continually coming to him with her problems.

He described his ideal mate in the idiom of feminist ideology but the clinical resume contained the following characterization: "He emphasizes personal pleasure and self gain. He takes pleasure in persuading others to follow his lead and may be inattentive to their needs. He appears to be acting out internal conflicts in an uninsightful, nonreflective way."

The problems of this youth stemmed from the stance of masculine strength which attracted women who wanted to lean on him. But whereas he "came on strong," he was too self-centered to provide the support they wanted, needing to be the recipient of attention and, perhaps, of nurturance. His feminist ideology (he wanted to marry a professional woman who would understand his problems and help him in decision making) might have been the expression of this need for supportiveness which he associated with independent women. These attitudes might have been the function of his youth or might remain permanent features of his personality.

MISTRUST OF WOMEN AS AN OBSTACLE IN THE SEARCH FOR SUPPORT

We have described some men whose psychic need for a supportive mate conflicted with their ideal of masculine dominance. In other instances similar needs were frustrated by different obstacles. The following case will describe a senior for whom a supportive mate was unattainable though such a relationship was culturally acceptable in his milieu in the guise of a doting wife. In Bob's case the yearning for a mother figure coexisted with hostility towards and mistrust of women.

Bob was a son of Jewish immigrant parents. His father, a blue-collar worker, was aloof and played a less important role in the family than did his mother. Bob was moving away from his dependence upon his mother at the cost of some depleted motivation for studying. He thought that he had worked hard in the past in order to please his mother. He would like to meet a devoted, intuitive woman who would know when he wanted to talk and when to leave him in peace.

Bob was too sure of his intellectual capacity to worry about intellectual rivalry with women. He was bright and articulate in discussion. But he was much less sure about his emotional relationships with women. He was tense even when he had to phone a new acquaintance. "I can't do anything the first time if I am not sure I'll do it well," he explained. He found the risk of failure a paralyzing fear. Although he attributed his virginity to moral principles, in another part of the interview he expressed anger at his mother for having influenced him against high school dating. He felt she had retarded his social development.

Much as Bob yearned for an early marriage he was mistrustful of women and "terribly jealous." He was "afraid of betrayal." He described himself as "a little masochistic—imagining women doing me dirt and wreaking mental vengeance upon them."

Bob expressed hostility and cynicism towards women. He resented their privileges: "If women are so hell-bent on equality why don't they pay their own way, call for a date, why are they exempted from the draft?" He was, incidentally, much less sensitive about his own ethical inconsistencies than about those of the feminists. He expected his future wife to be intellectually accomplished and stimulating. She was not to return to work until their children were in high school. As for helping her with domestic chores, he hated housework and wouldn't expect to be involved in it but, he added with some irritation, "If one is crazy about a woman you would do anything, I suppose."

Bob was one of some five seniors whose hostility towards women was undisguised. Another student summed up his image of the modern woman in these words: "The idea of 'man the king' is going out. Men feel emasculated these days. The woman is portrayed as a cool one, using sex to test a man and to make him prove himself through sex. This places a lot of pressure on men." Similar attitudes were expressed in answer to the question about the relative advantages and disadvantages of being a man (or a woman) in our society. Some men considered women to be powerful and pampered, as illustrated by the following views: "Women are used to being sought after"; "A woman is the center of attention without doing anything. She has it easy."

THE SEARCH FOR A WEAKER MATE: "A RELATIONSHIP I CAN HANDLE"

Another pattern of coping with a lack of masculine dominance was to seek out still weaker women who would not present any challenge to one's vulnerable sense of masculinity. The accounts of dating provided numerous illustrations of girls rejected because they were "too pushy" or "too aggressive," and occasionally "too bright" or "ambitious" or "not submissive enough."

The following case illustrates the more or less successful accommodation of an insecure man.

Peter, age twenty-two, is a Protestant whose parents were high school graduates. He described himself as having been plagued by self-doubt throughout his adolescence. Each time he went out with a girl in high school it was always the girl who "gave him the gate." When a high school steady broke up with him in his freshman year in college he "went into a real tailspin." He thought that he would never get a woman who really wanted to stay with him.

Fortunately, he received some help from the college counselor who lifted his great burden by reassuring him that, what he feared might have been a symptom of homosexuality (a friendship with a bisexual older man when Peter was still in high school), need not be so interpreted.

Finding a steady girl friend was only one of his problems. The other was coping with his "overpowering, perfectionist" father and his emotionally unstable mother (who had had several nervous breakdowns). His parents had, he felt, unrealistic expectations about his intellectual abilities. They conveyed to him their conviction that he would go far. He always tried hard but he feared failure. He remarked that seven years of being away from his parents in school and in college had not freed him of his dependence upon them. Asked about his current strains, he listed: "doing good work in my major" and "worry about being respected by my parents."

At the time of the interview Peter was engaged to be married to a young woman he had met in his sophomore year. He proposed marriage after several months of dating but she was not ready to make a commitment. Having experienced failure so frequently he was shaken by her indecision. In his junior year, after about a year of dating, they started having sexual relations. He was her first sexual partner, and she was his, though he concealed that fact from her for nearly a year.

Their sexual and other problems were working themselves out in a satisfactory way. Peter felt that he was "more forceful and aggressive than his fiancée." Her main defect was that she was not his intellectual equal and he missed intellectual companionship.

Peter's somewhat precipitious proposal of marriage, the pride he described in introducing an acceptable young woman as his fiancée to his parents, hint at some compulsive elements in his decision to marry, i.e., the wish to demonstrate to them and to himself that he was not the failure he feared himself to be. Marriage was a status conferring and reassuring accomplishment. He paid the price of intellectual compromise. Nevertheless, his problems were within the normal range and he was classified among the adjusted men.

Whereas Peter found in his fiancée a "relationship I can handle," another senior, similarly lacking in self-confidence and strength, failed to find such an adjustment because he refused to compromise. He continued to aim high and refused dates with girls who were not sufficiently challenging. "Why," he exclaimed, "that would be like digging up the kind of girls I knew in high school." His high expectations precluded the compromise that solved Peter's dilemma.

The men described above felt deficient in masculine strength, though some found more or less satisfactory ways of coping with this problem.

Among the self-confident men some were securely dominant over their satisfied female friends, and a few couples came close to an equalitarian pattern. Popular discussions of the "battle of the sexes" frequently assume that a struggle for dominance is unavoidable. Since equalitarian patterns may be presumed to become increasingly frequent, the next case history will portray such a relationship.

A PORTRAIT OF AN EQUALITARIAN COUPLE

Al and Timmy met when they were seniors in high school. They went to different colleges but, as college freshmen, were already sufficiently involved with one another to write daily, speak on the telephone twice a week, and spend vacations together. They began having sex relations during their sophomore year and got married in the summer following their junior year.

Timmy's application to the coeducational college which Al attended was rejected and Al transferred to an urban college in order to reside with his wife.

Al was twenty-one-years-old and Jewish, as was his wife. His foreign-born father had not finished college, his mother was an elementary school teacher. Al was an open and articulate respondent, who found it difficult to think of any costs involved in his early marriage, instead citing many advantages.

The equalitarian nature of this marriage is reflected in Al's liberal ideology concerning sex roles as well as his actual relationship with his wife, i.e., acceptance of her intellectual gifts, the sharing of domestic tasks, and his willingness to select a graduate school that suited her interests as well as his.

Al gave "liberal" answers to the standard questions on women's roles and masculine-feminine personality traits. His own experience did not confirm the familiar stereotypes: his father, for example, was more sympathetic than his mother and he himself felt more sympathetic than a lot of women he knew. As to emotionality, he denied the current notion that crying was unmanly. His wife saw tears in his eyes during a sad movie and she thought it was very nice that he could be so moved. In high school, after a fight with his parents he would close the door to his room and *make* himself cry: "It was a fantastic release." Now that he had Timmy to talk to, he had cried only a couple of times since his marriage. On the other hand, he considered himself more aggressive than Timmy.

Al had a high academic record which he maintained by dint of hard work. His wife's influence was helping him to overcome his excessive drive to achieve: "It was sort of unhealthy to be so upset if you get a B+. I used to think that the only thing I was allowed to do in life was to spend the day reading in the library. Timmy gave me confidence in myself. Today I just started reading for a final exam that is four days off. In the past I'd get a nervous breakdown if I had waited so long."

As to intellectual rivalry, they did compete during the first year of their dating. "I called her 'Lady Boss' and she hated it. But it seemed to me that she wasn't happy unless she won, mostly discussions, but also ping pong and everything. I tend to be argumentative and conduct arguments like a debate, i.e. 'it is perfectly obvious . . .' "

But these sparring matches were over. "Our interests are so different," he explained. "She is unbelievably apolitical, but interested enough to ask me questions. I don't enjoy English courses. I think she is brighter, able to grasp things more easily, especially in her fields of literature and art; she is keener about people. I remember more but she sees deeper into what she does observe." Al said that in high school his interests were languages and history and the girls were much brighter than the boys. Among his closest friends-confidants in high school was a girl. He was always opposed to masculine-feminine stereotypes.

He and his wife took only one course together: "It was fun studying together. We saw different things and we helped each other. Maybe we don't compete," he summed up, "because grades and achievement no longer matter to us as much as many other things." Al was the senior described on p. 53 whose disappointment over a B in a course was eased when, upon his return home, he found his wife elated by an A she received on a test. "Her being thrilled," he said, "made it up for me."

All housework was shared. There is no domestic task that he considers unmanly, whether it be cleaning the bathroom or doing the dishes.

Al felt quite confident about the future: "Everything I really wanted and tried for, I achieved. I think I can be a successful lawyer. It's something I really want, not something I chose because I couldn't think of anything else."

Al and Timmy intended to apply to several graduate schools and he was prepared to sacrifice his first, second, or even third choice in order to work out the best compromise for the two of them.

Their sexual adjustment was satisfactory: "She is as close to perfect as anyone could be." In response to some projective tests, Al said that there were no great differences in their sexual drives, that they did not have sex if she was not in the mood, and that it gave him tremendous pleasure to please her.

One unresolved problem had to do with his need to withdraw in periods of depression, generally brought about by unresolved conflicts with his parents.

"Timmy doesn't realize," he explained, "that I need a lot of time to be completely by myself, sometimes to take a walk by myself. Her attitude is 'I am your wife. I can help you.' Now that I am less tense and anxious about school, things have improved."

Al's respect for his wife's ability and delight in her academic success (even when it surpassed his own), his liberal ideology concerning woman's roles, his matter-of-fact sharing of housework, and willingness to select a graduate school in the light of her interests as well as his own—all these are elements of an egalitarian relationship. But Timmy's own attitude towards her future and certain features of her personality do not put Al's egalitarianism to its most severe test.

Timmy, Al felt, was not an ambitious career woman. She was very anxious to have children and looked forward to motherhood. He, himself, was equally eager to participate as fully in "the care of their young children as his work will permit." "Timmy is resourceful and will not sit around doing nothing," he said. "But if she does feel trapped by domesticity, she will always have her occupation to fall back upon. We'll hire a housekeeper. For all I know she may want a career of her own. If she does, we'll make an adjustment, just as I am prepared to compromise in the matter of graduate schools." Al read about some "house-husbands" in Sweden: "My initial reaction was 'great!' Not that I would want to sacrifice my career. That is the reason I could not ask a girl who enjoyed her work to give it up just because she is a woman. I feel confident that we could work it out."

As Al was describing his wife's keen and quick perceptions, the interviewer asked: "What are your special strengths?" "I am less easily thrown," he answered. "Not so many things look as great traumas to me. I can cope with situations."

But if he did draw upon this feature of their relationship for self-esteem he was apparently confident enough about his capacity for coping not to need her dependence. In fact, among the changes he would have liked to make in her he listed first, "not to get flustered so easily. I have to spend all my energy calming her instead of thinking about the solution of the problem."[4]

Apart from this equalitarian couple, we have included the foregoing cases to convey to the reader in richer and more vivid detail than a mere summary statement could accomplish, the experiences of the severely and moderately troubled youths. Moreover, by comparing troubled and adjusted cases we attempted to discern factors, social and psychological, that helped some men to assuage their feelings of inadequacy or to escape such feelings completely.

To shed light upon factors associated with strain we shall examine the seniors' religious affiliations, their ideologies as revealed by the Adjective Check Lists, and their scores on psychological tests. The most conclusive difference between the troubled and the adjusted men lies in their scores on psychological tests. The relation between ideologies and strain is too complex to be ascertained within the limits of our sample, but our data suggest some hypotheses.

RELIGIOUS AFFILIATION AND PARENT-CHILD RELATIONS AS FACTORS IN STRAIN

The Protestant and the Jewish students had nearly identical proportions of men who were troubled by their lack of dominance in relation to women: 39 percent of the former and 40 percent of the latter. This similarity between Protestants and Jews was equally true of the sons of college- and noncollege-educated fathers. The proportion of troubled Catholics was higher, 51 percent of all Catholics and this higher proportion characterized both educational categories.

We sought the explanation of the religious differentials in the quality of parental relationships. In all religious groups, anxiety about power vis-à-vis women was associated with unhappy relationships with both parents. Sixty-five percent of the troubled

4. Other features of this case are discussed on p. 104.

seniors had unsatisfactory ties with their fathers, as compared to only 43 percent in the total sample. The corresponding figures for maternal relationships were 48 percent for the troubled men as against only 26 percent for the sample as a whole. The unsatisfactory relationship with the first, crucially important woman in the life of the male might have contributed to his difficulties in later contacts with women. But the quality of paternal relationships proved equally significant in this particular strain.

Turning to the Catholic students we find (see Chapter 7, p. 198) the highest proportion of poor maternal ties of all three religious groups. The combination of a cold, punitive, and demanding mother was most prevalent among the Catholics. Of the ten troubled Catholics, only one had positive ties with his mother and six, at the other extreme, were highly dissatisfied sons. In the total sample of Catholics, the proportions of satisfied and highly dissatisfied sons were respectively, 22 percent and 44 percent. The paternal relationships of the Catholics did not differ from those of the two other religious groups.

We conclude that the relatively high proportion of poor mother-son relationships among the Catholic seniors might have been a factor in their higher incidence of anxiety over power in relation to women.

IDEAL NORMS AND COGNITIVE BELIEFS AS FACTORS IN STRAIN

The interplay between expressed norms of masculinity and actual experience is no doubt complex and circular. Conceivably, equalitarian values may relieve a man from the necessity of maintaining an ascendant stance, whereas traditional expectations may lead to strain.

But if the ideal of masculinity, by forming one's expectations, may exacerbate or relieve strain, the reverse causation is also plausible: experience may predispose a person to select some ideals and reject others. Our sample was not large enough to disentangle these complex relationships because the seniors as a group, on the basis of the Adjective Check List, showed pretty much the same ideals of masculinity.

The Adjective Check List for "my ideal man" served as an index of values. We assumed that the adjectives "aggressive," "dominant," "assertive," "strong," "courageous," and "masculine," as attributes of the "ideal man," expressed traditional values. The consensus with regard to these values was so high in the sample as a whole that values did not differentiate between the troubled and the adjusted men. Over 75 percent of all the seniors checked "strong," "courageous," and "masculine"; 68 percent checked "assertive"; and 59 percent "aggressive." The adjective "dominant" received the lowest ranking of only 43 percent. The majority of both the troubled and the adjusted men subscribed to much the same ideal of masculinity.

Case analyses, however, did indicate that the men involved in the most egalitarian relationships were relatively strong and self-confident. Within the limits of our small sample, egalitarianism appealed more to men who had nothing to lose by it than to those who needed it the more. All the same, one wonders whether these relatively strong and self-confident men were, at their stage of life, subjected to stringent enough tests of their egalitarian values and practices. These were also ambitious men and one can imagine them a decade later, caught in the the imperatives of occupational advancement and unable or unwilling to sacrifice economic or honorific rewards for the sake of their wives' careers.

However, if a few confident men were the exponents of egalitarianism, it is also true that some dependent men were attracted to supportive women under the guise of a doting wife when their milieu sanctioned a choice of nurturant and supportive mother-figure.

Equally complex is the relationship between experience and cognitive beliefs. In the group as a whole the troubled men were somewhat less likely to agree that "men are more aggressive than women."[5] Their reason was clear in at least a few extreme cases. Three men were sons of dominant mothers and weak fathers. These men were all too aware of their own lack of aggression and of the weakness of their fathers. Another youth acknowledged his own passivity and expressed scepticism about "global generalizations" concerning sex stereotypes.

But personal experience was not always congruent with beliefs

5. Eighty percent of the thirty-one adjusted men but only 59 percent of twenty-four troubled men endorsed the view that the men are the more aggressive sex.

concerning psychological sex differences. A few self-assured men, despite their own experience of ascendancy, opposed, as a matter of principle, all stereotyping of masculine and feminine personalities. All of these were sons of better-educated fathers. At the other end, some weak men endorsed the view that men are the more aggressive sex. Our data suggest the hypothesis that the sons of the less-educated fathers were more likely to cling to the traditional belief even when it ran contrary to their own experience.[6] If the explanation lies in the greater traditionalism of the less-educated families, it is an attitude that does not extend to all stereotyping of sex differences. The tendency to stereotype women negatively was similar in the two educational categories. The sons of less-educated fathers, for instance, were no more inclined than the sons of better-educated fathers to endorse the view that "It probably goes against the basic needs of men and women to place women in a position of authority over men."

Experience and beliefs concerning sex differences are not congruent within our sample. Some weak men endorsed the view that men are superior to women in aggressiveness. Moreover, a few secure men refused to subscribe to any stereotypes of sex differences in personality. The evidence is more adequate as we turn to psychological tests.

PSYCHOLOGICAL TESTS OF THE TROUBLED AND THE ADJUSTED MEN

Men who felt deficient in masculine power were compared with the adjusted men on thirteen psychological traits of the Gough Adjective Check List for "my real self." (See Table 5.1.)

The troubled men had lower scores than the adjusted group for Self-Confidence, Dominance, Heterosexuality, Aggression, Autonomy, Affiliation, Personal Adjustment, and Intraception (definition: "to engage in attempts to understand one's own behavior or the behavior of others"). On the other hand, and not unexpectedly, the troubled group scored higher than the adjusted men on Coun-

---

6. Of sixteen troubled sons of educated fathers, only eight thought that men were the aggressive sex. Of eight troubled sons of less-educated fathers, six believed in the superior aggressiveness of males.

seling Readiness, Self-Abasement, Succorance ("the need to solicit sympathy, affection . . . from others"), and Self-Control.

Table 5.1. Men Who Felt Lacking in Masculine Power and Adjusted Men (ACL for "My Real Self")

Percentage of scores falling at standard mean score and above (and below the mean) on specified traits

	Troubled Men (N = 22)		Adjusted Men (N = 34)	
	MEAN OR HIGHER	BELOW MEAN	MEAN OR HIGHER	BELOW MEAN
Self-Confidence	13.6	86.4	73.5	26.5
Dominance	18.2	81.8	76.4	23.6
Heterosexuality	13.6	86.4	67.6	32.4
Achievement	27.3	72.7	73.5	26.5
Aggression	40.9	59.1	73.5	26.5
Autonomy	45.5	54.5	67.6	32.4
Affiliation	22.7	77.3	44.1	55.9
Personal Adjustment	27.3	72.7	47.1	52.9
Intraception	63.6	37.4	82.4	17.6
Counseling Readiness	72.7	27.3	26.5	73.5
Self-Abasement	72.7	27.3	32.4	67.6
Succorance	50.0	50.0	29.4	70.6
Self-Control	50.0	50.0	32.4	67.6

The California Psychological Inventory, on the whole, does not present as strong a contrast between the troubled and the adjusted men as does the Adjective Check List. (See Table 5.2.) Nonetheless, the differences are in the same direction with regard to Dominance, Achievement via Conformity, Well-Being, Intellectual Efficiency, Self-Acceptance, Psychological-Mindedness ("degree to which the individual is interested in, and responsive to, the inner needs and motives of others"), and Socialization. The scores of the troubled men are relatively low on all of the above traits. However, there is hardly any difference between the two groups on Achievement via Independence and Femininity. The single inconsistent finding is the relatively high score of the troubled men on Achievement via Independence which aims "to identify those factors of interest and motivation which facilitate achievement in any setting where autonomy and independence are positive behaviors."

The psychological profiles of the troubled men are characterized by a lack of self-confidence. Granted that the low self-image may be in part the result of the failure to live up to the ideal of masculinity, it surely tended to create the problem in the first place. One telling finding suggests that the problems of the troubled men antedated their heterosexual relationships. Their relatively unfavorable parental histories suggest that their psychological traits may have been rooted in childhood experiences. Out of twenty-five troubled seniors 48 percent had unsatisfactory relationships with their mothers as compared with only 26 percent in the sample as a whole. The percentage of unsatisfactory relationships with their fathers was 65 percent for the troubled and 43 percent for the total sample.

If the psychological tests validly depict the troubled men as lacking in ascendancy traits, must we attribute their difficulties solely to personality factors? The very fact that nearly 50 percent of the sample experienced these particular strains points to some social determinants. The concluding section will examine the nature of the social challenges which so large a proportion of the seniors felt unable to meet.

Table 5.2. Men Who Felt Lacking in Masculine Power and Adjusted Men (CPI)

Percentage of scores falling at standard mean score and above (and below the mean) on specified traits

	Troubled Men N = 23		Adjusted Men N = 34	
	MEAN AND ABOVE	BELOW MEAN	MEAN AND ABOVE	BELOW MEAN
Dominance	47.8	52.2	85.9	13.1
Achievement via Conformity	34.8	65.2	61.8	38.2
Well-Being	17.4	82.6	44.1	55.9
Intellectual Efficiency	56.5	43.5	76.5	23.5
Self-Acceptance	73.9	26.1	91.2	8.8
Psychological-Mindedness	78.3	21.7	88.2	11.8
Socialization	34.8	65.2	41.2	58.8
Achievement via Independence	95.7	4.3	91.2	8.8
Femininity	69.6	30.4	70.6	29.4

CONCLUSION

It would be a mistake to assume that the strain examined in this chapter is nothing but the frustration of the near-universal desire of human beings for more power in interpersonal relationships. The troubled men not only felt dissatisfied but indicated that they violated their own (or their partner's) normative expectations.

The fact is that, despite some changes, the traditional ideal of masculinity was still the yardstick against which the seniors measured themselves. As was pointed out in Chapter 1, some machismo elements of masculinity were questioned. Moreover, the male ideal of masculinity now included some qualities such as patience, sensitivity, and artistic appreciation, hitherto defined as "feminine." The latter, however, had not so much replaced as augmented the familiar manly profile. As judged by the seniors' responses on the Gough Adjective Check List for "my ideal man," the latter was still "assertive," "strong," "courageous," "aggressive," and "masculine."

But when we turn from the "ideal man" to the self-description on the Gough Adjective Check List, it is clear that the self-concept falls short of the ideal. Of the traits attributed to the "ideal man," but most often missing from self-description, 40 percent fall into the cluster of the six manly traits listed above.

If we review the advantages males still enjoy in our society as described in the introductory pages of this chapter, it may appear surprising that nearly 50 percent of the seniors should feel inadequate vis-à-vis women friends. We have noted, for example, that boys are still socialized more strongly than are girls for independence and assertiveness and that the man's occupational aspirations take priority over those of his mate's. The prerogative of initiating contacts, though it exposes men to the risk of rejection, nevertheless implies and carries a degree of power. Again, the self-esteem of young women is probably still more dependent on their popularity with men than the reverse. Women's bargaining power declines more precipitously with age than is the case with men.

Given these and other masculine advantages, we might have expected a deviant minority but not nearly half the men to feel anxious about their inability to play the masculine role. But although the foregoing inventory of male advantages is no doubt accurate, this story has another side.

The men gave abundant illustrations of perceived inadequacies in intellectual and emotional relationships with women. After all, these women were generally also college students, if anything, more rigorously selected in terms of their high school performance (*Princeton Alumni Weekly*, 1971) and of nearly the same age. The trend towards earlier first marriages has been accompanied by smaller differences between the ages of the first married husbands and wives and the same presumably obtains for the courting couples. For example, in 1920 the husband's median age at first marriage was 3.4 years higher than that of the wife's. In 1971, the husband was, on the average, only 2.2 years older than his wife (Robert K. Kelley, 1974: 291). The narrowing of the age difference weakens the advantage of superior experience that the older man previously possessed. The trend towards earlier cross-sex interaction has increased the dependence of the young man on the emotional support of his female friend as against the male clique. Our study of self-disclosure revealed that in all areas especially the most sensitive, the closest female friend was the preferred confidante over closest male friends, siblings of either sex, or parents. The ability to grant or withhhold this expressive function gives some advantage to the female. Moreover, the increase in premarital sexual experience of female undergraduates creates stress because it may challenge the still dominant expectation that the male be the more sexually experienced partner (Kaatz and Davis, 1970, and Bell and Chaskes, 1970). Finally, the Women's Liberation Movement leads an increasing number of college women to challenge traditional male privileges, which are no longer ceded as a matter of course but must be contested and won by personal strength.

These challenges confront the male at a vulnerable stage of his life. He is still economically dependent on his family. Neither his role as student, nor as part-time worker can bolster his sense of manhood in a culture that identifies it so largely with economic independence and occupational success. Superior physical strength is not an effective resource in a milieu that censures its use with women. In time these men may in fact acquire superior power and status since present family life generally restricts the access of married women to independent sources of accomplishment, status, and economic power. These socially rooted advantages and privileges, later in life, will probably give many of these men the desired edge. But, for a large proportion of these college-aged men the ideal of masculine leadership was not yet attainable. The consequent sense of inadequacy not only created problems in relationships with women but had deleterious effects on other social relationships and on the seniors' capacity to study.

We have traced some power problems of the male college senior in the perspective of time. But structural features of various campuses make it more or less difficult for men to live up to traditional ideals or make the failure to do so more or less traumatic. The latter depends on the visibility of role performance to "significant others," or on the availability of cultural alternatives, i.e., other esteemed roles for those not successful in heterosexual relationships. Interviewed students who transferred from other colleges suggested several other structural factors (see p. 138) for illustrations) intensifying or muting the strain in question.

The final chapter of this book will consider some implications of our findings for public policy. We shall then defend the view that the alleviation of the strains here discussed does not lie in returning to the male his former advantages, but in a redefinition of the concept of masculinity in the direction of greater egalitarianism in interaction with women. Thoroughness was not the only motive that prompted the author to conclude the case studies in this chapter with the portrait of an equalitarian couple.

6

INTIMACY AND ISOLATION: A Study of Self-Disclosure[1]

The terms "instrumental" and "expressive" have become familiar since Parsons and Bales (1955) formulated the idea that small groups, in general, and families, in particular, are differentiated along "an instrumental expressive axis." Typically, instrumental roles, involving the achievement of tasks, are performed by men and emotionally supportive roles, by women. Since 1955, the universality of such sex-linked differentiation of roles has been questioned. Even more significant for our purposes is a shift in evaluation of these patterns. Parsons and Bales appeared to consider this role differentiation functional for the development of personality and for the social system. Current writings differ sharply. The "inexpressive male," "trained incapacity to share," the "inaccessible man"—these phrases, culled from the literature of the 1960s, convey a critical stance toward the lack of emotional expressiveness in men. The critics allege that the traditional ideal of masculinity is at the root of the problem. Men are admonished to

1. The author is indebted to the *Journal of Marriage and the Family* for permission to reprint sections of "Patterns of Self-Disclosure of Male Undergraduates" (Komarovsky, 1974).

be strong, tough, unemotional, competitive, and unsentimental. Conversely, they must avoid, at the risk of appearing "feminine," any expression of either weakness, hurt, dependence, or the softer qualities of gentleness and tenderness.

The need to maintain a "manly" facade, the fear of acknowledging "feminine" traits—all generate in the male a constant vigilance against spontaneous expression of feelings. As one senior put it, "I very seldom tell anyone what really hurts my feelings." His reserve extends to his parents: "I want my father to think of me as a responsible person; I want my mother to think of me as a man." Such guardedness adds stress to the ever-present external sources of tension (Jourard, 1964). Jourard (1964) argues that being manly requires men to wear a kind of neuromuscular armor against emotional expressiveness. He goes so far as to consider that the chronic stress thus generated is a possible factor in the relatively shorter life-span of men as compared with women. But the deleterious effects of such self-control do not end with stress. A man who does not reveal himself to others is not likely to receive their confidences. It is precisely in the course of such interaction, however, that a person learns to recognize his own motivations, to label emotions, and to become sensitive to the inner world of his associates. Without an experience of psychological intimacy a person becomes deficient in self-awareness and empathy (Jourard, 1971; Balswick and Peek, 1971). Still another recent writer (Marc Fasteau in Joseph H. Pleck and Jack Sawyer, 1974: 21) alleges that men are threatened by psychological probings of feelings. What passes for confiding in their relationships with women is nothing but their demand for uncritical reassurance.

A study of blue-collar marriage (Komarovsky, 1964) depicted the blue-collar husband as the "inexpressive man" par excellence. His lack of psychological awareness and his low interpersonal competence impaired his ability to cope with marital conflicts, or to receive and give emotional support in marriage.

The seniors of the current study differ from the blue-collar husbands in class, education, age, and generation. We studied their self-disclosure in relationships with various role partners in order to explore the social variables affecting the degree of psychological intimacy. The role partners included the senior's mother, father, closest brother and sister, and closest female and male friends. The selection of role partners enabled us to study generational, kinship, and sex factors in self-disclosure. The data thus bear on a variety of theoretical concerns: the generation gap, the relative importance of the family as against the peer group, and male "bonding" as contrasted with ties to the opposite sex.

This study of self-disclosure reveals only one side of what is generally meant by emotional intimacy. It docs not inform us directly of the receptivity of our respondents, that is, their ability to receive attentively the confidences of others.[2]

METHOD

The questionnaire on self-disclosure was adopted with minor modifications from the instrument constructed by Sidney M. Jourard and Paul Lasakow (1958).[3] It included fifty-six items, grouped under five major areas or topics: Work or Study, Money, Personality, Body (ten questions each), and Attitudes (sixteen questions). Respondents were asked to rate, using a scale from 0 to 3, the extent to which they had been open on each of the fifty-six aspects of self and to place an X, if they had presented a false picture of themselves to a given person on a given topic. Each respondent's disclosure score was the sum of the numbers he assigned to himself.

Illustrative of the questions included under Personality are the following: "The aspects of my personality that I dislike, worry about, that I regard as a handicap to me"; "The kind of things that make me feel especially proud of myself, elated, full of self-esteem or self-respect"; "What it takes to get me feeling real depressed and blue"; "What it takes to hurt my feelings deeply"; "My problems, if any, about getting favorable attention from the opposite sex"; "The facts of my present sex life—including knowledge of how I get sexual satisfaction; with whom I have relations, if anybody." The questions included under Body referred to the respondent's attitude towards his own body.

The self-disclosure questionnaire was filled out between the first and the second interviews. This gave the interviewer an opportu-

---

2. Jourard (1971) cites some evidence of the reciprocal nature of such communication.

3. The author is indebted to Dr. Jourard for the permission to use this questionnaire.

nity to discuss with the respondent his motivation for both disclosure and reserve in relation to certain topics and target persons. The qualitative material was thus obtained in the course of the interview, whereas Tables 6.1 and 6.2 were based on the self-disclosure questionnaire.

AN OVERVIEW OF SELF-DISCLOSURE
TO SIX ROLE PARTNERS

An overview of mean disclosure scores to six role partners for the sample as a whole is presented in Tables 6.1 and 6.2. The closest female friend emerged as the primary confidante in all areas but Money. Most of the seniors were economically dependent upon their parents, hence the latter were understandably the recipients of the fullest information about financial matters. The sums of the mean disclosure scores in all five areas for each of the six partners were, in order of magnitude: female friend (97.8), male friend (90.2), mother (74.1), father (63.7), brother (61.3), and sister (53.6) (see Table 6.1). Were it not for considerable communication with the fathers on the subject of Money, of the six target persons, father and sister would emerge as recipients of least information.

The high disclosure to the female friend was manifested especially in the areas of Personality and Body, which were shown to be the most guarded aspects of self.[4] To the extent, then, to which these young men were open about themselves, they experienced this intimacy most deeply not with their male buddies, siblings, or parents, but with their women friends. In this sensitive area of Personality the mean rates of disclosure in their order of magnitude were: female friend (17.5), male friend (15.0), closest brother (8.8), mother (8.6), closest sister (8.0), and, lastly, father (7.6.).

4. Within the area of Personality, strengths (e.g., "The kinds of things that make me feel especially proud of myself . . .") are shared, on the average, somewhat more fully with all role partners than weaknesses (e.g., "What it takes to get me feeling real depressed . . ." or "What hurts my feelings deeply . . .").

A low disclosure score for a particular topic may reflect its unimportance for the individual rather than its sensitive nature. But it is unlikely that the low disclosure of the items grouped under Personality (in comparison with Attitudes, Work, or Money) can be explained by lack of concern. These are more likely to be the private, guarded aspects of self.

Table 6.1. Mean Disclosure Scores to Six Role Partners in Total Sample

Area	Maximum possible score	Mother (N = 61)	Father (N = 58)	Closest brother (N = 39)	Closest sister (N = 44)	Closest male friend (N = 61)	Closest female friend (N = 60)
Attitudes	(48)	26.7	20.2	21.4	20.4	33.5	34.2
Work or Study	(30)	14.7	13.5	12.1	10.7	19.4	20.6
Money	(30)	14.8	14.3	10.2	7.5	12.4	13.3
Personality	(30)	8.6	7.6	8.8	8.0	15.0	17.5
Body	(30)	9.3	8.1	8.8	7.0	9.9	12.2
Total disclosure in all six areas per respondent		74.1	63.7	61.3	53.6	90.2	97.8

Table 6.2.   Mean Disclosure Scores to Six Role Partners
on Some Selected Topics for Total Sample
(Maximum Possible Score Is 3)

Topic	Mother	Father	Brother	Sister	Male friend	Female friend
Work						
"My shortcomings and handicaps"	1.26	1.08	.88	.84	1.85	2.10
"My strong points"	1.33	1.24	1.05	.94	1.69	1.90
Personality						
"Facts of my present sex life"						
"Attractiveness to opposite sex"	.51	.47	.58	.66	1.46	1.57
"What it takes to get me depressed, worried or hurt"	.79	.77	.80	.73	1.45	1.73
"The kind of things that make me especially proud of myself, elated, full of self-esteem"	1.33	1.18	1.18	1.00	1.56	1.82

The mean disclosure scores for Body were: female friend (12.2), male friend (9.9), mother (9.3), brother (8.8), father (8.1), and sister (7.0).

There is another way to convey the importance of the female as a confidante. In the sensitive area of Personality, twenty-seven of the sixty-two men in the sample, indicated that their closest confidante was a woman friend and for only seventeen men was the closest friend a male. Of the latter seventeen men, twelve were virgins. Interviews with virgins showed that most of them longed for a close relationship with a woman. Twelve men in the sample confided equally in a male and female friend (and more fully than to parents). Only the six remaining cases chose parents as primary confidants in the area of Personality. (Siblings were excluded from this comparison.)

THE FEMALE FRIEND AS THE PREFERRED
CONFIDANTE

Explaining the difficulty of sharing confidences with a man, a young wife in a study of working-class marriages said: "Men are different, they don't feel the same as us. That's the reason men are friends with men and women have women friends" (Komarovsky, 1967: 114). Male college seniors would hardly be expected to endorse, in word or deed, such an extreme view of psychic alienation between the sexes. We were not prepared, however, for the reverse finding, i.e., the discovery that the female friend was the closest confidante in all areas with the exception of Money. Our findings were all the more surprising since an earlier study of male undergraduates (Jourard and Lasakow, 1958) showed the male friend to be the target of their fullest disclosure.

We can approach the relative advantages of female versus male confidants by first noting some universal dilemmas in self-disclosure. On the one hand, the desire to escape loneliness, to find support, reassurance, appreciation, perhaps absolution—all generate the need to share feelings and thoughts with others. Pitted against these advantages are the risks of sharing, e.g., possible criticism, ridicule, loss of power, and the like.

Such universal dilemmas are shaped distinctively by male and female role definitions.

Women presented their characteristic impediments to free communication. Clearly, when men were occasionally unfaithful to their steady mates, they played a game that required concealment and deception. Others, unwilling to commit themselves to marrying their mates, had to be on guard when conversation turned to future plans.

The need to maintain the pose of masculine strength and, conversely, the fear of sliding back into a childish "little boy–mother" relationship, created another barrier to free disclosure to women. In the case to be cited next, these hindrances loomed so large that, contrary to the general rule, this senior channeled his fullest disclosure to his male, rather than female, friend. The vividness of the following illustration should not obsure the fact that this case was exceptional.

This senior, who concealed from his girl friend and sexual partner that he was in psychotherapy, found himself in a double bind. Soon after they met, the young woman told him that she was in therapy.

"I could not tell her," the youth said, "that I too was in therapy. That would show her how unsure and confused I was. A girl wants a strong man. I would be lowering my image in her eyes." But this concealment was a source of worry and guilt. He had been able to keep his secret for the first three months of their affair but felt that sooner or later she would discover the truth. Moreover, he passionately upheld the new values of authenticity, openness, and reciprocity in the male-female relationships, all of which, he felt, he violated by his concealment.

This man's attitude towards his closest male friend reveals even more clearly his sex-linked conception of friendship.

"My best male friend," this senior admitted to the interviewer, "knows that I am in therapy. Of course, I don't want to appear weak in front of him either; we are competing but still we confide in each other. Since we both occasionally admit weaknesses, this balances things out between us, neither feels permanently lowered."

A similar exchange of confidences with his girl friend, he explained, would not be equally acceptable because a woman is expected to ask for reassurance and a man is expected to be a "pillar of strength." Thus, unlike his male friend's confidences, his girl friend's admittance of weakness did not leave him free to reciprocate.

The senior just described had a close male friend and, were it not for his sense of guilt about his secret, would have been satisfied with his friendships. But several men were torn between their conception of masculine pride and their unfulfilled need for sharing worries. A plea for solace or reassurance, permissible for little boys and women of all ages, was not, in their view, appropriate for a grown man. To succumb to the temptation of confiding one's worries was to regress to a childish role, as illustrated in the following excerpt from an interview:

"I shall never forget," said one senior, "the mistake of telling one of my past girl friends about some of my problems. She became concerned and started offering all kinds of advice. From then on, she always treated me like a little boy, waiting for me to admit some problem and to seek her advice. Our whole relationship changed and I felt terrible that I had forced her into the role of an advice giver."

The final illustration is furnished by a senior whose closest female friend had "worried about her inhibitions, her timidity in talking in class, in standing up to her mother and to people in general."

"I could have made her feel better," said the young man: "If I'd told her that I had trouble speaking in class because I was very self-conscious. But instead of telling her (which would have helped me too), I didn't say anything. Trivial as it was, I couldn't bring myself to say that I, at twenty-one, a man who hoped to be a great writer, couldn't raise my hand in class."

This student characterized his relationship with his mate in the following way:

"I play the reassuring, protective father. She is my faithful, dependent child. Her faith and dependency are a form of reassurance and support for me. But there are days when I would like to come to her, as she comes to me, as a child, to tell her that I was hurt when my roommate didn't ask if I'd made Phi Bet (when he knew I'd heard) or that I didn't think my seminar professor liked me anymore—but I could never bring myself to talk about such sentimental drivel even though I wanted to."

Having described the psychic obstacles to free sharing of certain experiences with his closest woman friend, this senior nevertheless concluded that, on balance, his girl friend was his closest confidante. "The emotional outlet she provides could not be replaced by any friendship with a guy," he remarked. As he illustrated the unique rewards of this relationship, he stressed, not the sharing of weaknesses, but of aspirations. (In the total sample, the female received more information than the male friend about not only the strengths but also the weaknesses of the respondents.)

"I tell her," he explained, "that I want to be a great writer and go on about style, structure, imagery like a pompous ass. She listens and encourages me and accepts as a matter of fact that I'll be successful. She always builds me up. With my male friends, I'd feel silly and conceited to go on the way I do with her."

This senior, notwithstanding the fact that his ideal of masculinity stood in the way of disclosing dependency, need, or pain to his female friend, still found it easier to let his guard down with her than with male friends. In this he typified the majority of the seniors. The drawbacks of women as confidantes were, apparently, offset by the even more serious drawbacks of men as well as by certain advantages women confidantes offered.

The main disadvantage of a male friend, as confidant, was his threat as a competitor. "A guy means competition," one senior explained. "I have competed with guys in sports and for girls. Once you let your guard down, the guy can hurt you and take advantage of you. Your girl has your interest at heart." "Even your best [male] friend," remarked one senior wryly, "gets a certain amount of comfort out of your difficulty. A girl friend is readier to identify with your interests and to build you up."

The priority of the female over the male confidant was explained by a number of other factors. Those who had steady girl friends spent much of their leisure with them. In the words of one senior: "I see her a lot more than anyone else. Once I tell her something and get it out of my system, I have no particular need to talk to the guy." But if accessibility and high rate of interaction were the sole explanation, male roommates would have been equally important as confidants. Several men explained that sexual intimacy contributed to psychological closeness. Moreover, we cannot rule out the likelihood that women, socialized to perform expressive functions, make better listeners than men. The average disclosure scores to female friends were higher in four areas, but especially so in the sensitive areas of Personality and Body. The difficulty that males experience in sharing feelings (Jack O. Balswick and Charles W. Peek, 1971) may, incidentally, give the female friend a certain power in the relationship. For example, one not untypical senior admitted his inability to confide: "My mother says, 'talking to you is like talking to a stone wall.' " He is most open about himself with his girl friend. She, on the other hand, confides in several persons. She wields a certain advantage over him because, at least in respect to confiding, he needs her more than she needs him.

This is not to deny that a few seniors have rejected the traditional view that an admission of weakness was unmanly. As one student indignantly explained: "I don't believe that masculinity means being made of granite." Our data did not permit a study of the relative consistency between the newer ideal of masculinity and actual emotional expressiveness of the respondents.

The higher disclosure to the female than to a male friend repeats the typical pattern of disclosure within the family, where the mother was the recipient of more information than the father. This was explicit in the comment of a senior who admitted he was a leaner. Explaining his desire for an early marriage, he said: "I like to have someone to tell my problems to and I don't want to wind up telephoning my mother." Possibly as a consequence of the typically distant relationship with one's father (see p. 190) these seniors have developed a preference for a female confidante. Some support for this hypothesis comes from the disclosure patterns of seniors whose relationships with their mother were "unsatisfactory." Though even they exhibited a somewhat higher disclosure to a female than to a male friend, the difference in favor of the female was narrower than for the sample as a whole. The disclosure scores on Personality of the seniors with unsatisfactory relationships with their mothers, were 16.3 and 17.6 to male and female, respectively. For the sample as a whole, the comparable figures were 15.0 and 17.5 (see Table 6.1).

Finally, still another factor channeled confidential disclosure to women when the relationship reached a certain level of mutual commitment. The fiancée of one senior was hurt to discover how open the youth continued to be with his male friend. That both shared the normative expectation of being each other's closest confidant was apparent from his apologetic comment: "I offered some lame excuse, but I still wanted a male point of view about certain matters."

The primacy of the female friend as the target of disclosure is the major difference between the current study and the previous study of Jourard and Lasakow (1958) who found that the closest confidant was a male friend. The importance of the female friend may, perhaps, be explained by the trend towards earlier cross-sex interaction and the related decline in segregated subcultures of adolescent males and females. This trend has been documented for the period between the 1930s and 1960s (J. Richard Udry, 1966). Replication of the 1958 study in the same college would test the hypothesis that the transfer of psychological intimacy to a female friend occurs now earlier in the life cycle than was the case in the 1950s.

THE EXCEPTIONS: THE FAVORED CONFIDANT
OTHER THAN THE FEMALE FRIEND

Not all seniors chose the female friend as their closest confidant in the protected area of Personality. Out of sixty-two students, seventeen gave fullest information about Personality to the closest male friend. Significantly out of these seventeen men, twelve were virgins (virgins constituted only 26 percent of the total sample). An association between sexual experience and psychological intimacy with a woman is further confirmed by the fact that of the ten highest disclosers on Personality in the sample as a whole none was a virgin, but five of the ten lowest disclosers were virgins. The virgins communicated less fully than the sexually experienced men not only with female but with male friends as well. Their mean total disclosure to male friend was only 72.8 as compared with 90.2 for the total sample.

This is not to say that sexual intimacy guaranteed full disclosure to a female friend. One sexually experienced senior explained his reason for choosing a male confidant: "Guys relate better to guys, a woman cannot understand how a man feels." Despite an active sex life, he did not find relationships with women fully satisfactory. He remarked that he generally wished that the girl would leave "just about after I reach orgasm." This senior's relationship with his mother was classified as "unsatisfactory" on a threefold division of "satisfactory," "average," and "unsatisfactory" parent-child relationships. This senior was one of six black sons of college-educated fathers whose general disclosure scores were lower than those of comparable white students, as seen in Table 6.3.

The twelve seniors whose scores to male and female friends were equally high (and higher than to either parent) represented several types. Some showed this symmetry because of a general reserve or, conversely, a general openness in communication. Three of the twelve were among the ten lowest and three among the ten highest disclosures on Personality and Body in the total sample.

Of the remaining six, three belonged to what might be termed male subcultures on the campus—one to a fraternity, one to an athletic team, and one to a male drug-using group. The last was represented by a senior who took drug trips with male friends and who had had one homosexual experience with an older man. But none of these six men was a virgin and all six had female, as well as male, confidants. One other senior with equally high disclosure scores to female and male best friends, was an articulate leader of a campus pacifist group who was separated from his wife shortly before the interview. The female confidante on his self-disclosure was his wife.

Of the sixty-two men in the sample, six named one or both parents, rather than a person of their own generation, as their closest confidant. In other words, for some 90 percent, the closest relationships in terms of self-disclosure were with their peers and only 10 percent turned to their parents.

COMMUNICATION WITH PARENTS

The sons, at the modal age of twenty-one, were considerably more open about themselves with their mothers than with their fathers. The mean total disclosure scores to mother and to father were, respectively, 74.1 and 63.7 (see Table 6.1). Scores were nearly identical in some areas because these were equally withheld from both parents. "The facts of my present sex life," as we shall show, was one striking example of such reserve.

The higher disclosure to the mother was associated with a generally more satisfactory relationship with her than with the father. Conflict might, of course, result in a high level of communication, even if filled with acrimony. In comparison with other types of communication, however, self-disclosure was apparently facilitated by feelings of warmth towards the target person. Several schedules, used in this study, were intended to measure the quality of parent-son relationships and all of them portrayed the mother as the closer and the warmer of the two parents. For example, asked to rate the proposition "My mother (my father) made me feel wanted and needed," only 10 percent of the sample checked "tended to be untrue" or "very untrue" for the mother; the corresponding figure for the father was 27 percent. Again, rating relationships with each parent on the scale from "very tense and strained" to "very close and intimate," the seniors gave their mothers a higher rating. Seventy-four percent checked the two highest ratings for their mothers and only 50 percent rated their fathers as highly.

The relationship between affection towards a person and self-disclosure has been studied previously. Jourard and Lasakow (1958) found a significant positive correlation between parental cathexis (attachment) scores of thirty-one nursing students and their self-disclosure to each parent.

The reign of silence between the sons and their parents on the subject of sex created some estrangement but the majority felt that avoidance provided a tolerable adaptation to a potential conflict, one tacitly preferred also by the parents. "My parents never wanted to know," remarked one youth in describing his sexual life, "I believe they preferred it that way." The degree of reserve was confirmed by the average scores in the area of sex of the forty-three sexually experienced seniors (the virgins and the few married students were excluded). Of the eighty-six scores to parents, 70 percent consisted of 0's (no information) or X's (deception).

Fuller disclosure on the subject of sex did not always betoken a harmonious relationship between sons and parents. One nineteen-year-old senior (described on p. 73) defiantly announced to his conventional parents his intention to move from his own room to the apartment of his girl friend. It was both a rebellion and a plea for absolution. His twenty-two-year-old brother, present at this conversation with parents, was incredulous. "You just don't tell certain things to your parents," he admonished his younger brother.

FATHER'S EDUCATION AS A FACTOR IN SELF-DISCLOSURE

Some previous studies have demonstrated that lower educational and socioeconomic status tended to be associated with lower level of verbal communication, in general and of self-disclosure, in particular (Murray A. Straus, 1968; Komarovsky, 1967). The seniors of this study represented an educationally homogeneous group but one recruited from diverse educational and therefore, undoubtedly also, class backgrounds. This combination provides an opportunity to inquire into the impact of early family socialization on communication. If this effect is persistent, the sons of the less-educated fathers (those with twelve or fewer years of schooling) would exhibit lower disclosure scores than the sons of better-educated fathers. On the other hand, a similarity between the two groups of seniors would argue that the common college experience erased whatever differences might have stemmed from their diverse family backgrounds.

In order to refine the educational comparison, the cases were cross-classified by the father's education and the senior's religion. Despite the small number of cases, the educational differences present so consistent a pattern as to warrant presentation in Tables 6.3 and 6.4. Included in these comparisons were four areas of disclosure (Attitudes, Work and Study, Personality, and Body) and four role partners (mother, father, closest male and female friends).[5]

Table 6.3 shows the total disclosure scores for each educational and religious subgroup. Turning to the white students first, the sons of better-educated fathers indeed show higher total disclosure scores in each religious group, as seen in Table 6.3. The more detailed presentation in Table 6.4 confirms this finding. Of forty-eight possible comparisons between sons of better- and less-educated fathers (in the four areas and to four role partners), the scores of the former were higher in twenty-nine and lower in fifteen, and in the remaining four, the two educational categories had nearly identical scores.

On balance, the sons of better-educated fathers had not merely higher total self-disclosure rates but communicated with a wider variety of role partners as compared with upwardly mobile sons.

The hypothesis, presented earlier, that socialization in a lower-class family[6] may impair the capacity for self-disclosure, is not, however, supported by our findings. Whatever blocked the communication of lower-class seniors, did not block it in all relation-

Table 6.3.   Total Disclosure Scores of Seniors by Race,
Education of Father, and Religion*

White	Fathers, 12 years of schooling or less	Fathers, over 12 years of schooling
Protestants	224.3 (N = 6)	296.3 (N = 11)
Catholics	228.2 (N = 8)	302.7 (N = 9)
Jews	257.8 (N = 6)	261.6 (N = 12)
Black Protestants	239.3 (N = 3)	216.2 (N = 6)

*Each score is the sum of average scores in four areas (Money excluded) and to four target persons (siblings excluded) for the specified subgroup.

5. The small number of cases in some cells led to the exclusion of siblings in this cross-classification by religion and father's education. Because of the small number of black students the comparison in Table 6.4 is limited to whites.
6. As measured by the education of the father.

Table 6.4. Self-Disclosure Scores of White Seniors by Education of Father and Religion

Area and Direction of Self-Disclosure	Protestants Education of Father		Catholics Education of Father		Jews Education of Father	
	12 years or less (N = 6)	Over 12 years (N = 11)	12 years or less (N = 8)	Over 12 years (N = 9)	12 years or less (N = 6)	Over 12 years (N = 12)
Attitudes						
To mother	16.8	27.2	13.8	27.4	22.0	23.3
To father	17.3	25.7	12.5	28.1	15.6	22.9
To male friend	25.1	35.0	30.1	38.6	34.5	32.7
To female friend	31.3	30.7	34.3	36.2	36.7	31.6
Total	90.5	118.6	90.7	130.3	108.8	110.5
Work						
To mother	10.5	18.7	8.4	15.2	18.8	16.0
To father	10.8	17.3	7.3	16.2	10.2	15.0
To male friend	14.8	19.0	17.0	21.2	21.2	23.4
To female friend	18.8	17.4	20.5	18.2	21.3	21.2
Total	54.9	72.4	53.2	70.8	71.5	75.6

Table 6.4 (continued)

Area and Direction of Self-Disclosure	Protestants Education of Father		Catholics Education of Father		Jews Education of Father	
	12 years or less (N = 6)	Over 12 years (N = 11)	12 years or less (N = 8)	Over 12 years (N = 9)	12 years or less (N = 6)	Over 12 years (N = 12)
Personality						
To mother	6.0	12.6	5.9	9.8	8.5	8.4
To father	6.3	10.6	5.6	10.3	3.8	8.9
To male friend	10.1	17.6	14.7	11.8	11.7	13.8
To female friend	18.5	16.2	20.9	19.8	20.0	14.8
Total	40.9	57.0	47.1	51.7	44.0	45.9
Body						
To mother	8.2	12.7	6.9	12.4	7.8	6.9
To father	6.8	11.2	6.4	11.9	4.4	4.4
To male friend	7.5	12.7	9.3	11.8	9.5	8.8
To female friend	15.5	11.7	14.6	13.8	11.8	9.5
Total	38.0	48.3	37.2	49.9	33.5	29.6

ships. The low total self-disclosure scores of these seniors were caused by the striking meagerness of their communication with their mothers and fathers. These relationships show the greatest contrast with sons of better-educated fathers. The seniors from less-educated families also shared their attitude and feelings less fully with their male friends, though in this case the difference between the two groups of seniors was not as striking or as consistent. The unexpected result concerns relationships with female friends. If the essence of psychological intimacy consists in sharing the sensitive topics of Personality and Body, the lower-class seniors exhibited it quite fully in relationships with female friends. Their disclosure to female friends was generally higher than that of seniors from better-educated families. The proportion of virgins, who tended to be reserved, did not differ in the two educational categories, but the lower-class seniors had a relatively higher proportion of committed men. Such men may be expected to be more open with their women friends than men who are still playing the field.

Another possible explanation of the relatively high disclosure to women friends is the minority status of the lower-class seniors on this campus. This may have created some social distance in relation to the students with college-educated fathers. The social distance from both their classmates and their parents may have channeled communication of the lower-class seniors, in a compensatory fashion, to their female friends.[7] This result is all the more surprising because sex-role socialization (and segregation in male and female subcultures) tend to be more marked in lower socioeconomic strata (Komarovsky, 1967). The upwardly mobile seniors in our sample may have represented a selected group, or, again, four years of college may have modified their behavior.

In sum, the relatively low total self-disclosure of seniors from less-educated families did not stem from any generalized inability or reluctance to be open with associates. It reflected mainly their meager communication with their parents. Father-son relationships were less satisfactory in the lower stratum. Only 19 percent of the twenty-two sons of less-educated fathers, as compared with 31 percent of the thirty-six sons of better-educated fathers, enjoyed

---

7. Indeed, when it comes to Attitudes, the sons of educated fathers chose male friends as their primary confidants. Only the lower-class seniors shared Attitudes more fully with their female friends, thus pushing up the mean score for disclosure of attitudes to closest female friend for the sample as a whole.

satisfactory relationships with their fathers.[8] The gap in education between fathers and sons admittedly inhibited communication in some cases. But the fathers were perceived also as especially deficient in warmth and understanding (see pp. 190–91).[9]

RELIGIOUS AFFILIATION AND RACE AS FACTORS IN SELF-DISCLOSURE

The breakdown of disclosure scores by education of father, race, and religion results in a set of numbers too small for conclusive findings. There does exist some consistency in the tables, and we present them for their suggestive value. On balance, religious affiliation appears to be less decisive than education of father in degree of self-disclosure. Contrary to Jourard's (1961) finding, none of the religious groups in our sample is uniformly high or low in communication. The influence of the religious affiliation varies with the educational background of the respondent, the area of disclosure and, the role partner. On the other hand, our results confirm an earlier study by Jourard and Lasakow (1968) with respect to the relative reserve of our small sample of black students.

An earlier study of the effect of religious denomination on self-disclosure (Jourard, 1961) found that Jewish male (but not female) college students had higher total scores than Methodist, Baptist, and Catholic males of comparable socioeconomic status.

Our results suggest the need to take account of the education of the father in future studies. In our study, as indicated in Table 6.3, it was only among sons of less-educated fathers that Jews exceeded Protestants and Catholics in self-disclosure. The total disclosure scores of Jews from better-educated families were, in fact, lower than those of other religious denominations.[10]

8. The fathers of the remaining four respondents were deceased.
9. Data did not permit the comparison of disclosure scores by mother's education.
10. The lower scores of disclosure to female friends of better-educated Jews in the area of Personality may be explained in part by the relatively higher proportion of virgins among them. Virgins in general tended to have lower disclosure scores to female as well as to male friends than sexually experienced seniors. Among the better-educated seniors, the disclosure scores to women were, respectively: Jews, 14.8 (39 percent virgins); Protestants, 16.2 (27 percent virgins); and Catholics, 19.8 (22 percent virgins).
Among the seniors from less-educated backgrounds, neither these disclosure

The small number of black students makes the comparison by race and education of fathers inconclusive. The six black sons of college-educated fathers, were much lower disclosers than white Protestants of similar educational background in every area. The only exceptions were Attitudes and Work to female friend. There were no virgins among either the six better-educated black seniors or the three blacks with less-educated fathers. By contrast, of the eleven white Protestants with college-educated fathers, three were virgins. But the sexual experience of the black seniors did not raise their scores of disclosure to women (in the areas of Personality and Body) to the level of the white Protestants.

Our case studies do not offer a ready hypothesis for the reserve of black students. Blacks constituted a small minority on this campus and at least one black senior attributed his limited social life to the fact that there were few black majors in his field of study.

The next section compares the psychological profiles of the ten lowest and the ten highest disclosers in the area of Personality (see Table 6.5). Among the ten lowest disclosers, three were black, although black students constituted only 11 percent of the total sample. Unlike the white low disclosers, the three black students had relatively high scores on Heterosexuality and Dominance and low scores on Succorance and Self-Abasement on the Gough Adjective Check List. The reserve of the black students, thus, is not associated with the psychological profile typical of white low disclosure and may, therefore, reflect a different combination of influences.

---

scores nor proportions of virgins varied as widely by religion as among the upper-class students. The scores and percent of virgins by religion follows: Jews, 20.0 (33 percent virgins); Protestants 18.5 (33 percent virgins); and Catholics, 20.9 (25 percent virgins).

In the areas of Attitudes, Work or Study, Personality, and Body, the religious differences must be considered separately for each educational category. Among the better-educated, Jewish students have lower disclosure scores to their mothers (54.6), fathers (51.2), and male friends (78.7) in comparison with the two other religious groups. The corresponding figures for Protestants are 71.2 (to mother), 64.8 (to father), and 84.3 (to male friend). The Catholic rates for disclosure for the three role partners are, respectively, 64.8, 66.5, and 83.4.

The low disclosure to mothers on the part of less-educated Catholics—35.0 as against 41.5 (Protestants) and 57.1 (Jews)—may be associated with the higher proportion of unsatisfactory mother-son relationships among the Catholic seniors. In the sample as a whole, 44 percent of Catholic, 20 percent of Protestant, and 16 percent of Jewish mother-son relationships were assessed as "unsatisfactory" (with "average" and "satisfactory" as the other two categories).

Table 6.5. The Ten Lowest and Ten Highest Disclosers (ACL)

Percent of each group falling above the mean score for the total sample on specified trait.

	Lowest Ten		Highest Ten*
TRAIT	BLACK	WHITE	
Heterosexuality	100	14	44
Affiliation	67	43	67
Personal Adjustment	67	43	67
Achievement	67	57	78
Intraception	100	71	89
Succorance	67	28	44
Autonomy	33	43	56
Self-Abasement	0	57	67
Aggression	33	43	33
Dominance	100	57	67
Self-Confidence	67	57	67
Self-Control	33	57	56
Counseling Readiness	33	43	44

*There was only one black student among the highest disclosers and three black students among the ten lowest disclosers.

PSYCHOLOGICAL PROFILES OF LOW AND HIGH DISCLOSERS

Using disclosure in the area of Personality as possibly the most sensitive index of psychological intimacy, we compared the lowest with the highest disclosers. Certain sociological correlates of self-disclosure, discussed earlier in this chapter, were confirmed. Five of the ten lowest disclosers but none of the ten highest were virgins. Three of the ten lowest and only one of the ten highest disclosers were black. Some negative results were also confirmed. Neither religion nor education of the father was associated with the two extremes.

The Gough Adjective Check List for "my real self" permits the comparison of the two extremes with regard to thirteen selected psychological dimensions.

The data suggest the general hypothesis that neither the lowest nor the highest disclosers represents a homogeneous group. Put in other words, it is likely that different combinations of factors may converge to produce either of the two extremes. If this is the case, it has some implications for the relationship between mental health and self-disclosure. Current literature assumes a high positive correlation between these two factors. This view needs to be qualified by the possibility that high self-disclosure may, in some cases, reflect a troubled personality.

The low disclosers among white students were characterized by relatively low scores on Heterosexuality, Affiliation (defined in this test as the need "to seek and sustain numerous personal friendships"), Personal Adjustment, Achievement, Intraception (defined as the "attempt to understand one's own behavior or the behavior of others"), and Succorance ("dependent on others," "seeking support"). These were predictable differences with the exception of Succorance. The high scores on Succorance of the fullest disclosers suggests the possibility that at least some of them may be motivated by an unusual need for support and for external bolstering of a relatively low self-esteem. Among the indicative adjectives for Succorance are "immature, whining, self-pitying." The existence of this type may account for the fact that the total group of high self-disclosers is only slightly more "self-confident" and "dominant" than the low disclosers.

The ten lowest and ten highest disclosers were compared also on the ten dimensions of the California Psychological Inventory. Table 6.6 presents the results.

Table 6.6. The Ten Lowest and Ten Highest Disclosers (CPI)

Percent of each group falling above the mean score for the total sample on specified trait

	Lowest Ten		Highest Ten*
	BLACK	WHITE	
Socialization	33	29	60
Self-Acceptance	100	71	100
Dominance	67	57	80
Feminity	67	71	90
Psychological-Mindedness	100	86	100
Well-Being	33	57	70
Achievement via Conformance	67	57	70
Self-Control	33	57	60
Intellectual Efficiency	33	71	70
Achievement via Independence	67	100	100

*There was one black student among ten highest disclosers.

The full disclosers (nine of whom were white) had higher scores than the white low disclosers on Socialization, Self-Acceptance, Dominance, Femininity, and Psychological-Mindedness. High scores on Femininity were described in the test manual as "appreciative, patient, as behaving in a conscientious and sympathetic way." The low scorers were "outgoing, hard-headed, ambitious, active, robust, restless . . . impatient with delay . . . and reflection." The total sample of seniors was skewed in the direction of high scores on Psychological-Mindedness and Femininity in comparison with the standard scores in the test manual. This may account for the fact that the differences between the two groups of disclosers were not any higher.

CONCLUSION

In contrast to earlier studies of male undergraduates (Jourard and Lasakow, 1958) the seniors of this study experienced psychological intimacy most fully in cross-, rather than same-, sex relationships. This primacy of the female friend was documented by the questionnaires and interpreted by the qualitative materials of the interviews. We suggest that the transfer of psychological closeness from a male to a female friend may occur earlier in the life cycle of males who attend college now than was the case in the 1950s.

Looking towards the future, one might speculate whether the Women's Liberation Movement with its ideology of sisterhood, seeking to heighten women's solidarity and militancy, might reverse the trend towards earlier cross-sex psychological intimacy. Such a reversal would be strengthened should men, in turn, react with anxiety and hostility to the women's quest for equality. Still a third development might have a similar impact. Should the "Men's Liberation Movement" grow in influence, its emphasis on male expressiveness might also foster same-sex sex solidarity.

Among other divergent or novel findings are the influences of father's education and religion on self-disclosure which were shown to be more complex than previously reported, and to vary with particular relationships.

On the other hand, the results of this study are consistent with previous findings in several respects. Confirmed is the higher disclosure to one's mother than to the father and to peers than to

parents. Information about Personality and Body was more spar-
ingly given than about Attitudes or Work or Study, consistent with
earlier studies.

Since this study was limited to male undergraduates, there is no
yardstick with which to assess the sample as a whole. The seniors
themselves rated their disclosure considerably below the maximum
possible scores, as shown in Tables 6.1 and 6.2. Moreover, the
seniors admitted that their lack of self-disclosure was a grievance,
occasionally voiced against them, by their closest women friends.
Of 82 complaints from women friends reported by the seniors, 13
percent referred to excessive reserve. On the other hand, "lack of
full self-disclosure" comprised only 5 percent of the 171 criticisms
the seniors themselves listed in describing their closest female
friends.[11]

Despite this sex difference in patterns of dissatisfaction, we shall
propose a hypothesis that departs somewhat from the familiar
emphasis on male inexpressiveness. Our analysis of the sons from
less-educated families suggests a distinction which may be applicable to sex differences in self-disclosure of college-educated men
and women. The upwardly mobile seniors had lower total disclosure scores and a narrower range of recipients of disclosures in
comparison with upper-class seniors, but in the area of Personality
their disclosure to close female friends was equally full. Similarly,
we propose the hypothesis that college-educated men may disclose
the sensitive aspects of their personality in fewer relationships than
do women, with consequently lower total scores on disclosure tests.
On the other hand, if the capacity for intimacy is measured not by
total scores but by the depth of the closest relationship, college-
educated men may not rank below women in self-disclosure. At
least one study of a small group of married couples did indeed show
similarity on the part of the sexes in disclosure to the spouse
(Jourard, 1971).

Two other studies, though not concerned with self-disclosure,
offer some support of the proposed hypothesis. Jerald S. Heiss
(1962) found females more expressive than males with casual dates
but not with the persons they were committed to marry. Robert K.

11. In a study of working-class marriages, the complaint "mate doesn't reveal
worries" was expressed by 26 percent of the wives and only 9 percent of the husbands
(Komarovsky, 1967). Granted that disclosure of worries does not exhaust emotional
expressiveness, among both the blue-collar and the student couples, dissatisfaction
with the mate's excessive reserve was stronger among women than among men.

Leik (1963) reported that males were more instrumental and females more expressive with strangers, whereas in family interaction the difference between the sexes diminished. The hypothesis that the total self-disclosure of college-educated males is indeed lower than of females but that, in their most intimate relationships, the sexes do not differ in the extent of self-disclosure, remains to be tested.

The comparison of the ten highest and ten lowest disclosers suggests the probability that neither extreme represents a homogeneous group. A high disclosure rate may be associated with personal adjustment, heterosexuality, self-acceptance, and also, on the other extreme, with an exceptional need for succorance and support. The implications of self-disclosure for mental health or interpersonal relationships, consequently, present a more complex pattern than is sometimes assumed and require further study.

Finally, apart from the cited female grievance over the excessive reserve of some seniors, we do not know how the female confidantes would characterize or assess the quality of their communication with the men in this study. For example, would they have characterized the men as self-centered in their confiding or as sympathetic listeners as well? Case studies presented throughout the book illustrate a variety of patterns of communication but definitive answers could come only through interviewing the female confidantes.

7

THE SONS JUDGE
THEIR PARENTS

As its title indicates, this chapter is written largely from the stand-point of the sons. The familial satisfactions and strains are those reported by the sons. The fathers and the mothers are known only as portrayed by their offspring—with all the selective perceptions and distortions that inhere in such one-sided presentation of human interaction.

The felt strains, or, indeed, the denial of them, tell us something but not all we want to know about the son's attitudes towards his parents. Occasionally the picture presented by the respondent appears to be belied by the indirect evidence of the total case. More significantly, the respondent may not be aware of the consequences of his parental relationships for role performance in other statuses. For example, one youth, who spoke glowingly of his parents, appeared to have come by parental approval too easily. His psychological profile suggests an inflated self-image and an inability to cope with restrictions, all of which will certainly stand in the way of his grandiose occupational plans. Such latent consequences of parent-son relationships are illustrated in various case histories (see, for example, p. 188, p. 194).

We used several methods to get at parent-son relationships. The introductory overview is based upon four schedules. The bulk of the data was derived from other sections of the interview. For example, in discussion of family relationships seniors were asked to list the three most, and three least, favorable characteristics of each parent as a parent and as a person, apart from family roles. Parental attitudes were investigated in most areas of the senior's life. His attitudes towards his future paternal role said much about the fathering he had received himself.

AN OVERVIEW OF PARENTAL RELATIONSHIPS

All schedules portrayed the mother as the closer and the warmer of the two parents. Asked to rate their relationships with each parent on the scale from "very tense and strained," at one pole, to "very close and intimate," at the other, the seniors gave their mothers a relatively higher rating. Seventy-four percent of the group gave their mothers the two highest ratings but only 50 percent rated their fathers as highly. The mother emerges as the closer of the two parents on another schedule, summarized in Table 7. 1. For example, 58 percent of the sons checked "very true" that "my mother made me feel wanted and needed," with only 10 percent checking "tended to be untrue" or "very untrue." The corresponding percentages for the fathers were only 35, endorsing the positive statement and as much as 27, giving the two negative ratings.[1]

As judged by the schedules, maternal love was not "unconditional." The responses to the propositions reflecting control and demand for achievement (see propositions 2, 4, 6, 8, 9, and 10 in Table 7. 1) on the average reveal that the mother is seen as the more "overprotective" and controlling parent than the father.[2]

Only six seniors felt that they were closer to their fathers than to their mothers. One son spoke admiringly of his physician father as "not only a good father but an intellectual colleague." His mother, a high school graduate, was described as "ignorant and prejudiced." Thus, a father who combined a warm interest in his son

1. Leonard Benson (1968: 176) cites five studies confirming that the mother is perceived as the more loving parent and the one for whom children of both sexes have, on the average, greater affection.

2. Our findings do not support Ruth E. Hartley's (1959) summary of previous research to the effect that "fathers in general seem to be perceived (by boys) as punishing and controlling agents." Possibly, the research cited by Hartley covered a wider class spectrum than our sample. Lower-class fathers have been reported as harsher disciplinarians than college-educated fathers (Donald G. McKinley, 1964).

Table 7.1.   Parent-Child Relationships*

Relationship to mother in childhood

1. She made me feel wanted and needed
   <u>36</u> very true   <u>20</u> tended to   <u>6</u> tended to   <u>0</u> very untrue   62
   be true   be untrue

2. She set very few rules for me
   <u>8</u> very true   <u>14</u> tended to   <u>31</u> tended to   <u>8</u> very untrue   61
   be true   be untrue

3. She praised me when I deserved it
   <u>29</u> very true   <u>32</u> tended to   <u>1</u> tended to   <u>0</u> very untrue   62
   be true   be untrue

4. She never let me get away with breaking a rule
   <u>9</u> very true   <u>25</u> tended to   <u>27</u> tended to   <u>1</u> very untrue   62
   be true   be untrue

5. She ridiculed me and made fun of me
   <u>0</u> very true   <u>1</u> tended to   <u>11</u> tended to   <u>50</u> very untrue   62
   be true   be untrue

6. She wanted to have complete control of my actions
   <u>2</u> very true   <u>15</u> tended to   <u>22</u> tended to   <u>23</u> very untrue   62
   be true   be untrue

7. She acted as if I didn't exist
   <u>1</u> very true   <u>1</u> tended to   <u>5</u> tended to   <u>55</u> very untrue   62
   be true   be untrue

8. She pushed me to do well in school
   <u>25</u> very true   <u>18</u> tended to   <u>14</u> tended to   <u>5</u> very untrue   62
   be true   untrue

9. She was overprotective of me
   <u>12</u> very true   <u>20</u> tended to   <u>20</u> tended to   <u>9</u> very untrue   61
   be true   be untrue

10. She tended to keep out of and withdraw from family situations that
    might be unpleasant
    <u>1</u> very true   <u>8</u> tended to   <u>23</u> tended to   <u>29</u> very untrue   61
    be true   be untrue

Relationship to father in childhood

1. He made me feel wanted and needed
   <u>22</u> very true   <u>23</u> tended to   <u>15</u> tended to   <u>2</u> very untrue   62
   be true   be untrue

2. He set very few rules for me
   <u>8</u> very true   <u>26</u> tended to   <u>20</u> tended to   <u>7</u> very untrue   61
   be true   be untrue

*The author expresses her gratitude to Kenneth Kammeyer for the permission to use this schedule, originally adapted from Anne Roe's scale.

3. He praised me when I deserved it
   <u>22</u> very true   <u>33</u> tended to   <u>6</u> tended to   <u>1</u> very untrue   62
                   be true   be untrue

4. He never let me get away with breaking a rule
   <u>8</u> very true   <u>27</u> tended to   <u>24</u> tended to   <u>3</u> very untrue   62
                   be true   be untrue

5. He ridiculed me and made fun of me
   <u>0</u> very true   <u>2</u> tended to   <u>20</u> tended to   <u>40</u> very untrue   62
                   be true   be untrue

6. He wanted to have complete control of my actions
   <u>1</u> very true   <u>12</u> tended to   <u>16</u> tended to   <u>33</u> very untrue   62
                   be true   be untrue

7. He acted as if I didn't exist
   <u>0</u> very true   <u>4</u> tended to   <u>15</u> tended to   <u>43</u> very untrue   62
                   be true   be untrue

8. He pushed me to do well in school
   <u>16</u> very true   <u>23</u> tended to   <u>19</u> tended to   <u>4</u> very untrue   62
                   be true   be untrue

9. He was overprotective of me
   <u>4</u> very true   <u>13</u> tended to   <u>19</u> tended to   <u>25</u> very untrue   61
                   be true   be untrue

10. He tended to keep out of and withdraw from family situations that
    might be unpleasant
    <u>2</u> very true   <u>12</u> tended to   <u>27</u> tended to   <u>20</u> very untrue   61
                    be true   be untrue

with a markedly superior education to that of his wife, scored especially high.

Another type of a close paternal tie was found in a strained marriage in which each parent formed an alliance with one of the children, in this case a father-son versus a mother-daughter team. Four out of the six fathers who were favored by their sons were professional men, married to less-educated wives; the remaining two did not attend college, nor did their wives. One of these less-educated fathers was enthusiastically described by his son (see p. 193) as "the greatest man on the face of the earth" and the other, deceased, was still mourned by his son. The son missed most the emotional support provided by his father, who always sensed when his son was upset and would take him for a ride to talk over the disturbing problem.

The father's intellectual competence played a part in those six close father-son relationships. But a more constant feature was a warm understanding of the sons' experiences. In only a couple of these cases was the relationship with the mother strained so that the son turned, as it were, to his father for the nurturance and warmth lacking in his mother. More frequently the mother-son relationship simply did not match the stimulation and satisfaction provided by the father. But, to repeat, this supremacy of paternal versus maternal ties characterized only some 10 percent of the sample.

The sons were asked to compare themselves with each parent, with regard to three features: "personality and temperament," "intelligence," and "outlook on life."

Despite warmer relationships with their mothers, the sons felt that they resembled their fathers more closely with regard to all of the above features (see Table 7.2). For example, twenty-one sons gave the father an edge with regard to resemblance in intelligence as against only eleven who felt they resembled their mothers more. As to personality, twenty-eight checked "father more" as against only nineteen who identified more closely with the mother. Nineteen men indicated their greater resemblance to their fathers in "outlook on life," the equivalent figure was only eight for mothers. We have eliminated from the above comparison those who checked "neither" or "both equally," as specified in Table 7.2. Greater perceived resemblance to the same-sex parent was to be expected. The surprising finding was the considerable proportion of seniors who thought they resembled their mothers more, or equally as much, as their fathers. Forty-six percent fell into the above category with regard to "personality and temperament" and 50 percent with regard to "intelligence." There may be some connection between this acknowledged identification with their mothers and the refusal of the men to stereotype sharply male and female personalities as documented in Chapter 1.[3]

Resemblance to their mothers in personality was particularly frequent in mother-dominated marriages (as assessed by sons). Sixty-five percent of sons in such marriages checked "equal" or "mother more than father" for resemblance in personality, as against 46 percent for the sample as a whole. The mother-domi-

3. Leonard Benson (1968: 181) cites two studies showing that boys perceive themselves to be more like their fathers, while girls claim greater resemblance to their mothers. But Ruth E. Hartley (1959) cites a number of studies showing that (while boys may perceive themselves to be more like their fathers) boys tend to resemble their fathers in personality and attitudes much less than girls resemble their mothers. The closer attachment to the mother, the lesser interaction with the father and his aloofness may be factors accounting for this difference between sons and daughters.

nated families included a disproportionate number of strained mother-son relationships. Within the limits of our small sample, this finding emphasizes power as a factor in identification with a parental figure.[4]

Table 7.2.   Responses to the Question: Which of Your Parents Do You Take After?

| | Number of Students Giving Specified Answers | | |
| | *In Personality, Temperament* | *In Intelligence* | *In Outlook on Life* |
Responses			
Neither	3	3	20
Mother only	3	1	4
Father only	5	4	4
Both, but mother more	16	10	4
Both, but father more	23	17	15
Both equally	9	20	5
Don't know	2	6	9
Totals	61	61	61

The greatest divergence between the sons and their parents appeared in "outlook on life," with nearly 50 percent of the respondents indicating that they resembled "neither parent" or checking "don't know." But this divergence in outlook was not, as we shall see, the feature of parent-son relationships which the sons found most stressful.

The schedules presented a more favorable portrayal of family relationships than the qualitative sections of the interview which disclosed many dissatisfactions. It is apparently only a seriously aggrieved son who is prepared to check the most unfavorable rating on a schedule.

Using the total case as the basis for classifications, we distinguished three categories. "Highly satisfactory" were relationships the sons characterized by positive statements and an absence of serious dissatisfactions. These, we repeat, were the assessments of the respondents. In some cases our own judgments were less favorable. For example, among the twenty-three sons "highly

4. For the role of each parent in sex-role differentiation of daughters and sons in "instrumental" and "expressive" traits, see Alfred B. Heilbrun, Jr. (1965). Leonard Benson (1968: 166–87) summarizes the literature on the son's identification with his father.

satisfied" with their mothers, we included seven youths whom we judged to be overindulged and overprotected, though they themselves failed to perceive these shortcomings.

At the other extreme were the "highly unsatisfactory or ambivalent" relationships, so classed because the sons disclosed serious grievances with overt or covert conflicts. The intermediate group, the "average" parent-child relationships, were lacking both in positive assessments and strong criticisms.

Once again, the mother was seen as the favored parent (see Table 7.3). Thirty-seven percent of mother-son relationships were judged to be "highly satisfactory" on the evidence the sons presented throughout the interviews as compared to only 26 percent of such father-son ties. The contrast is even sharper at the other extreme. The percentages of "highly unsatisfactory" relationships were 26 for the mothers and 43 for the fathers.

Fewer sons were satisfied with their fathers than with their mothers but the satisfied sons in each relationship were satisfied for the same reasons. The criteria applied to mothering and fathering were nearly identical as judged by the three most favorable qualities attributed to each parent. The happy sons praised each parent for the same virtues. The prized qualities were only rarely task-oriented parental functions. "Worked hard to support the family," "good homemaker," "always made breakfast for me," and the like, were listed relatively infrequently. At the top of the list of "three most favorable qualities of your mother (father) in relation to you" was, for both parents, a cluster of qualities containing love, devotion, warmth, availability, and involvement. A near second in terms of frequency was another cluster consisting of supportiveness, understanding, and encouragement. "Fostered indepen-

Table 7.3. Sons Rate Parental Relationships
(Based upon Total Case)

	Fathers		Mothers	
Parental Relationships	*Number*	*Percent*	*Number*	*Percent*
Highly satisfactory	15	26	23	37
Average	18	31	23	37
Highly unsatisfactory and ambivalent	25	43	16	26
Totals	58	100	62	100
Fathers deceased	4			

dence," "was reasonable," "liberal," "permissive" was the third-ranking category of qualities. Finally, there were some scattered votes for "stimulating," "intelligent," "has good values," and others. Thus, the qualities ranked highest were love and supportiveness.

The section of the interview dealing with parents as individuals, apart from their parental roles, is meager in content. We had expected the seniors to be especially concerned and articulate about parents in relation to themselves, but the contrast between the two sections was striking. Loyalty could hardly be the explanation for the reticence because in describing parent-son relationships, arrogance, selfishness, sadism, and alcoholism were among the defects sons felt free to express. The shallow portrayal of parental personalities may signify a lack of psychological distance on the part of young men, still struggling with emotional dependence and therefore unable to view parents as personalities in their own right.

We have seen that the satisfied sons gave nearly identical reasons for their favorable attitudes towards their mothers and fathers. This is not true of the dissatisfied sons whose grievances against their parents differed. We shall first present the case against the fathers.

FATHERS AND SONS: THE SONS' DISSATISFACTIONS

The flood of current writings on the generation gap would have led us to expect that conflicts of values and outlook would be one of the major problems vis-à-vis fathers. Such differences did exist. Table 7.2 reveals that 42 percent of the sons disclaimed any similarity between themselves and their fathers in "outlook on life" and an additional 13 percent answered "don't know." A father's feeling that draft avoidance was cowardly, pitted against his son's determination not to fight in Vietnam; a father's bewilderment at his son's contempt for "jocks"; clashes in political ideologies; paternal anxiety over a son's lack of occupational commitment —these and other differences occasionally caused overt conflict and pain for the son. Granted such symptoms of the generation gap, the latter did not appear as significant as popular pronouncements claim. Possibly a random sample of male undergraduates demonstrates less radical departures from parental values than do writings specifically addressed to newly emerging trends. For example, for every senior who rejected the occupational success goals of his father on ideological grounds, there were several who, unsure of their occupational goals, regarded their confusion as a personal failure.

Whatever may be said about the generation gap, the most intense dissatisfaction expressed by the seniors with their fathers centered upon other problems. Using the total case as the basis for the assessments, the most frequent grievance, reported by 44 percent of the sample, was the father's lack of warmth, involvement, and closeness. Taking the sons' testimony at face value, what the sons missed in their fathers most were expressive qualities: i.e., intimacy, warmth, understanding, and acceptance. Occasionally this lack of warmth was coupled with sporadic outbursts of temper or ridicule, and with "irrational" acts of discipline.

It may be argued that estrangement between fathers and sons was in itself the product of their differences in outlook, indeed a means of avoiding overt conflict. "I don't bring up this subject at home, it would only lead to an argument" was certainly a familiar refrain throughout the interviews. Nonetheless, this unhappy feeling of distance from their fathers was not in the main caused by the generation gap. The sons declared themselves closer in outlook to their fathers than to their mothers (see Table 7.2) but when it came to emotional closeness and intimacy, the mothers held the advantage. In self-ratings of family relationships, exactly one half of the men described ties with their fathers as "neutral" or "strained." The corresponding figure for the mothers was only 27 percent.

Lack of paternal warmth thus headed the list of expressed dissatisfactions. Next in frequency was the failure of the father to present a suitable model of masculinity. Occupational failure or educational inadequacy was indicated by 17 percent of the sample, and the father's weak masculine posture vis-à-vis the mother, by 12 percent. Despite the attention the weak father–strong mother syndrome has received in clinical literature, this situation was perceived as a problem by only 12 percent of the sons, as contrasted with 44 percent who complained about the lack of paternal warmth and closeness. Some latent difficulties involved in weak father–strong mother situations are considered on pp. 197 and 215.

Fear of a respected but aloof father was expressed by 9 percent of the sons and another 9 percent felt that their major problem was to realize the inordinately high goals set for them by their admired fathers. For example, one troubled youth felt that his father did not love him, other than as "a machine grinding out high grades." The pressure to achieve in school was ever present and the son's success was the condition for his father's, at best, somewhat niggardly response. This problem was presented by the son of a businessman who had had to interrupt his own college education for economic reasons. The son complained that he could never discuss his problems with his father: "All my father wants of me is achievement. In high school, if I got ninety-five on some test, he would ask at dinner time what happened to the five missing points. He was quick with sarcasm. I was welcome only when I did well in school."

This senior neatly summed up his relationship to his father with the following remark: "Yesterday, I got a letter that I made the dean's list. The first thing I did was to call my father, just so that I could get close to him."

In summary, the single largest deprivation the sons lamented was insufficiency of expressive qualities in the fathering they had received. A relatively small proportion blamed their fathers for defects in instrumental qualities, that is, failure to live up to traditionally masculine roles.

This lack of paternal warmth was, of course, the sons' complaint; the fathers' side of the story is missing. But at least one youth perceived his own share in creating the estrangement. This senior described his father as a brilliant and dominant man who, however, "cannot relate to people . . . and neither can I," the son added. He suspected that his aggressive and independent brother might be respected by their father whereas he himself had failed to win his father's approval, despite his obedience. His father's approval was so deeply desired by the respondent that he dared not risk his displeasure. For example, he did not want to attend the college picked for him by his father but remained silent and obedient. As to communication with his father, the son had this to say: "Every so often in the last couple of years he'd try to talk to me. It's difficult for him, since I don't talk very much. It's like pulling teeth, I guess. But I was glad he wanted to talk to me. He was talking about my personal life more than it's usually talked about in my family. I didn't share my problems with him. He had as much trouble talking with me as I had with him."

FATHER'S EDUCATION AS A FACTOR IN FATHER-SON RELATIONSHIPS

The college-educated fathers, on the average, enjoyed better relationships with their sons than fathers with only twelve years of schooling or less. Thirty-one percent of the college-educated but only 19 percent of the less-educated fathers had "highly satisfactory" father-son relationships. At the other extreme, strained relationships were reported by 38 percent of the sons of college-educated fathers as against 50 percent of the sons of less-educated fathers. Again, the sons of the better-educated fathers exhibited, on the average, .75 major grievances per son as contrasted with the 1.13 rate for the sons of the less-educated fathers.

The economic and educational deficiencies were understandably more characteristic of the less-educated fathers. "Not a shining model," "ignorant," "limited in outlook," "his lack of education hurts our relationship" were complaints voiced by their sons. But the less-educated fathers were perceived also as especially deficient in warmth and understanding, and were accused of sporadic outbursts of authoritarianism. In fact, the economic and educational inadequacies were held against the less-educated fathers, by and large, only when combined with lack of warmth, a tendency to ridicule, or authoritarianism. A couple of sons held their uneducated fathers in some resentful contempt despite their fathers' good nature—but these sons were the exceptions. Thus, a son of a construction worker explained that his father was not a person "to model your life after." "He never used his mind and was a poor disciplinarian. He worked hard but had no sophistication whatever and was tactless and intolerant. Talking to my father is like talking to a stone wall—our communication is nil," he added. With all this criticism, the son admitted that his father had some good features: "He would always do what I asked him to; even if tired he would drive me before I learned to drive. I had a whip hand over the old man. Of course, I gave him no grief. I did well in school. Still I have to hand it to him, his attitude always was, 'if you want to do it, O.K.' "

This son indicated on the family relationship schedule that he felt closer to his better-educated mother and resembled her in personality and temperament.

This, then, was one of very few cases in which the father's low educational and occupational achievement appeared the decisive and sufficient element in the son's censure despite the father's good nature. More typically, the father's low level of achievement was resented only when accompanied by harshness and indifference towards the son. Previous studies have reported that lower-class fathers are harsher disciplinarians (Donald G. McKinley, 1964) and participate less in child care and leisure activities with children (Melvin L. Kohn, 1969: 117) than college-educated fathers. Possibly, the lack of continuous involvement made occasional acts of discipline appear especially tyrannical.

Apart from harsh discipline and indifference, a combination of contempt and fear on the part of the son occasionally caused friction with the less-educated father. A senior, who both despised and feared his father, explained, "My father is two generations away from me in his values." But his real dissatisfaction was directed at his own "hypocrisy" and his efforts to "smooth over disagreements" at all costs. For example, before returning on holidays to his small-town, midwestern conservative family, he usually got a haircut and he hated himself for this submission to his father's "outmoded" outlook. Meakness and avoidance of conflicts characterized all of this youth's social relationships.

The less-educated father can offset his deficiencies by certain personality characteristics that evoke the son's affection. A senior with a high academic record and a commitment to a demanding professional career had long since surpssed his Southern Baptist father in education. The son disclaimed any resemblance to either parent in "outlook on life." But neither the father's very modest occupational attainments nor his poor education and his "puritanical" views lessened the admiration and the love this youth felt for his father as is demonstrated in the following excerpts from the interview:

Asked to list his father's three best qualities, this senior put "understanding" first. He is often amazed at the "uncanny understanding" his father has of his son's experiences. His father seems to understand what his son "goes through." Next to understanding, "rarely ever volunteers advice, waits for me to ask," was the second quality, and the third was: "He really showed more affection than most fathers show to their children." In conclusion, the son exclaimed: "He is the greatest man on face of the earth!"

When the interviewer turned to the three paternal limitations, this senior listed two and could not think of a third one. "His morals are more puritanical than mine though he does not try to impose his values upon me" and "a slight tendency to protect me when I was younger" were the two faults the son acknowledged. The only hassle he ever had with his father, "if you can call it a hassle," was his father's waiting up for him till three or four o'clock in the morning and then calling from his room: "Are you alright?" The son tended to keep late hours and did not like the idea that his father worried and stayed up for him.

Another illustration of a warm interpersonal relationship between a less-educated father and his son was provided by a twenty-two-year-old black student, a son of a room-service waiter with only one year of high school. The student was the eldest son in a family of seven children. Were it not for the burden of supporting so large a family, his father, we were told by his son, would have gone a lot farther.

"Devotion to his family," "hard work," and "persistence" were listed as qualities most admired in his father, who despite his long working day, signed up for a correspondence course in electronics. The son respected his father for refusing to allow the boy's mother to go to work. "I felt as my father did at the time," he explained. "I wouldn't want to see my wife going out to work for money." As to his father's limitations, he had a temper, "but his temper didn't fool us. We knew he cared for us." As the boy became older he started staying up late in order to talk to his father and to help him in repairing TV and radio sets for neighbors. Both parents trusted his judgment and gave him a lot of freedom. His mother was a calm, even-tempered woman. He was the first of the siblings to go to high school. "I was made into a wise man at the age of eighteen," he added. Both parents made him feel "wanted and needed."

Despite his educational superiority over his father and his four years in an urban college, this youth had not departed from his father's basic outlook. He acknowledged their similarity in attitudes. He felt that he fully justified the trust his parents had had in him and the freedom they granted him. He apparently never had to struggle for their approval. This happy adjustment may have lost him some insight into himself. It is even possible that this approval was too easily won in the sense that it fostered grandiose aspirations and, according to his psychological profile, an impatience with constraints and requirements.

Notwithstanding the greater overall satisfaction on the part of the sons of college-educated fathers, two complaints were registered more frequently by them than by sons of less-educated fathers. The sons of college graduates accused their fathers of excessive demands for achievement. In some of these cases the burden was clearly self-imposed through the internalization of paternal goals.

The resentment of the father's weakness vis-à-vis a strong mother was mentioned more frequently by sons of college-educated fathers although the proportions of mother-dominated marriages were nearly identical in the two educational categories. Possibly sons had higher expectations of college-educated fathers and hence their weaknesses were all the more obtrusive.

The alienation between the less-educated fathers and their sons are strikingly manifested in the preceding chapter on self-disclosure. These sons disclosed little about themselves to their fathers in all areas and particularly in the guarded sphere of Personality (see pp. 160–62). The low father-son communication was particularly true of Catholics and Jews. Among Protestants the sons of the less-educated fathers also showed lower disclosure scores but the difference between the two educational categories was smaller. The following section on the influence of religion on father-son relationships may offer an explanatory hypothesis.

RELIGION AND FATHER-SON RELATIONSHIPS

Religious affiliation does not appear to play a crucial role in the degree of satisfaction with the paternal relationship but the small number of cases makes this generalization inconclusive. The one possible exception is the prevalence of strained relationships among Jewish and Catholic sons of less-educated fathers. The explanation may lie in the fact that Protestant fathers were all native born, but of the eight Jews and Catholics in this category, four were immigrants with, according to their sons, old-world, authoritarian attitudes. The fathers *demanded* respect that their college-educated sons felt they had not earned. One of these sons, a Jew, said wryly: "We are not a grateful family; Father puts in seventy hours a week of hard work with little reward." But he went on to describe his father's lack of friendliness, bad temper, and narrow-mindedness. He concluded: "One cannot have an intelligent conversation with my father."

THE CASE AGAINST THE MOTHERS

If the fathers were accused of giving too little of themselves, the mothers were blamed for giving too much, at least too much protection and inquisitiveness. The standard questions of the interview included: "List three most favorable qualities of your mother as a mother in relation to you," and "List three limitations of your mother as a mother in relation to you." The most frequently cited maternal failing was "overprotection." These sons described their mothers as "nosy," "bossy," continuously interfering, warning, pushing, managing. Occasionally, mothers were alleged to hinder spcifically masculine development such as athletic skills, physical courage, and heterosexual social life.

The anger at the over protective mother derives, no doubt, from the son's ambivalence and his struggle against the pull of the dependent, infantile role. Several sons admitted as much. We cannot always explain why some sons, having described their mothers as overprotective, did not consider this a failing and apparently accepted the role of an indulged and dependent son, whereas others were in conflict. For one thing, overprotection is not a single trait and represents a variety of motivations and behaviors. For another, the personalities of the sons differed. These varieties may be exemplified by two cases. One, an admittedly overprotected son, talked light-heartedly of his mother's inquisitiveness. He continued to live at home and did not resent her "faults." The praise with which she rewarded his academic achievements served, he felt, to motivate him to work harder. A very different mother-son relationship was reported by another youth who also described his mother as overprotective. This rebellious Jewish youth was determined to break with the religious and cultural milieu of his lower-middle–class parents. Characteristically his need to rebel was associated with an ambivalent dependence upon his parents. An external situation contributed to the intensity and form of his rebellion. His acceptance by an upper-status group at the Ivy League college aroused longings for upward mobility. (See pp. 201–3 for a fuller description of this case.)

In describing maternal faults, second in frequency to the overprotective mother came the cold and punitive one. "My mother did all the punishing in our family," said one senior, and there was no mistaking the bitterness of his references to her "scathing" remarks and rigid rules. "She never hugged me and I never hugged her," said another senior. Still another man in this group of dissatisfied sons referred to his mother as "cold and pushy."

Of the sixteen most dissatisfied sons, ten came from wife-dominated marriages, whereas of the twenty-three most satisfied sons, only four came from wife-dominated marriages. Underlying the bitterness of the dissatisfied sons may have been the struggle to free themselves from their identification with the mother as the dominant figure in the family. The sons were explicit in their dissatisfaction with the lack of maternal love.

The third most frequent complaint against mothers concerned deficiencies in what were traditionally viewed as masculine qualities of intellect and achievement. These are exemplified by such statements as: "She just hangs around without accomplishing anything"; "No capacity for abstractions"; "no interests"; "not interested in any cultural things." One senior had difficulty in deciding which parent he resembled in "outlook on life" because he never thought of his mother as having *any!*

The contempt for the mother's lack of intellectual quality was sometimes accompanied by other grievances, making it difficult to determine the most basic one. For example, one son described his mother as "intellectually limited and narrow-minded," adding "my mother is just a backdrop for Dad." His father was described as "terribly selfish and uncaring" and "energetic and driving." The son perceived himself as closer to his mother than to his father in personality and temperament. The anger and contempt expressed towards his mother may have been caused less by her intellectual limitations than by the fact that she yielded to her husband and did not protect her children from him. This may have disturbed the son all the more because he recognized in himself his mother's weakness.

Another son, whose contempt for his mother's intellect was combined with other grievances, declared himself alienated from both parents. He referred to his father as a "thick, sadistic man. Still, if I just met him I'd like him better than I would my mother." Having described her lack of cultural interest and her intellectual laziness, he added that she was "cheap about money." In this case as in the foregoing one, one suspects that the son's dissatisfaction with his mother's intellect was accentuated by other deprivations.

RELIGION AND MOTHER-SON RELATIONSHIPS

As in the case of the fathers, the findings on the influence of religious affiliations are inconclusive because of the small size of the subgroups. Nevertheless, the similarity between the Protestants and the Jews and the relatively high degree of disatisfaction among the Catholic sons is suggestive. Forty-four percent of the Catholic sons had strained relationships with their mothers, as contrasted with only 16 percent of the Jews and 20 percent of the Protestants. The syndrome of the cold, punitive, and demanding mother was reported in nine cases. Six out of the nine were Catholic although Catholic students represented only 29 percent of the sample. At the other pole, 48 percent of the Protestants, 37 percent of the Jews, but only 22 percent of the Catholics described their maternal relationships as "satisfactory." The remaining cases in each religious group fell into the "average" category. The Catholic mother-son relationship was equally unsatisfactory in the two educational categories (based upon the education of fathers).

THE STRUGGLE FOR INDEPENDENCE

Independence from parents and the ability to assume responsibility for one's own life is a central component of the masculine role in our society. The manifest goal in the socialization of male children is to ensure their emotional and economic emancipation from the parental family.

The struggle for emancipation was carried on quite consciously by some sons. "I deliberately refused to answer certain of my mother's questions in order to establish my right to privacy," explained one student. Several men who lived away from home reported that home visits reawakened dependency. For one thing, as one senior put it: "When at home I am not the one to provide the choreography—who gets the car, when meals are served, even when one goes to bed or gets up." But the socialization for independence may be hindered by circumstances of modern life and by psychodynamics of family relationships.

Excessive dependence upon one or both parents was a problem for over 36 percent of the sample. In the great majority of these cases the evidence came from the direct testimony of the sons who worried about their ignominious submissiveness to parents or their stormy and, as they suspected, ambivalent rebellion against the family. Still others perceived that strong attachment to their parents stood in the way of their social life outside the family. In a minority of the dependent cases the judgment was based not upon the diagnosis of the respondent himself but upon the indirect evidence of the interview and the psychological tests. The degree of dependence was judged to be excessive when it hindered the respondent in the performance of other roles he and his social milieu considered appropriate and obligatory at his stage of life.

The varieties of parent-son relationships from the point of view of the degree of dependence upon parents is presented in Table 7.4, for the sixty out of sixty-two cases we were able to classify.

Table 7.4. Degree of Dependence upon One or Both Parents

Relationships	Number	Percent
Dependency a manifest or latent problem	22	36.7
Independent and alienated sons	9	15.0
"Average": no evidence of excessive dependence or strong independence	10	16.7
Independent with fair or good parental relationships	15	25.0
Miscellaneous (e.g., responsibility for an unstable mother widow, the son's serious psychological impairment, and others)	4	6.7
	60	100.1
Unclassifiable	2	
Total	62	

VARIETIES OF DEPENDENT SONS

The dependent sons—those who so defined themselves and others, fewer in number, whom we so designated—represent a variety of types. Occasionally, the excessively strong tie to the parents was forged by an exceptionally rewarding family and a timidity in novel social situations. For example, one senior spoke enthusiastically of his large and warm family and the security and approval he found at home. He visited his nearby parental home frequently. At the same time he expressed some anxiety over his lack of male and female friends. He was a virgin ("good old Protestant ethic") and confessed that he might be afraid to expose himself to risks of new relationships. It would appear that the solace he received from his frequent visits to the parental home served to weaken the incentive to venture into the social world of the college community.

Among the dependent sons in happy families we included an only child who felt satisfied with both parents, though he admitted that his mother was overprotective and still treated him as a child by demanding to know details of his activities, including his social life and even his bowel movements. He did not find this surveillance too great a price to pay for the comforts and personal service he received at home. He was searching, not incidentally, for a mate who would serve his needs and whose life would revolve around him. His psychological profile, sketched solely on the basis of psychological tests, stated in part: "There is also something of the little boy in X, a tendency to feel inferior before authority and to put himself down, a tendency to look for and solicit unqualified emotional support and sympathy and to be self-centered in ways that are self-aggrandizing and disruptive. He also tends to give in to impulse without reflection."

Another senior, who lived at home throughout his college years although he could afford an apartment of his own, was so exceptionally awkward and unpopular with male as well as female friends, that his home, not especially happy, was nevertheless the only refuge where he could relax at all. He resented the overprotection of his mother but, again, did nothing to escape it.

The dependent sons discussed so far were emotionally locked into dependence by rewards received within the family as against the threatening world outside the home. But, paradoxically, a somewhat larger group of seniors was dependent in unhappy rather than in happy families. Sons who complained about their cold, unsympathetic fathers occasionally remained intimidated by the latter to the extent that they abdicated their own will in what appeared to be a futile yearning to win paternal love and approval. One such youth felt that his brother "beat me out" in competition for his father's approval. His brother was the "clever one" and he himself was the "good boy." He had long lost whatever admiration he had for his intellectually limited father but he had not lost his fear of him. "Father will make fun," he said bitterly, "where a guy is vulnerable." The son was still afraid to antagonize his father and still hoped to win his praise.

A cold, unloving mother, though rarer in our sample than a cold father, had in a few cases a similar effect of binding her son to her in a continuing but futile struggle to win her love.

The dependent sons cited above were characterized by submissiveness to parents at the sacrifice of personal autonomy or ventures into the outside world.

Dependence can take forms other than such abject submission. Several sons were as fully tied to and even oppressed by parents, but all the while carried on an open or covert warfare. Their dependence was manifested by their overriding concern with parental relationships, a concern that stood in the way of other role requirements of twenty-one- to twenty-two-year-old males. The following case will illustrate a covert or "passive" rebellion.

A senior has internalized the high achievement goals of his parents. In his own words: "The keynote of my parents' creed is accomplishment! I agree with them one hundred percent. My father is very bright and very quick. The word for my father is 'controlled.' He never put any pressure upon me to perform well in school. He always said, 'you do the best you can.' But I am a failure."

This youth is conducting a passive, self-punishing rebellion against his parents the nature of which he apparently does not perceive. He is still a virgin. His sexual inhibitions are described on pages 6 and 16. The parental expectation of high achievement are now his own, generating a great fear of failure. The "reasonableness" of the parents offers him no target for overt anger or rebellion. Nevertheless, through internally motivated sabotage, he denies his parents what they want, insures his continued dependence upon them and escapes decisive tests of his ability to achieve. Throughout his college career he had never handed in a paper on time and has delayed an application for a graduate fellowship, despite repeated telephone reminders from home, until the deadline had passed. He expressed his worry about the continued financial dependence upon his parents but the delay in applying for the fellowship (which he had a chance of obtaining) may tell another story of his real motives. He leads a quasi-hippie life, in his appearance and love of folk music but does not use drugs (perhaps because of his fear of loss of control).

Unlike this senior who conducted the conflict with his parents underground and at a great cost to himself, other dependent sons were involved in an overt struggle with one or both parents, the very passion of which bespoke their unresolved conflicts. Many of these sons stressed the vexing fact of economic dependence upon their parents, both as symbol and cause of their dependence. Jim, a nineteen-year-old Jew (a son of a college-educated father) was one of the two most rebellious sons, in both cases the major conflict was with their mothers.

Jim was one of the few respondents who was too angry to list more than one favorable feature of his mother: "She loves me and wants the best for me as determined by her." By contrast, her faults were fully inventoried: "her comments about my friends, her complete lack of understanding of the life I am leading at the college, her temper, her limited range of experience. I can't respect my mother. She is a very forceful person, a lot stronger than my father." Jim has, he admitted, some of his mother's stubbornness and temperament, "but I like to think myself milder than my mother."

The thing that makes Jim furious with his mother is that she still treats him like a child. She doesn't suggest, she orders vociferously. He gets angry and shouts: "Stop it, stop it, stop it!" He exists "in a limbo." On the one hand, he lives in an apartment of his own and works as a mature, independent person. He hates to visit his home but he does visit it about twice a month (they live in the same city). There is nothing happy about these visits—"I go back home as a child."

Among his father's limitations are an excessive dedication to his work, too little time spent with the family, and the lack of forcefulness in the family. Jim hopes to spend more time with his own children and to be an "informed adviser" to his son. On the credit side is his father's intelligence and good temper. His father is more likely than his mother to offer suggestions rather than to issue orders.

There was a note of desperation in Jim's speculations about the means of escaping the role of the child, thrust upon him by his mother. The pull was, apparently, strong and was not offset by the independent role he felt he enacted in the college community.

Jim reflected aloud, half asking for the interviewer's counsel: "I think I may continue to be a little protected child unless I take some drastic step to break with them completely. The root of my problem is my economic dependence. Maybe I should ask them to set money aside for me (Jim was to embark upon many years of professional training upon graduation from college) so that I wouldn't have to ask for money like a child. If I had a car of my own I would not be forced into the role of a child, asking to have a car for the weekend. Perhaps I should announce that I'll see them only on holidays—a few times a year." Jim added at one point: "I wouldn't want to feel pressured to marry just to escape my family"—apparently assuming that marriage might provide some shortcut to a secure sense of adulthood.

Jim felt "contempt" for his older brother, his limited aspirations and education, and he disclaimed knowing anything about his siblings' feelings about the family. His first sexual partner was a non-Jewish girl. His flaunting announcement at a family dinner that he was moving into his girl friend's apartment succeeded in shocking his conventional parents (see pp. 86–87 for additional discussion of Jim's sexual life).

Part of Jim's rebellion against his family appeared to stem from upward mobility as he perceived it. He sometimes called himself Unitarian instead of Jewish. When questioned, he explained that this was a philosophical reaction to his discarding of religious dogma in college. When the interviewer asked whether he might like to "pass" as a non-Jew, he responded that he didn't look Jewish, adding that perhaps there was indeed an element of social mobility in his attitude.

The youth just described was not the only one plagued by economic dependence upon his parents. "The check from home is a monthly reinforcement of dependence. Parents send the check and then ask all kinds of questions: how are the classes going, what you are doing. The check is a kind of a blackmail. You come here and it is really something. You have to decide whether you are using your time and resources properly. You can hardly explain it to yourself and there are all those letters and questions."

Sons of affluent parents were occasionally caught in the dilemma of resenting the power parents derived from economic support but being unwilling to forego accustomed conveniences or even luxuries. One respondent presented a moving account of the way economic dependence upon his parents pulled him back into a younger and less mature role and, conversely, hindered his growth. But he spent the summer following his junior year traveling in Europe. Much as he resented his dependence he obviously had no intention of foregoing travel to take a summer job (during the years when summer jobs for college students were available).

The expense and duration of education makes complete financial independence from parents well nigh impossible. All the same, some sons, who both resented their parents and doubted their own courage, expressed self-contempt for not confronting the challenge of self-support. The anguish of one such youth, exacerbated by the criticism of his girl friend is described on pp. 117–18.

In the next case, the process creating the son's dependency involved an especially strong sense of personal inadequacy. The crucial element in the son's dependence was the anxiety and foreboding with which he faced the world. The need to win parental approval and the rewards of the role of a nurtured child are secondary ties to parents. This youth perceived himself as weak and undeserving. The psychological summary includes the following: "His behavior is often self-punishing, perhaps in the hope of forestalling rejection from outside."

Several features characterized Tim's unhappy family life: a cold, rigid, and domineering mother; a strained, religiously mixed marriage; a weak father; and Tim's poor health since early childhood.

Tim could think of only two favorable traits of his mother: "She took care of my physical needs: made my bed, fixed my breakfast, and she praised me when I did well in school." The list of maternal limitations is longer: "She was afraid of expressing her emotions. For example, I never embraced her. She never embraced me. She had too many 'rigid rules.' For example, I came home once and said that some exam was dull and boring. 'Don't say that,' she scolded, 'it shows lack of respect.' She has a tendency to be very anxious and tense, and she is bigoted against Negroes and Jews."

His father was more approachable. "He listened to me more than my mother did but there is little friendship between us. He is not strong enough in personality. My mother did all the punishing in the family. He's subservient to her. I felt disgusted. He had no integrity and failed to make his religion the religion of the family. He tends to be tyrannical in a petty way."

Partly because of Tim's chronic illness and partly because he was "the smart one," and his sister "the rebel"—his parents, he thought, were overprotective and at the same time more demanding of him. His father has been tenderer towards his sister who moved away from the parental home. Tim feels anxious about getting into the real world, paying bills, coping with an apartment lease, living alone. He actually felt relieved when his parents opposed on financial grounds his request for an apartment of his own.

Tim thinks he is smarter and certainly more liberal than both his parents but admitted that his mother's and perhaps even his father's approval still "matters a little." He argues with his mother "quite a bit." He is not frightened of what his mother may do to him but "a little frightened of what she may think" of him. She makes scathing remarks, calling him a sheep for following the "hippie radicals" and she considers opposition to the draft to be unpatriotic and unmasculine. He tries not to make his mother's views matter but they do.

We have illustrated a variety of dependent sons whose need for parental control, support, and approval was perceived by the respondents (or judged by us) to be excessive for their age. Some of these sons attempted to rebel openly, others conducted an unconscious passive rebellion.

The emphasis upon dependence does not mean that all the independent sons were invariably free from the scars of parental relationships. Among the "independent and alienated" sons (see Table 7.4), for example, was a senior whose life style dismayed his parents. This was a depressed youth who viewed his own future and, indeed, the future of the world as completely bleak. He told the interviewer in a bland tone, that he could not think of even a single good quality of his mother. The nearly complete break with his parents, economic independence from them and his persistence in a deviant (from the parental point of view) style of life—all have excluded this senior from the "dependent" category. Possibly a psychiatric analysis would discover that suppressed anger at his parents and a passive rebellion against them constituted both the cause of his depression and his rejection of parental values. He differed from the dependent sons in the well nigh complete break with his parents.

The sons of the less-educated fathers might have been expected to be freer of parental control. Not only had they surpassed their fathers (and generally, their mothers as well) in education, but also they were more likely than the sons of college-educated fathers to have scholarships and part-time jobs and hence to enjoy a degree of economic independence from their families. These expectations are supported by the data. Of the thirty-nine sons of college-educated fathers, 16 or 42 percent were judged to be psychologically dependent upon one or both parents. The comparable figure for the upwardly mobile sons was five out of twenty-three, or only 22 percent. Among these five dependent sons, three were dependent upon their strong mothers. Superior education did not always supply the son with a powerful enough weapon. One uneducated but strong father could still dominate his son by directing his ridicule at his son's vulnerable traits.

The saliency of family relationships and the high incidence of unresolved problems with one or both parents may appear surprising when all around us voices proclaim the weakening of the family and the predominance of the peer group.

The psychological struggles twenty-one-year-old men may still carry on with their parents have, no doubt, been exacerbated by certain social factors. This is especially true in college-educated and, presumably, more affluent families. College seniors from such families experienced considerable ambiguity in their relationships to parents. Their thrust towards independence and autonomy was strongly encouraged both in theory and in practice. Unlike working-class youth attending a local college, middle-class men were likely to have a separate apartment even when the parental home was within commuting distance. Their sexual life, although it generally violated parental standards, was, nevertheless, not subject to parental surveillance or control. If the sons decided to marry while still in college, this decision was not seriously challenged. In the past, marriage symbolized the full assumption of the adult role and, in our society at any rate, an independence from the family of orientation. Much of this ethos of independence remains despite changes which make its realization difficult. The prolongation of education, the diffusion of birth control, general affluence, the acceptance of the fact that marriage need not necessarily demand of the young man the role of the provider—these have all contributed to the declining age at first marriage since the turn of the century. But some survival of the traditional role definitions can be seen in the senior's outrage at some parental pressure: "I am a married man. You can't tell me what to do." The cost and prolongation of professional training, however, made sons economically dependent upon parents. Even when money was not used by parents as a means of control, the fact of economic dependence was irritating and, above all, a symbol of immaturity. All in all, dependence in some sectors, autonomy in others, and ambiguity in still others created an unstable and troublesome masculine self-image.

8

THE FUTURE: Occupational Plans, the Draft, and Politics

Not every senior had made an occupational choice at the time of the interview and those who had were not always free of misgivings. But students uncertain about their occupational goals were no carefree vagabonds. The extent of their unhappiness is reflected in their psychological profiles (see Tables 8.2 and 8.3). The overwhelming majority approached the role of worker and family provider as one of the touchstones of masculinity. To be unsure about one's choice of work was tantamount to asking: "What am I going to do with my life?" Only three or four spoke of jobs as an indifferent means to a modest livelihood, with the meaning of life centered upon interests other than work.[1]

---

1. We considered and had to discard the hypothesis that students who were attracted to the hippie, communal form of life or to radical politics may have dropped out from this intellectually traditional and demanding college and consequently were underrepresented in the senior class of 1970. The proportion of dropouts (calculated as percentage of entering freshmen who did not graduate at the conclusion of their senior year, in June, September, or February) was about the same as in the preceding five years. The class of 1972, on the other hand, showed a higher proportion of students who failed to graduate on time.

THE OCCUPATIONAL FUTURE

The attitudes of the sixty-two seniors towards their future occupations are summarized in Table 8.1.

At one pole were 26 percent of the sample, whose occupational goals were firm and who had no conflicts or misgivings about their choices. Another 29 percent had also chosen their future careers but were greatly anxious about making the grade or experienced other conflicts to be illustrated presently.

Table 8.1.   Attitudes towards Future Occupational Roles

	Number	Percent
Occupational choice made, with reasonable confidence and with no serious strains	16	26
Occupational choice made but serious anxiety about making the grade, including other strains	18	29
Uncertain, pessimistic, and depressed about future goals	15	24
Lowered original occupational aspirations with some sense of defeat	7	11.3
Undecided but with strong resources and achievement goals	2	3.2
Unrealistic occupational goals, exceeding resources	2	3.2
Miscellaneous	2	3.2
	62	99.9

At the other pole, 24 percent of the men were "in limbo," as one of them put it: confused, lost, uncertain as to what they wished to do, pessimistic, and depressed about their outlook. Thus, about one out of four seniors suffered major stress in the role he perceived to be significant for his masculine identity. Eleven percent had lowered their aspirations because they realized they lacked the ability or drive to pursue their original goals, and felt some sense of defeat over this failure.

The remaining six men, or about 10 percent presented special problems. Two had goals we judged to be grandiose in the light of their modest resources. Another two seniors were still torn between various choices, but both had a high academic average and a strong need for achievement. Finally, two students dropped out of college after the interview and were working.

THE "LOST AND DEPRESSED" SENIORS

Among the various types in this category were the "social rebels" who despised the establishment and its success values without, however, finding in radical politics a full-time occupation. When social criticism is in the air, personal problems tend to be rationalized in expressions of social alienation. But we included among the social rebels only those who were seriously involved with ideological and social issues or political activities—whatever other personal influences may have contributed to their indecision about work.

One social rebel (the son of a Jewish immigrant father with less than eight years of schooling) considered himself a pacifist. He was a leader in radical politics on the campus but limited his rebellion to nonviolent protest. He was prepared to go to jail rather than accept the draft. In some ways he was closer to the hippie culture than to radical activism. At one time he considered an academic career. "I could really groove with it," he said, adding that he would never get tenure because he would get involved in student politics and would probably write poetry instead of scholarly articles. Moreover, he rejected the "package-deal establishment" careers and had "more respect for freaks than for conformists who move from college to graduate school in a lock-step progression." All the same, he would have to make a living and was worried about his future. He thought he might start a restaurant with some friends.

At the time of the interview his main problem was to regain his emotional equilibrium shattered by his wife's infidelity and desertion. He had a straight-A record in high school and did well in college until his marital problems, in the beginning of the senior year, made class attendance impossible and graduation problematic. His ethical qualms about chances for a good life in our society, as well as his emotional crisis, depleted him of all motivation to study and created anxiety and pessimism about the future.

Another senior (a son of a college-educated Catholic father) who had returned to college after two years in the Peace Corps, was also critical of our society. The central evil was the Vietnam war, he asserted. Once he saw how wrong that war was, he lost faith in all the institutions and materialistic values that kept the awful war machine going. A man who was oppressed by forces he cannot control, he added, was incapable of playing the dominant masculine role.

His parents, and especially his mother, had too much reverence for professional careers. In his freshman year, when he hardly knew anything, his parents badgered him about his choice of a major. In order to stop the inquiries, he picked economics. As for himself, he did not glorify professional careers. "Writing a good philosophy paper is a game, just another skill like playing a guitar," he said with restrained anger. "I don't believe that being a General Motors executive is necessarily better than being a bartender." He had no idea of his future: "I'll just try to get some kind of a job that won't drive me completely crazy."

Still another senior (a son of a Jewish high school graduate, recently deceased) became "politicized," as he put it, and lost all interest in his major, physics, which he came to consider irrelevant and meaningless. He had stopped attending classes and described himself as "lost and confused." He was torn between his responsibility to his widowed mother and his conviction that, faced with the draft, he should either go to jail or leave the country. He despised success values and conventional careers but at the same time doubted that any activities to change society would be effective and worth his effort.

Apart from the social rebels (all of whom, incidentally, maintained at least a B average in college before they became politicized) the "lost and depressed" category included men who had suffered a major defeat in their chosen field, which made their original occupational goal patently unattainable. (Two other students in this situation persisted unrealistically to aspire beyond their capacities and seven were able to compromise and lower their aspirations but not without some sense of defeat [see Table 8.1].) The student about to be described was crushed by his failure.

This was a black student (a son of college-educated Protestant parents) who had a good academic and athletic record in a private high school. He had intended to become a physician but did so poorly in his freshman and sophomore premed courses in college that he abandoned his plans. In the interview he reported his major strain as "having no goal in life. Nothing has any meaning. College has put a dent in my ego. I lost my place on the roster." He became so depressed in his sophomore year by his poor academic record that he stopped going to classes. He described the vicious cycle: "Instead of telling myself that I'll do the best I can, even if it is only a C, I just didn't do any work and wound up with, like, thirty points of Incomplete." He could not face getting mediocre grades. The academic defeat coincided with an unhappy love affair. He was not attracted to any field and, were it not for the draft, would have taken a couple of years off to find himself.

This youth made some reference to the racial problem but his psychological profile offered a more plausible explanation of his paralysis of will. His passivity and restlessness were manifested in other areas of life apart from college work. Despite his "success" with women he was obviously hostile to them. They all wanted more of him than he could give, he explained. For example, he would like the girl to leave right after sex, he would like to be left alone. He will marry a "warm, serving woman who would love me," even if he himself is not in love with her.

He described his childhood as an unhappy one. His driving, cold, career-oriented mother was more successful than his father (who was absent from home for long periods, in a job that demanded traveling). The son felt that his mother was as poor a wife to his father as she was a mother. The clinical psychologist spoke of a "failure of masculine identification." Be this as it may, there was ample evidence of resentment against his mother and women in general, combined with a search for support. Prior to college he had never been confronted by failure. Combined with his psychological difficulties, the deflation of the ego suffered in the sophomore year depleted his motivation to study.

Whereas the youth just described maintained adequate motivation when his high school efforts won him recognition, others with similar family backgrounds had a long history of passivity.

Among the lost and depressed seniors were some characterized by passive and disorganized rebellion against cold but demanding mothers and weak fathers.

One such youth said that he tended "not to want to do anything much." He is a son of a Catholic college-educated father. Neither politics, religion, nor sex mean much to him. He flunked out of college and was readmitted after a year's leave. He escapes problems by taking acid trips with a "bunch of guys" and he has dealt in drugs. He has had some homosexual fears and several heterosexual affairs. The psychological profile described him as immature, looking for easy gratification by manipulation rather than through hard work, and looking for affection without being able to give much in return.

The parental marriage was an unhappy one. Both parents drank and if the son had some contempt for his father for failure to make anything of his life, his attitude towards his mother was one of anger. His mother was the intellectually and emotionally dominant spouse, who "pushed us all." "She acted," the boy said, "like an asshole when she was drunk." His father was too weak. Were he in his father's place he would "crack his mother or split, she inflicts shit on him." But his father was "easily hurt and too lenient."

Anger at a cold, demanding mother, who pushed children to do well in school, characterized another floundering youth, a son of Catholic college-educated parents. He was on probation and had lost interest not only in his studies but in his longtime hobby, photography. He described himself as always anxious, depressed, with the future—a "complete blank." The psychological profile tells of a young man, too depressed and self-involved to have any vital energy for academic work. "My mother," he explained bitterly, "thinks that the only learning is in a library. She would dismiss a factory job as a learning experience." He appeared to be passively rebelling against his mother, who demanded achievement without rewarding her children with sufficient love.

Still another type among the lost and depressed was represented by students whose exceptional need for scholastic achievement was combined with low self-esteem. These students had not discarded achievement as a value. In fact, achievement mattered so much that they were paralyzed by the fear of failure. One student felt that he could write a good paper if only he were not so afraid of grades and of teachers' criticism—"If only I could relax." But he feared that he "would write or say something stupid" and, being so dependent upon the approval of others, he was afraid to take risks. Teaching, he thought, would be a good way to avoid the draft but the fear of talking before groups ruled out even this expedient choice. He delayed applying for a teaching job beyond the deadline.

Another youth (a son of a Protestant professional man) may have also been petrified by a fear of failure. Much as he admired his successful father, he hoped that his own children would respect him less and love him more. His father expected so much of him, he said, that he would not have been able to satisfy him even had he performed "terrifically well" in college.

The discrepancy between high aspirations and a low self-image, or between an ideal of dominance and a gentle personality must have played a part in depletion of occupational ambition in the case described by the clinical psychologists as follows: "This student defends himself with a show of confidence and self-assurance but he has suffered hurt and disillusionment in himself. A gentle, moderate temperament coexists with a desire to be assertive and influential." Although he had been admitted to an excellent law school, he was consulting a psychiatrist about his "total lack of direction."

The lack of occupational commitment in the last group of cases may have also stemmed from passive rebellion against parental pressures for achievement. But unlike men completely depleted of motivation, these students did not consciously reject success goals even though their lack of confidence made the outcome doubtful in their own eyes.

OTHER STRAINS IN OCCUPATIONAL ROLES

The problems that immobilized one out of four seniors, also plagued, if to a lesser extent, other seniors. The difference is one of degree. Indeed, only 26 percent of the total sample were firm and free of conflicts about their occupational goals. Anxiety about one's ability to make the grade in the chosen field was not uncommon. One senior, planning to enter law school, acknowledged the strength of his ambition to be rich and successful. But he was not overly optimistic about his ability to put out the effort his aims required. He would like, he admitted, to control others but felt that he "came on too wishy-washy." The psychological profile described him as "rigid, constricted, and overcontrolled, trying to fit into a set structure and lacking in originality, spirit, and spontaneity."

Ethical problems seriously disturbed 13 percent of the sample. "Self-advancement versus integrity" and "financial remuneration versus service to society" were mentioned as dilemmas of occupational choices. A black student, for example, wondered how he was going to serve the black community with his French major. He did not want to bring up his children in a roach-and-rat-ridden apartment but neither did he wish to separate himself from the ghetto.

He was worried that teaching French would not make much of a contribution to his people.

Among those torn by moral conflicts, a few suffered less guilt than shame in the face of peer disapproval of self-serving careers. One son of college-educated Protestant parents looked forward to material rewards of a business career. The "amorality of the business game" bothered him a little, he confessed, but not nearly as much as did his friends' criticisms of his opportunistic and overambitious character. In order to avoid the draft, he considered teaching in a prep school, though he agreed with his parents that a lifelong teaching career was "small potatoes and would be a waste of my talents." All the same, he savored the reaction of his critical friends should he decide to teach for a year or two: "It would be a slap in their faces."

Apart from such moral conflicts, a nearly identical number of seniors, 12 percent of the sample, had sacrificed serious interests, sometimes under parental pressure, to more financially profitable or more prestigious occupations. These interests varied from composing songs, playing musical instruments, writing fiction, painting, and high school teaching (not as a temporary means of avoiding the draft, but as a permanent career). Some of these students blamed themselves for lack of courage "to chuck the career drive," others were resigned and invoked their future responsibilities as family providers.

Finally, some science majors remarked that they were not "too psyched up" about graduate school because they felt "cut off from life" in the laboratory. Others than science majors occasionally expressed the same feeling of being cut off from life and hinted that, were it not for the draft, they would have dropped out of college.

As the following section on the draft will show, its effect upon the choice of occupations was considerable. Students, vacillating between two or more graduate schools, decided in favor of those carrying deferment. Others intended to take certain jobs for the duration of the Vietnam war in order to avoid the draft with full intent to change occupations thereafter.

SOME FACTORS IN DEGREE OF OCCUPATIONAL COMMITMENT

The case histories of students who were uncertain and depressed about their occupational future suggested that parental relationships played a part in their depression. This hypothesis is strengthened by the comparison of this alienated group with the students who were firm and happy about their career choices. The percentages of highly unsatisfactory paternal relationships were only 31 for the sixteen occupationally committed students free of conflicts, but nearly 67 for the fifteen floundering students. Similarly, the unsatisfactory maternal relationships in the two groups were 31 percent and 53 percent, respectively. Moreover, mother-dominated marriages were more frequent among the occupationally uncommitted than in the total sample, the figures being 40 percent for the former but only 19 percent in the sample as a whole.

Upon further scrutiny this association between unsatisfactory parental relationships and the absence of occupational goals was found to characterize only the Protestant and the Catholic students, the Jews constituting an exception.

Case histories suggest the hypothesis that the lack of occupational direction had different origins in different religious groups.

The six floundering Catholics all had resentfully referred to their mothers as demanding and cold. It is plausible that their occupational problems may be traced to rebellion, overt or passive, against their mothers, who demanded high academic performance but did not reward it with love. By contrast, none among the four uncommitted Jews reported this syndrome of a demanding but cold mother. Their difficulties stemmed from other causes. Two of the floundering Jews had become politicized, as described earlier in this chapter, turning against establishment careers but seeing no future for themselves in radical politics. Two others suffered from a discrepancy between high aspirations and low self-esteem. One of these two wanted to be tough, powerful, and successful. However, he scored low on the law school aptitude tests and had to give up the hope of a career in law, without finding a suitable alternative.

Thus, the uncommitted Jewish students, unlike the Protestants and the Catholics, did not consider their parental relationships to be unhappy. The depleted occupational ambition appeared to be related to ideological factors or to the discrepancy between aspirations and low self-esteem. These phenomena may have also been the by-products of some aspects of familial relationships; other than those covered by this study.

The effect of father's education upon the degree of occupational commitment can only be surmised because of the small number of cases in a cross-classification by father's education and religion.

Nevertheless, the data enable us to put forth the following hypothesis. The sons from less-educated and lower-class backgrounds appear to be overrepresented among both extremes; the purposeful career-bound group and the lost and depressed students. On the one hand, the drive for upward mobility inspired the lower-class youth with a sense of purpose, relatively lacking in sons of better-educated, more affluent families. But other youths from lower-class backgrounds (in some cases, perhaps, because of a lack of adequate preparation) encountered special problems of adjustment to college, in comparison with sons from more advantaged homes and were discouraged by their failure to make the grade.

The psychological profiles of the fifteen uncommitted were compared with forty-two of the rest of the students. The results are reported in Tables 8.2 and 8.3. The Adjective Check List for "my real self" vividly presents the poor self-image and the markedly lower scores of the uncommitted on Self-Confidence, Self-Control, Personal Adjustment, Achievement, Dominance, and Heterosexuality. The uncommitted were relatively high on Succorance. The California Psychological Inventory confirms the psychological type of the uncommitted on Dominance, Well-Being, Socialization, Self-Control, Achievement via Conformance,

Table 8.2. Uncommitted Students Compared to the Rest on the ACL for "My Real Self" (Percentage of Scores Falling at Standard Mean Score or Above)

Trait	Uncommitted (N = 15)	The Others (N = 42)*
Self-Confidence	21.4	59.5
Self-Control	14.3	47.6
Personal Adjustment	21.4	45.2
Achievement	21.4	66.7
Dominance	28.6	61.9
Intraception	50.0	83.3
Affiliation	14.3	42.9
Heterosexuality	28.6	52.4
Autonomy	57.7	59.5
Aggression	57.1	61.9
Succorance	64.3	28.6
Self-Abasement	57.1	45.2
Counseling Readiness	57.1	40.5

*Five personality tests were missing from the case studies.

Table 8.3. Uncommitted Students Compared to the Rest on the CPI (Percentage of Scores Falling at Standard Mean Score or Above)

Trait	Uncommitted (N = 15)	The Others (N = 42*
Dominance	53.3	76.2
Self-Acceptance	80.0	85.7
Well-Being	13.3	40.5
Socialization	13.3	47.6
Self-Control	13.3	40.5
Achievement via Conformance	26.7	40.5
Achievement via Independence	93.3	92.9
Intellectual Efficiency	53.3	73.8
Psychological-Mindedness	86.7	83.3
Femininity	60.0	73.8

*Five personality tests were missing from the case studies.

and Intellectual Efficiency. On the other hand, the average score of the uncommitted on Achievement via Independence is high, suggesting some potential that was not realized.

The fact that the uncommitted were both lower on Heterosexuality (ACL) and on Femininity (CPI) is not the contradiction it might appear to be. The low-scorer on Heterosexuality is described in the ACL manual as dispirited, inhibited, aloof. The low-scorer on Femininity (CPI) is one who is not patient, persevering, respectful, and accepting of others, etc.

THE DRAFT

It will come as no surprise to the reader that the great majority of the seniors in this 1969–1970 study opposed the Vietnam war and were ultimately ready to take almost any step to avoid fighting in a war they felt to be immoral. A student, expressing the dominant attitude, said: "Even lying to avoid the draft is better than shooting at people who aren't shooting at you." Among the opponents of the war, some would stop short of going to prison or fleeing the country. But they generally cited pragmatic (e.g., damage to future careers) rather than moral or patriotic reasons for eschewing such drastic steps.

Only 10 percent of the sample were resigned to serve if drafted and if no legitimate escape were available. Another 10 percent were members of the ROTC or planned to join the reserves. Eighty percent either expected graduate school, occupational, or health deferments and, in the absence of such avenues of escape, were severely disturbed by the problem of the draft. Even students who expected an occupational deferment were not always free of problems. In a number of cases the occupation was chosen precisely as a hedge against the draft and in spite of other, more genuine occupational interests. High school teaching was accepted by many seniors only as the lesser of two evils and was resented by some as an interruption of long-range career interests. Even so demanding a career as medicine was chosen under duress by some students to whom other occupations were more congenial. The threat of the draft spread a shadow over the earlier college years. Several students spoke of their anxiety over grades because what was at stake was not merely admission to graduate school but the risk of being drafted.

To have described 20 percent of the students as resigned and 80 percent as resentful and searching for some escape from the draft does not convey the ambivalence and the conflict students underwent in arriving at the final decision. Indeed, asked to list major sources of current strains, one out of every four seniors in the sample said: "the draft."

The ambivalence sometimes stemmed from guilt over occupational exemption and the fact that "others will fight and may die for me." Some students had brothers in Vietnam and experienced even greater guilt over their own refusal to serve. Ideological conflicts with parents were mentioned by many. The generational gap in attitudes was apparent since it was generally the parents, despite their concern for their sons, who stressed the patriotic duty to serve the country and were shocked by the sons' talk about jail or fleeing the country. "My parents are gung-ho about military service and would be humiliated to face their friends were I to resist the draft," explained a senior. Another senior reported: "I try to explain my position to my relatives and they are sort of revolted. They say: 'Aren't you going to be a man and stand up and fight for your country? Where's your patriotism and your courage?' Then I nonchalantly explain that I don't have the courage or patriotism and that I don't consider these things particularly desirable. I can't stand this cult of masculine toughness but still I don't like this hassle with my relatives."

A few students, under cross-pressures from their families and their antiwar friends, had not been able to resolve the inner conflict. For example, one youth vacillated between the disturbing suspicion that he opposed the draft out of fear and, on the other hand, that his refusal to serve was a brave moral stand. "I wish I could stop thinking about it," he added.

Finally, some youths, deferred on grounds of health, fantasized about missed opportunities for a heroic gesture. "I wish I were eligible," said one of this group, "so that I could resist."

THE ROLE OF THE CITIZEN

The campus on which this study was done was the scene of a major political upheaval during the junior year of our respondents. Students occupied college buildings, the academic community was torn by political strife, the confrontation between students and the police (called in by the administration to get the students out of the occupied buildings) was a bitter and a bloody one. This section is based upon the reports of the seniors about their behavior and their attitudes during that turbulent period. The political role referred to in the title of this section is one played out on the campus, with only occasional references to society at large.

The power of passionately committed minorities in political movements is confirmed anew in this study. Only about 20 percent of the sample could be described as "active participants" in the struggle, either "on the left" or in support of the administration. Active participation was defined as any activity, other than merely signing a petition, e.g., "sitting in" in the student-occupied buildings, joining collective action to strike or prevent the strike, attending meetings of partisan groups, and the like. We were careful to inquire into actual activities and attitudes at the time of the upheaval, rather than retrospective appraisals, and we classified as activists those who were involved at least for a time and not necessarily throughout the crisis. Thus, for example, a self-confessed "wishy-washy liberal" testified that he became active at the end of the period, having been "radicalized by police brutality."

At the other extreme from the "activists" were some 15 percent of the group who managed to detach themselves completely from the dramatic events and who spoke with no embarrassment whatsoever about their detachment. Some left the campus for the duration of the trouble, others took a job. One senior explained: "I needed the time to study, sleep, and to catch up in general." If they volunteered any explanation for their seeming indifference, it was to cite preoccupation with future careers or, in a few cases, with serious psychological problems having nothing to do with politics. Not counted among the "indifferent" was a reporter for the student radio station who described the troubled period as "probably the best time of my life." The nostalgia for the excitement of the past centered around his own successful performance as a reporter with only casual comments upon the issues. He agreed with the need for some reforms but opposed the methods of the militants.

It is no exaggeration to describe the great majority of the students, some 65 percent of the sample, as uneasy, guilty bystanders. Degrees of felt guilt varied, as did the sympathies with one or another of the polarized minorities at different stages of the events. The explanations for noninvolvement ranged from brief and straightforward admissions, such as "I was afraid of getting my head bashed," to involved psychological self-dissection or elaborate political analysis.

Some men who attributed their lack of participation to psychological inadequacies included a senior who signed two contradictory petitions because he lacked the courage to refuse. Less self-loathing but still self-disparaging was another student who said that he generally tended to tone down his opinions so as not to "cause static." Among the psychological sources of inaction, in addition to the admitted lack of moral courage, was depression. For example, one antiwar and anti-Establishment senior, in sympathy with leftist militants in theory, felt too dejected to enter the melée. He felt the future to be bleak and meaningless.

Most explained their nonparticipation in ideological terms. Some believed in the need for reform but were repelled by the militant methods and rhetoric. Others were disillusioned by both the student militants and the violence of the police summoned to the campus by the administration. Still others were outraged by student riots but felt that no group on the campus provided leadership for dealing effectively with the militant students. "A plague on

both your houses," summed up the position of several "bystanders."

Associated with the intellectual arguments of the nonpartici-
pants was a familiar social phenomenon. Many of them were
members of social networks which generated ambivalence and
cross-pressures. We have too few militants to test the hypothesis
that theirs was a relatively more homogeneous social milieu. But
students who found themselves on the fence during the upheaval
referred with great frequency to their marginality. "I had friends in
both camps" became a familiar refrain. One self-styled "jock"
roomed with conservative fellow athletes but maintained his association with some radicalized friends. When he was about to join
the conservative opposition, he was "clobbered in the discussion"
with his radical friends and in consequence did nothing. Several
seniors, close to their families, described themselves as more liberal
than their families and more conservative than their friends. "I am
stigmatized by my friends for taking the side of the administration,"
remarked one senior, "but my family is so conservative that I have
to defend the SDS and then I am criticized by my mother for my
radicalism."

The most striking conclusion concerning student reaction to the
historic political upheaval on their campus during their junior year
was the small minority of participants on either side of the political
spectrum. Some 15 percent were completely detached, to the point
of leaving the campus for the duration of the trouble. The great
majority, as we have pointed out, 65 percent of the total, were
uneasy, ambivalent bystanders.[2]

2. Student politics have been recently studied perhaps more extensively than any
other topic covered in this book. Among the relevant books containing bibliogra-
phies are Amitai Etzioni (1968: 398), Kenneth Keniston (1965, 1968), and Seymour M. Lipset, ed. (1967).

9

A THEORETICAL
SUMMARY

It is not the purpose of this chapter to recapitulate the findings presented in the book. This conclusion aims at a more general theoretical overview.

A REVIEW OF AREAS OF STRESS

This study did not undertake to examine the lives of the seniors in all their concreteness and fullness. Since our focus was on role strains, the portrayal is one-sided because it minimizes the delights and satisfactions of life. But if, in one way, the study presents too dark a picture, in another, it is not dark enough. Though emphasizing role strains, we did not attempt to cover them all. For example, we did not study systematically relationships with professors, employers, or with relatives beyond the immediate family. Moreover, our quest centered upon the distinctively masculine role strains, rather than problems men and women might have in common at this stage of life. This was the case also when what was distinctively masculine referred only to a unique form or intensity of some common human problem. We also tended to emphasize strains which stemmed from changing sex roles and which were at least potentially susceptible to social control. Finally, idiosyncratic psychological difficulties were discussed only when they impinged upon role behavior or attitudes.

Even had elementary sociological principles not forewarned us, common knowledge would have led us to expect that role strains were inescapable for youths living in our rapidly changing, complex, and relatively unintegrated society. Over 80 percent of the sample did experience difficulties, ranging from mild to severe, in fulfilling role obligations in one or more statuses covered by the study. The "adjusted" 20 percent included a disproportionately high number of "low disclosers," suggesting the possibility that we judged these men adjusted only because we failed to penetrate their reserve. The extent of strain may have been underestimated for another reason. Apart from problems studied by means of schedules, scales, and standardized psychological tests, a degree of subjectivity, no doubt, entered into the distinction between the "no strain" and the "mild strain" categories. We required explicit evidence of difficulty and, therefore, some latent problems may have escaped detection. All in all, the figure of 80 percent, if anything, underestimates the proportion of seniors troubled by some degree of role strain.

Classified by the concrete areas of stress, the highest proportion of seniors, 72 percent, experienced in the past, or at the time of the interview, some problems in the sexual sphere. This includes the 24 percent of the sample distressed by the fact that they were still virgins, and the 48 percent who, though sexually experienced, reported one or more of the specific difficulties discussed in Chapter 3.

The next highest proportion of all seniors, 53 percent, were worried about their future role as workers. Among these, 24 percent were uncertain, depressed, and pessimistic about occupational goals, and the remaining 29 percent had a higher-than-average anxiety about their capacity to reach the chosen vocational objectives. The importance of these concerns reflected something else than the need to earn a living. Neither the "lost and depressed," nor the "ambitious but insecure" men doubted in the spring of 1970 that they could find some means of livelihood upon graduation. Clearly, work, and success in it, still symbolized the essence of manhood for these youths. Even men who expressed disdain for the "lock-step" careers of the establishment were tormented by their sense of void and the absence of appealing alternative life styles.

Next in incidence of strain came family relationships. Over 33 percent of the men had not attained the degree of independence from their parents they deemed to be a touchstone of manhood. An additional 15 percent were independent but at a cost of estrangement from or a complete break with their parents.

Problems in relation to parents were summarized also under other headings. Highly unsatisfactory of painfully ambivalent father-son relationships plagued 43 percent of the sample. Equally unsatisfactory relationships with the mother characterized only 26 percent of the group. [1]

In relation to women, apart from the sexual sphere, the failure to attain the ideal of masculine leadership or dominance caused the most severe strain. Forty-five percent of the sample felt deficient in assertiveness. This proportion included a few who blamed women for perpetuating a perninicious social norm by expecting males to be dominant.

Less prevalent than the sense of failure with regard to the ideal of masculine leadership, was the experience of intellectual insecurity in contacts with women. Thirty percent of the seniors reported such feelings in relation to former or current women friends. Several of these seniors were explicit in affirming the norm of male intellectual superiority. It was, however, not always clear whether feelings of anxiety were aroused only in the face of marked intellectual superiority of one's female associates, or whether even equal female intelligence sufficed to create stress.

Of the sixty-two seniors, only six, or 10 percent, experienced role strains in nearly every sphere of life covered by the study. Such general maladjustment strongly suggests a psychologically impaired personality handicapped in coping with life. This across-the-board stress, however, was the exception, not the rule. Clearly we cannot rest with an explanation that would attribute observed problems exclusively to psychological impairment.

In the following section we shall attempt to classify, from a sociological point of view, the varieties of pain experienced by the seniors.

1. Since the categories of dependency and ambivalence occasionally overlapped, we presented each variety of familial problems separately.

MODES OF ROLE STRAIN

Role strain was defined in this study as felt or latent difficulty in role fulfillment or the experience of low rewards for role conformity.

Viewed from a sociological perspective, each case of role strain may be usefully analyzed in terms of at least five attributes: what, how, where, who, and how much. More precisely, a case of role strain: 1) involves certain components of roles, i.e., norms, beliefs, values; 2) exemplifies a particular mode of difficulty (see the discussion of modes of strain below); 3) occurs in a given structural, institutional, or situational context (e.g., intrarole, role-set, status-set, economic institution or a crisis situation, such as an earthquake); 4) is experienced as an intrapsychic or an interpersonal conflict with particular role partners; and 5) exhibits various degrees of intensity.

The use of the scheme may be illustrated by applying it to two or three illustrations of role strains in recent studies. For example: a school superintendent accepts the norm that school personnel must be selected on merit but is asked by an influential local politician, as a personal favor, to appoint a poorly qualified teacher. The elements involved in this strain are legitimized role obligations and pressures. The mode is that of conflict; the locus is a single role enmeshed in an educational institution; the personnel is exemplified by an interpersonal conflict with a single role partner (Neal Gross, et al., 1964). Again: an officer-instructor in the staff school of the Air Force Academy is troubled because the typical military interaction between him and the other teacher-officers is not the kind which he feels should prevail among colleagues in an educational institution. In this case the elements involved are two normative expectations; the mode is conflict; the locus—a status-set of officer and teacher; the personnel—intrapsychic. In the same study, some officer-instructors were troubled because the assignment to teaching was felt to be detrimental to their advancement in the air force. Here, the role element is behavioral obligation; the mode—low rewards for role conformity; the locus—a military role; the personnel—intrapsychic (J. W. Getzels and E. G. Guba, 1954).

Existing classifications of role strains occasionally fail to distinguish the five above-named attributes and base their types haphazardly upon diverse dimensions. The proposed paradigm may, through "substruction of property space" (Allen H. Barton, 1955), bring to light the assumptions underlying various typologies, point out the lacunae and the inconsistencies.

The attribute here termed the "mode of strain" has been least fully developed in the existing literature and hence particularly requires elucidation.

Six modes of role strain were distinguished in the experiences of the seniors: 1) ambiguity (or anomie); 2) lack of congruence between the idiosyncratic personality and role requirements; 3) socially structured scarcity of resources for role fulfillment (apart from problems of allocating the actor's energy and time); 4) low rewards for role conformity; 5) role conflict; and 6) overload of role obligations (see William J. Goode, 1960).

MODE 1: AMBIGUITY OR ANOMIE

The components of complex social roles tend to range from mandatory to discretional. In dating, for example, the seniors enjoyed a degree of legitimized free choice in ways of initiating contacts, topics of conversation, kinds of activities and others. Some negotiation with the female partner was expected, but both parties recognized the matter as a "free zone" for mutual accommodation.

This legitimized free zone contrasts with ambiguity. The latter was characterized precisely by the uncertainty as to whether any norm regulated the situation and, if so, which? Ambiguity is likely to arise when some established norms are weakening. For example, the expectation that the male invariably pays the expenses of a date has been undermined by numerous social changes, e.g., the increased interaction of the sexes in college and at work, more informal dating customs, the initiative permitted women to suggest some joint activity, the weakening of the concept that the man pays and is to be recompensed by sexual favors, etc.

An ambiguous situation may eventually turn into a culturally defined "zone of discretion" to be negotiated in terms of the relative bargaining power of the parties and the exigencies of situations. On the other hand, the breakdown of a uniform norm, e.g., "the male pays," may be followed by a process of differentiation, in which the prior single norm is splintered into numerous injunctions, contingent upon varieties of specific conditions: how well the parties know one another, which one has the cash to sponsor a given event, how informal is the occasion, at whose initiative was it undertaken, and so on.

Whatever the future will bring, the present situation with regard to paying for joint activities was one of uncertainty which disturbed men and women, especially in early stages of the relationship. The women wondered: "Does he *expect* us to go dutch or will I offend him by suggesting it? Do I give him the money in a restaurant or ask for a separate check?" One of the seniors, having invited a woman he had been dating for a few weeks to a restaurant, found himself two dollars short. She gave him two dollars, but he was indignant to discover, when they met again, that she expected him to repay her. In such unstructured situations, both the male and the female are likely to worry, not only about violating the expectations of the other but, depending upon personality, about reciprocity: "Am I allowing myself to be exploited?" or "Do I tend to exploit others?"

Sexual relationships presented many ambiguous situations, as was illustrated in Chapter 3. "The biggest strain," remarked one senior about sexual approaches on a date, "comes from not knowing what is expected of you. With each girl it is different."

Two other major areas of ambiguity were revealed in the interviews. In the case of student marriages, what, if any, were the obligations of the two parental families for the support of the young couple? The absence of clear normative guides is, occasionally, a cause of conflict because the situation is open to unregulated play of interests, sometimes rationalized by appeals to conflicting values. Similarly lacking in clear definitions was the allocation of domestic tasks between men and women students living together, whether unmarried or married. This is not to say that some degree of accommodation never emerged, but generally a trial and error period was required.

The distinction between ambiguity and conflict as modes of strain may be analytically valid but difficult to confirm empirically. Ambiguity is neither a legitimized zone of discretion nor an instance of clear-cut, if conflicting, norms. The actor's problem is precisely to find out which norms are applicable in an ambiguous situation. Ambiguity is experienced as a confusion with the consequent need to play it by ear, guessing the normative expectations of the role partner or experiencing mental conflict between alternative possibilities. The contrast we propose, then, is between ambiguity (i.e., problems of an actor who has to ad lib in a relatively unstructured situation) and conflict between two legitimized expectations or clearly defined pressures. The operational criteria for determining how low the degree of consensus and how weak the moral commitment must be for a role to be rated as ambiguous—in other words, for distinguishing between confusion and conflict—must be developed in the course of research. An operational index of ambiguity consists of a high proportion of "don't know" in response to a question as to appropriate behavior in a given relationship, as well as a wide scatter of responses with low moral commitment to any. As stated earlier, a historically novel, rapidly changing, or crisis situation tends to exhibit this mode of strain.

To designate ambiguity as a role strain is not to prejudge its functional significance for the actor or the social system. Whether ambiguity eventually results in a free zone or evolves into a complex cluster of contingent norms, for all its stress, it provides a degree of flexibility for the actor. Similarly, the social system acquires a margin of flexibility required for optimal adaptation. This is, of course, the theme of Durkheim's *Suicide*. In recent years it has been treated in studies of the relationship between degree of role consensus and a number of dependent variables. How much ambiguity in specific role definitions in a given social system may be excessive, insufficient, or optimal is a problem requiring a complex balancing of functions and dysfunctions for clearly specified ends.

MODE 2: LACK OF CONGRUITY OR "MALFIT" BETWEEN IDIOSYNCRATIC PERSONALITY AND SOCIAL ROLE

Every mode of strain has a subjective side. It is the individual who acts, doubts, or suffers. When the discussion is limited to the sociological plane, the subjective counterparts of sociologically defined elements are generally left implicit.

But there is a mode of role conflict in which the psychological component is not merely such a subjective counterpart, but plays an independent role. If a short, physically weak youth experiences role strain in relation to his dates, the conflict is one between certain idiosyncratic aspects of personality (here physical and physiological) and the masculine ideal which dictates that the male should be taller and stronger than the female. This square-peg-in-a-round-hole mode may be further exemplified by the problems of an insecure man placed in a position of responsibility, a compulsive perfectionist in an unstructured situation, a highly ambitious and high-powered personality placed in positions requiring execution of simple orders, and the like. The intention here is to distinguish between psychodynamic personality patterns, on the one hand, and the internalized values and social attitudes, on the other. The practical difficulties of the distinction may be illustrated by a full-time homemaker whose need for achievement is frustrated by housewifery. Is it a case of a "malfit" between personality and social role or does she exemplify a conflict between the high cultural value placed upon achievement and housewifery? The answer lies in the origin and intensity of her "achievement drive." If it is the product of socialization in a society which values achievement, then the drive is an internalized value. On the other hand, if the roots of the drive lie in the rejection of femininity and the need to compensate for feelings of inferiority, it might be classed as an idiosyncratic personality trait. A personality trait that is deviant in nature or intensity from modal patterns of a given society suggests psychodynamic roots. But the distinction we are proposing may be difficult to make in practice, not merely because it requires a thorough knowledge of the ego's personality, but also because the malfit between personality and social role and the mode of conflict may coexist as aspects in one and the same case. In a heterogeneous society with a variety of values and distinct subcultures a deviant personality may bolster its psychological tendencies with appeal to some values. In the case of the frustrated housewife, it is likely that psychodynamic needs led to the selective acquisition of achievement values among existing cultural alternatives and these values in turn served to intensify the conflict. The malfit of personality and role is likely, then, to exist as a component in role strain, side by side with the mode of conflict and separable from it only analytically.

The most patent examples of strain caused by the lack of congruence between personality and role were presented in the chapters on the virgins and on power relationships with women. In each case, seniors, troubled by their inability to conform to the masculine role, differed from the adjusted men in scores on the two personality tests. The psychological traits of the troubled men were precisely those that would plausibly make role conformity difficult. We considered the possibility that the traumatic deviation from the accepted role might have been the cause (and not the result) of the traits in question. However, the troubled men had relatively unsatisfactory parental relationships in comparison with the adjusted men. This suggests that these psychological traits developed early in childhood, antedating heterosexual relationships and creating obstacles to role fulfillment.

Other statuses of the seniors also illustrated personality as an impediment to role conformity. The psychological profile (see pp. 203–4) of the senior tormented by his dependency upon his family is a case in point. His fear of leaving the parental home and his terror in the face of the demands of independent existence (generally met as a matter of course by a significant proportion of the seniors) point to some deviant psychological traits.

The diagnosis of a current strain as a malfit between role requirements and personality does not, of course, rule out social factors in the shaping of personality. Indeed, in a period of rapid change, patterns of familial socialization are likely to impair the ability of the adult of either sex to fulfill the expected role. This assumes that parents, affected by the socialization they received in their own childhoods, tend to perpetuate traditional attitudes. By contrast, the impact of economic, demographic, and cultural change may require modification of gender roles.

MODE 3: SOCIALLY STRUCTURED INSUFFICIENCY OF RESOURCES FOR ROLE FULFILLMENT (OTHER THAN THAT CAUSED BY PROBLEMS OF ALLOCATION OF THE ACTOR'S ENERGY AND TIME)

As Goode (1960) has noted, role strain is frequently caused by the overdemanding character of total role obligations. In this sense, insufficiency of resources may be due to the competing or conflicting claims upon time and energy. Insofar as the insufficiency of resources is attributable to the idiosyncratic inadequacies of position-occupants, the case falls under the Mode 2 of role strain, the malfit between personality and social roles.

But socially structured inadequacy of resources may exist apart from the overload of obligations and pressures. The strain of the doctor called upon to treat a disease for which contemporary medicine has no cure is a case in point. His failure to fulfill his role is caused neither by competing obligations nor by personal inadequacy. The modern male socialized to demand of himself superior intellectual ability vis-à-vis his wife may be subjected to strain because his society no longer provides him with special privileges and advantages to ensure such superiority.

We are dealing here, of course, with the now familiar thesis of the germinal "Social Structure and Anomie" (Merton, 1968: 185 ff.). In Merton's essay, the disjunction is posited between widespread aspirations in a given society, and differences in access to legitimate means of realizing them at various levels of social stratification. In our case, the normative aspirations are those linked to a given role, with difficulties tending to be experienced by a sizeable proportion of actors in that role. The frustrated goals of the doctor treating an incurable disease are not universal in a given society, they are peculiar to physicians. The lack of technical facilities for role fulfillment is universal, experienced, in this case, by all occupants of this particular status at a given time.

Various positions in a given society might be compared in this respect to account for differential rate of role strain. What are the utopian elements in various role definitions? Given the state of technical skills, the inherent risks, and other problems of scarcity of facilities, which social roles show the widest gap between the prescribed ends and the available means?

A dominant theme of Chapters 2 and 5 was the idea that the seniors were hard put as a group to live up to certain features of traditional masculinity. Their social milieu demanded superior assertiveness and intellectual prowess vis-à-vis women, while no longer providing privileges and advantages which previously supplied resources for such role attainment. Additional references to Mode 3 of role strains are to be found in the section on the uses of psychological tests (see p. 244).

The masculine role in our society carries more power and privilege than the feminine role. Thus, one would expect that the problems confronting the seniors were those of living up to their own or their partners' ideals of masculinity. Indeed, such were the more prevalent difficulties. But Mode 4, the feeling that conformity to the masculine role brought low rewards, was not absent from the seniors' testimony.

MODE 4: LOW REWARDS FOR ROLE CONFORMITY

This mode of strain, unlike the preceding two, does not derive from barriers on the road to role fulfillment but from the actor's feeling that role conformity does not carry desired rewards in personal satisfaction, material benefits, or social esteem.

Every instance of role fulfillment implies some costs in time and effort and the sacrifice of rewards, which some alternative use of one's resources might yield. Under what conditions does the actor feel that the rewards of conformity are not commensurate with the effort?

The dissatisfaction with the rewards linked to role fulfillment may stem from a comparison between the actor's role with some other existing alternative. "I am just a housewife," reflects the speaker's view that her role carries less social esteem than does professional status. In one study of blue-collar workers, a man complained that his friends holding factory jobs "always rib me about being a dirty old garbage man" (Komarovsky, 1967). These illustrations refer to achieved roles within a generally accepted system of stratification.

As contrasted with the above, the seniors occasionally stated that some aspects of the masculine role were frustrating and irrational. The contrast in this case was not between two existing alternatives but between an ascribed role and an imagined reform. These men began to question the validity of some features of traditional masculinity, without being able to liberate themselves from them. The ideal of machismo, some seniors bewailed, not only put an intolerable burden upon them but hindered more humane and rewarding relationships with women and with men (see Chapter 5). The senior described in Chapter 6 (see p. 165) perceived correctly that the ideal of the "strong silent type" robbed him of the emotional reassurance he desired and could have received from his woman friend.

Other criticisms of current definitions of the masculine role were made in response to questions concerning perceived disadvantages and advantages of the feminine role in contemporary society. "What do you think a man, and more particularly *you*, might envy in the woman's role?" was the concluding question of this section of the interview. We did not ask directly: "Did you ever wish you had been born a girl?" Not a single respondent volunteered that he wished he had been born a female, unless one so interprets the statement of the senior who said that he envied women "having children and bringing them up." Other men envied women's freedom from the pressure to prove themselves through achievement and their more passive role in courtship. There were elements of idealization and of hostility in the words of a senior who said: "Women are courted, they don't have to do anything or to put their pride on the line. A beautiful girl comes into a room and without doing anything she has a lot of attention and goodwill expressed to her." Critical as men were of some elements of the current definition of the masculine role, on the whole they perceived it to be superior in freedom and power to the role of women.

We have limited the Mode 4 of role strains to felt dissatisfactions with low rewards of role conformity. As observers we occasionally perceived dysfunctional consequences for the individual of those roles he internalized and played out uncritically. For example, for one senior the ideal male had "physical strength, maturity, and control over his emotions." He failed to recognize the price he paid in trying to live up to this ideal. His girl friend's major dissatisfaction with him was his lack of emotional expressiveness. "She says," he remarked dejectedly, "that even my voice doesn't go up and down, as if I am bored all the time. I guess I am usually kind of blah." He accepted his girl friend's criticism of his emotional blandness. But he lacked the insight to relate his defects to his "John Wayne" ideal of masculinity.

MODE 5: CONFLICT

The mode of role strain which is by far the most frequent subject of research is conflict. Role conflict exists whenever we encounter any clash, opposition, or incompatibility between normative or socially structured role phenomena. Studies which carry the title of "role conflict" appear to have singled out for emphasis conflict involving the manifest, institutional components or roles. But a richer body of materials on role conflict may be found under other rubrics, in the studies of latent structures of industrial plants, armed services, schools, churches, families, and so on. These studies show that given the situational contexts, functional problems, formal definitions of roles, social composition of the personnel, and other factors—there emerge typical patterns of role conflict which cannot begin to be subsumed under "conflicting sets of legitimized role expectations."

For example, the ambivalence built into the role of the professional has been analyzed by Merton and Barber who distinguish the situational and structural sources of conflict. The former refers to the typical conditions under which persons obtain professional help; the latter deals with the unintended by-products of norms defining professional roles (Merton and Barber, 1963).

Another illustration is provided by Lennard and Bernstein who show that in a therapeutic situation the new patient and the analyst are likely to have dissimilar expectations, the patient expecting the analyst to be more active than the analyst himself expects to be (Henry L. Lennard and Arnold Bernstein in Biddle and Thomas, 1966). Again, when an indignant student comes in to complain about a low grade the teacher is placed in a typical dilemma. The teacher must criticize the inadequate performance but in such a way as to avoid doing unnecessary damage to the student's self-respect. This dilemma may be exacerbated by the defensiveness of the teacher whose judgment has been challenged by his student. In an illustration cited by Goffman, the surgeon in charge of a critical operation must correct his subordinates but in such a way as not to destroy the self-confidence required for their performance during the operation (Erving Goffman, 1967). The latent character of these dilemmas is attested by the fact that it takes perceptive and laborious effort to bring them to light. The richest mine for the study of role conflict may lie precisely within these latent structures of roles.

From a purely formal point of view conflicts may be classified as follows:

a. Conflict caused by problems of allocation of time, energy, or other resources between alternatives which are not intrinsically conflictful.
b. Conflict caused by presence of alternatives which not only may compete for time or resources but are intrinsically conflictful. This type may in turn be divided into:

1. The alternatives represent two conflicting choices, such, however, that a compromise may be made between them, optimizing
   the advantages of each and minimizing their costs. The adminis-
   trator who wants order but realizes that the means of securing
   order may hinder his other goal of fostering the creativity of
   subordinates might conceivably resolve the dilemma by some
   compromise.
2. The alternative represents two contradictory choices which are
   mutually exclusive. If the ego is to act at all, the choice must be
   made between them. Whereas order and spontaneity may be
   conceived as a continuum, this variety of conflict represents two
   discrete choices. For example, free expression of sexuality in an
   adulterous relationship conflicts with the value of marital faith-
   fulness.

Another criterion of classifying conflicts concerns the congruence
between the ego's perception and reality. When the ego perceives
the existence of the conflict correctly the latter is a *manifest* one.
When ego does not perceive the role partner's conflictful expectations, we have the *latent* variety. *Pseudoconflict* refers to the ego's
misperception of the alter's position, falsely attributing to him
conflicting attitudes.[2]

There is hardly a chapter of this book that does not contain
examples of the varieties of conflicts here distinguished. For example, a youth told his male friends of his "scoring" with a beautiful
girl, only to discover, as their relationship developed, that he felt
increasingly disloyal to her and unhappy about revealing too much
about her to his male friends. The clash is between the norms
linked to the status of the male friend (more specifically, the
prestige acquired by frequent scoring) on the one hand, and the
norms of loyalty and privacy linked to the status of the mate, on the
other. In this case the conflict was intrapsychic. The devastating
jealousy experienced by another senior, a radical who had endorsed the ideal of an open relationship, offers an illustration of an
intrapsychic conflict between sentiment and ideology. Again, the
senior who concealed from his sexual partner that he was in
therapy, exemplifies an intrarole conflict between two ideals, i.e.,

2. Preiss and Ehrlich (1966: 95) make a somewhat different distinction between
contradictory expectations "in which all cannot be fulfilled and . . . all cannot be
ignored" (in which, in other words, expectations are "mutually exclusive and
exhaustive of the acceptable pattern") and, on the other hand, contrary expectations
which though they cannot all be fulfilled *can* all be ignored.

of masculine psychological strength as against sincerity and openness in close relationships with women.

MODE 6: OVERLOAD OF ROLE OBLIGATIONS

This mode of role strain was described by Goode (1960). He claimed that given the multiple statuses occupied by an individual his total role obligations are overdemanding, in the sense that he cannot meet all the demands to the complete satisfaction of all his role partners (or to his own satisfaction, we might add). The interviewers received the impression that whether or not the overload was a pervasive problem, references to it were *de rigueur.* Occasionally there was the ring of unmistakable sincerity in a remark such as the one cited on p. 103: "If I don't go out, I go crazy, but if I do . . . I can't get my work done" (a senior science major with twenty-five hours of laboratory work a week).

In conclusion, a warning must be sounded about the danger of introducing value judgments into the classification of modes of strain. Lawrence Podell (1966) called attention to such evaluations when he stated that "male ball-and-chain grumbling is only griping, female diaper-and-dishes dissatisfaction is role-conflict." Especially susceptible to such distortions is the distinction between Mode 2—malfit between personality and role—and Mode 3—the socially structured scarcity of resources for role conformity. As long as the role definition itself is not called into question, the tendency will be to look for psychological deficiencies in explaining role strain. For example, college seniors are expected to become at least moderately competent providers and certainly not welfare recipients. Hence, the aimless and pessimistic students will tend to be classified under Mode 2. The need for a remedy aimed at individual adjustment is implicit, be the remedy psychological counseling or educational measures to provide opportunities for vocational experiences for such unmotivated students.

On the other hand, the men who failed to realize their ideal of masculine dominance were cited as examples of Mode 3. This classification was based on the assumption that male dominance is not easily attainable for college youth, and should, on other grounds as well, be eradicated as an ideal.

If values do play a role in classifying modes of strain, they should, at the very least, be made explicit. Another path to objectivity lies in discovering the incidence of the strain in a given population. The presumption that deviant personalities are involved would be reasonable if the sufferers constitute only 10 or 15 percent of a given population. By contrast, the fact that nearly 50 percent of the seniors, by their own admission, fell short of the ideal of masculine ascendancy points to some shared social roots of the difficulty.

The foregoing typology of modes of strain was meant to be exhaustive and, indeed, we found no instance of strain that fell outside it. The theoretical dimensions that underlie it consist of the following: Normative expectations, their lack of clarity (Mode 1) or complementarity (Mode 5); Normative (or socially structured but not legitimized) expectations and pressures, their lack of clarity (Mode 6) or complementarity (Mode 5); Socially determined resources, their insufficiency as instrumentalities for role fulfillment (Mode 3 and Mode 6), or their inadequacy as rewards or inducements (Mode 4).[3]

Finally, the idiosyncratic personality enters into the typology when it is incongruous with role expectations (Mode 2).

The six modes of role strains are separately identifiable as proximate sources of stress. Occasionally the proximate mode can be linked to another as its cause. The familiar problem of the gainfully employed mother is one of conflict within the status-set of worker and mother. Should we choose to pursue the cause of this conflict further, the judgment may be made that the conflict is caused by the lack of child-care centers and part-time jobs, by the social expectation that the obligation of child rearing falls exclusively upon the mother, and the like—all of these conditions may constitute "socially structured insufficiency of resources for role fulfillment." Again, proximate mode of strain may be to conflict between role-set obligations. The conflict may be exacerbated by ambiguity as to priorities of demands on the part of various role partners. Institutionalization of such priorities would in turn reduce the conflict.

3. The author expresses her gratitude to Edward Lehman for his helpful comment on the theoretical dimensions of the typology of modes of strain.

SOCIAL CHANGE AS A FACTOR IN ROLE STRAINS

Though we have emphasized social change, the six modes of role strain may also be found in relatively static societies. For example, discontinuities between successive statuses the individual occupies from one stage of life to another may create conflict. The same is true of conflict within a role-set. Even ambiguity, characteristically associated with breakdown of old norms, may be endemic in some relatively stable social structures.

Similarly, strains which on the face of it are unrelated to social change may in fact be its result. The low rewards for role conformity and the overload of obligations were so perceived by the seniors only when new ideologies of women's and men's liberation movements opened up the possibilities of alternative social arrangements. The objective situation must be distinguished from the definition given it by the person. The perennial struggle of young adults for independence from parents has been given new poignancy by the confused status-set of the young adult, with its new liberties and dependencies. The only substantive areas of strain which we have not explicitly linked to social change (though they no doubt could be so linked) are some other aspects of parent-child friction and the problems of occupational choice.

ROLE STRAIN AS A FACTOR IN SOCIAL CHANGE

That role strain may be a source of social change has been recognized by many sociologists (e.g., Parsons, 1951: 280–83). However, the overriding interest of writers on role conflict has been in mechanisms that hold conflict in check.

As in other areas of role analysis, here also some distinctions will open the way for productive investigations. The first such distinction is between the existence of social disorganization, and the strain experienced by the actor. So far, we have limited our summary to problems acknowledged by the students themselves. As observers, however, we noted many cognitive and ethical inconsistencies and potential conflicts which at the time of the interview caused the seniors no perceptible distress. Although sociologists have long recognized that similar objective stimuli may evoke different reactions, this recognition has not been systematically applied to the case in point. Writers have been too ready to identify the objective condition of malintegration (status inconsistency versus status crystallization, conflicting obligations, ambivalences, and the like) with felt strain (Donald J. Treiman, 1966). Once the distinction is explicitly made between the objective fact and the actor's definition of it, relative deprivation and reference group theory may prove a fruitful source of explanatory hypotheses.

Merton's analysis of social mechanisms for the articulation of roles in a role-set also illuminates differential outcomes of potentially conflictful situations.

But if similar forms of disorganization may be differently experienced, it is also true that forms of disorganization vary in their potential for stress. For example, dissensus over norms regulating the interaction of role partners would presumably be more disruptive, and hence more stressful, than similar dissensus in attitudes peripheral to such interaction. It is not surprising that Preiss and Ehrlich found relatively low consensus in such attitudes held by policemen about their occupational role as advancement opportunities, freedom to express feelings, and the like. The same research revealed higher consensus on instrumental than on expressive role expectations (1966: 170).

Similarly, the normative components of most roles range in importance from mandatory to discretional. Insofar as mandatory elements tend to be more deeply internalized or more severely sanctioned than the discretional elements, difficulties in conforming to the former will be more stressful.[4]

So much for a few illustrative hypotheses suggested by the distinction between the existence of social disorganization and the actor's actual experience of stress (Komarovsky, 1973b: 658).

To return to the seniors, we shall attempt to account for their apparent equanimity in the face of what the observer perceived as disorganization.

To begin with, an apparent inconsistency may not in reality be one. Attitudes are occasionally labeled contradictory because they are not ideologically consistent. For example, a person may endorse the principle of "equal pay for equal work" but demand that, in a period of economic depression, men be given priority over

4. In addition to such socially mandated priorities, there are, of course, individual and idiosyncratic hierarchies (Ralph Turner, 1968).

women in employment. There is no logical requirement that answers to these two issues be either both feminist or both anti-feminist. The degree of ideological consistency in attitudes may constitute an interesting problem, but an absence of such consistence is not necessarily a contradiction.

More relevant to the problem at hand, are true cognitive or ethical contradictions.

Occasionally, the actor felt no discomfort because he failed to recognize his contradictory stand. One youth claimed to admire women who aspired to be doctors or lawyers. However, when asked to list repellent unfeminine traits, he put "excessive grade consciousness" on the top of the list. It may be argued that a man, admiring achievement in women, may still be attached to the stereotype of passive, unstriving femininity. Nevertheless, this man acknowledged that excessive grade consciousness is an unfortunate necessity for premed male students. Were he confronted with the fact that this necessity exists also for women who seek admission to medical schools, he could have hardly failed to perceive his inconsistency. At the very least he would have had to concede that he puts more stringent restrictions upon the means that a woman may use in the pursuit of her career than he allows a man. The original endorsement of the universalistic ethic as far as feminine aspirations were concerned made his restriction of means morally inconsistent. A sexist attitude towards both goals and means, however reprehensible on other grounds, would have the merit of consistency.

Another case of unconscious ambivalence was that of a self-centered, achievement-oriented senior who wants to have an affair with a truly "feminine" woman—soft, gentle, and sweet. But at this particular stage of life he didn't want a demanding affair that would interfere with his studies. "She would have to have interests of her own," he commented, in order, one supposes, to accept the narrow slot he allocated to his future love in his life. He might be lucky and find a masochistic woman, satisfied with this restricted type of relationship. But he half-realized that the soft and vulnerable "feminine" woman might not have the sturdy self-sufficiency to allow him the freedom he wanted. The cognitive dissonance here involves the wish for an unlikely combination of qualities in a woman. The dissonance is reduced by suppressing the realization of how rare such a love object is likely to be.

Nevertheless, many ethical inconsistencies, fully acknowledged by the seniors, still failed to produce any significant discomfort. For example, the double standard of sexual morality was upheld with the accompanying sentiment, "I know I shouldn't feel this way but I do." The application of universalistic standards to both sexes coexisted with the expectation that their future wives would sacrifice their own aspirations to their husbands' career interests. These illustrations suggest that human beings can tolerate considerable ethical inconsistency as long as their self-interest is not threatened. In other words, if ethical inconsistencies rebound to the advantage of the actor and his role partners do not press their claims, rewards tend to assuage whatever stirrings of guilt occasionally arise.

If ambivalences caused no current strain, they nevertheless represented precarious and unstable adjustments. The young men appeared unrealistic in describing the future. All too frequently, for example, wishing to enjoy the best of both worlds, they did not foresee that the zestful, competent, independent women they hoped to marry might not easily fit into the semitraditional roles they preferred for their future wives.

Finally, whether or not an experience of stress will induce a change in norms is affected by the actor's "definition of the situation." The tendency to place blame for role strain on personal inadequacy has, no doubt, a conservative affect. On the other hand, deflecting the blame from self to some feature of the social order activates the potential for change (Komarovsky, 1973b: 659). As we shall note in Chapter 10 the seniors who fell short of their traditional ideals of masculinity tended to attribute the failure to personal inadequacy. Only a few made reference to the need for changes in role definitions.

RELIGION, FATHER'S EDUCATION, AND PARENT-CHILD RELATIONSHIPS AS FACTORS IN STRAIN

The main purpose of the book was to set forth the attitudes and the role strains of a group of men randomly chosen from the senior class of an Ivy League college. The factors determining the presence or absence of strain within our sample could not be ascertained with equal conclusiveness because of the small size of the subgroups. In some cases, the consistency of the findings and the interview data offset the limitations of small numbers and provided suggestive and novel leads.

Religious affiliation did not play a major part in the presence and absence of the role strains studied in this book. Since we did not investigate the religiosity of the seniors, the operative elements in the religious family background consisted of ethnic differences or distinctive religious values. Apparently the four-year college experience muted whatever relevant differences the three religious groups brought to college as freshmen. For example, the tendency to stereotype women negatively was similar among Protestants, Catholics, and Jews. The consensus with regard to the ideals of masculinity was so great within the sample that religious differences couldn't be ascertained. The proportion of virgins was slightly higher among Jews and lowest among Catholics. The Catholic seniors had a somewhat higher proportion of men worried about dominance in relation to women. This particular strain was associated with the relatively high ratio of unsatisfactory mother-son relationships among Catholics.

Father's education, may have been on balance, a more significant independent variable than religion but less so than we had anticipated. The sons of less-educated fathers (and, hence, we may assume, of lower socioeconomic origins) did not, for example, exhibit, as a general rule, a more traditional sex-role ideology. On the other hand, their self-disclosure to parents was lower than that of the sons of college-educated fathers. The father-son relationships of Jews and Catholics among the less educated were particularly unsatisfactory, representing in a number of cases cultural conflicts with immigrant fathers.

Lest the negative results are interpreted as a sign of general insignificance of class in sex-role attitudes and strains, the reader must be reminded of the relatively narrow class spectrum represented in the senior class of a private, Ivy League college. Public opinion surveys representative of the country as a whole have reported class and educational differences in verbally expressed sex-role attitudes, although studies dealing with actual experiences of various socioeconomic strata remain to be done.

Of the three variables—religion, father's education, and parental relationships—the latter was most frequently associated with degrees of strain. In some cases, as for example, in anxiety over dominance, unfavorable father and unfavorable mother relationships were equally significant. In other situations, e.g., the incidence of virginity, unsatisfactory ties with the father played a predominant part. Intellectual insecurity vis-à-vis women was not associated with the excess of unhappy maternal or paternal relationships.

THE USES OF PSYCHOLOGICAL TESTS

As stated in the Introduction, the sociological analysis was supplemented by the use of two psychological tests. A clinical psychologist prepared, on the basis of these tests, a psychological résumé of each of the sixty-two cases. This double sociological and psychological perspective enriched our findings in several ways.

First of all, psychological data occasionally supplied the intervening nexus explaining a discovered association between two sociological phenomena. For example, Chapter 4 revealed that the virgins reported less satisfactory relationships with their fathers than did nonvirgins. In the absence of psychological tests, one could only speculate about the meaning of such a finding. However, both psychological tests—the California Psychological Inventory and the Gough Adjective Check List—portrayed the virgins as deficient in self-esteem relative to sexually experienced seniors. Two previous studies, cited in Chapter 4, showed that unsatisfactory father-son relationships tended to lower the son's self-esteem. It is likely that an unfavorable self-image, in turn, would drain the son's confidence to take an initiative in sexual advances to women. Thus, we can conclude that unfavorable father-son relationships tended to be associated with virginity by lowering the self-esteem and self-confidence of the son.

The contribution of psychological data was not limited to providing a fuller explanation of the dominant tendencies. Some deviant cases were likewise illuminated by psychological tests. For example, in the sphere of sex, the deviant cases were virgins with satisfactory father-son ties and, conversely, sexually experienced seniors with tense father-son relationships. Ed (see pp. 133–36) shied away from sex, although he rated his ties with his father highly. A nonvirgin who described his paternal relations as highly unsatisfactory is cited on pp. 62, 98. In these deviant cases the clinician's summary offered some hypotheses as to the psychological dynamics involved in resultant behavior.

Psychological data played also another and quite a different role in our analysis. In Chapter 5 on "Emotional and Power Relationships with Women," for example, psychological tests provided an additional, independent variable, increasing the explanatory power of the study to account for observed behavior. Nearly 50 percent of the seniors were troubled because they felt unequal to the demands of the traditional ideal of masculine psychological strength and assertiveness. Though definitive comparative data are not available, there are grounds for the judgment that changes in the status of women, among other conditions, present new challenges to the traditional expectation of masculine dominance, in comparison with earlier periods of this century. We argued in Chapter 5 that social changes made the traditional ideal of masculinity out of reach for a sizeable proportion of the seniors in this study. If the purpose of the analysis is to account as fully as possible for the observed experiences, psychological tests supplied a supplementary explanation. The seniors, troubled on the score of power, rated lower than the adjusted men on the whole cluster of traits of ascendancy, competence, leadership, and the like. In sum, sociological analysis pointed to increasing difficulty in role conformity, whereas psychological tests revealed which psychological traits enabled some men but not others to overcome these new obstacles.[5]

Another illustration of the use of psychological tests as independent, additional variables is to be found in Chapter 6, dealing with self-disclosure. The bulk of the chapter was focused on social factors influencing the extent and direction of self-disclosure. In conclusion, however, we compared the psychological tests of the ten lowest and ten highest disclosers. These extremes were found to differ on some dimensions of personality, showing that extent of self-disclosure is affected by both social and psychological factors. The psychological profile of the ten highest disclosers suggests also

5. The reader may be reminded that the 55 percent of the seniors who were adjusted with regard to power did not always live up to the ideal of dominance. Some of the men were able, for cultural and psychological reasons, to accept the emotional support of stronger but nurturant women.

the hypothesis that divergent personality types (some characterized by strength and others by extreme need for succorance) may be found among persons who are exceptionally open about the sensitive aspects of self.

The psychological tests were not equally significant in all the areas covered by the study. Students holding different beliefs concerning sex differences did not vary as sharply on psychological scores as those differing in actual behavior. We may infer that cognitive beliefs are not rooted in the deepest layers of personality to the extent true of typical behavior patterns. Moreover, the correlations with distinctive psychological traits varied in magnitude from one sphere of behavior to another. Students intellectually insecure with women did not differ from the adjusted men with regard to most psychological tests. By contrast, much sharper psychological differences distinguished virgins from nonvirgins, occupationally committed men from those still floundering, men troubled on the score of power vis-à-vis women from men who were adjusted.

We have also raised without being able to answer, a problem in the social psychology of changing gender roles. In this period of change, what psychological types are "the first to take up the new" or "the last to give up the old?"

We entertained two contradictory hypotheses. According to one, men, unable to conform to the traditional ideal of masculinity and reap its rewards, might, to use A. K. Cohen's (1955) phrase, be in the market for a solution and therefore be receptive to egalitarian values. By contrast, it has been suggested (see, for example, Joan Aldous, 1974; Mirra Komarovsky, 1940) that it is not the defeated individual but a person with a "fairly high self-esteem, flexibility—and some sense of controlling his own destiny" who would be more likely to engage in behavioral improvisation or "role making" (Aldous, 1974: 232) in a period of social change.

The difficulty in testing these conflicting hypotheses stemmed, first of all, from the fact that, as formulated above, they proved too general. For example, men with high self-esteem are not a homogeneous group for our purposes. Some men are so achievement oriented that they use their interpersonal skills and flexibility in the pursuit of a career rather than in innovative behavior within male-female relationships. This would militate against their hospitality to an egalitarian ideology of marriage roles. Contrariwise, men unable to live up to the traditional ideal of masculinity were occasionally so deeply attached to it that they were unable to make use of the succor egalitarian values might have provided. Instead, they clung to the traditional ideology all the more stubbornly and defensively. The interplay between persistent personality traits, experience, cognitive beliefs, and values proved too complex to be definitively resolved within the limits of our small sample, though nearly every chapter raised these issues and, occasionally, provided some suggestive leads. For example, seniors who were "the traditionalists" on the subject of working wives, had lower scores on Well-Being, Intellectual Efficiency, and Personal Adjustment than the nontraditional students. The traditionalists were also more troubled on the score of power in relationships with women. This would suggest that some personal maladjustment may have made for resistance to the more liberal preferences as to future marriage roles. Among the few couples who came closest to egalitarianism, the men were relatively strong and self-confident. One wonders, however, whether these men, at their stage of life, were subjected to stringent enough tests of their egalitarian values and practices. These were also ambitious men and one can imagine them a decade later, caught in the imperatives of occupational advancement and unable or unwilling to sacrifice economic or honorific rewards for the sake of their wives' careers.

We conclude the summary of our use of psychological analysis with one final observation. The clinician's profiles, based on the psychological tests, often illuminated the psychodynamic processes which, in a given case, explained either the individual nature of the strain or the particular mode of coping with it.

AFTERWORD:
The Author's Envoi

It is difficult to conceive of a society completely free of human suffering—painful dilemmas, frustrated goals, conflict, regret, or guilt. This book, however, examined a sample of college seniors at an Ivy League college mainly for difficulties of a particular order —those related to changing gender roles in attitudes and behavior. I did not disguise my values but, I trust, neither did I allow them to "distort the logic of evidence" in presenting both the dominant and the variant experiences of this group of young men.

In this final personal assessment of the findings, it is noteworthy that nearly every chapter of this book illustrated in its own sphere the lead-lag character of social change and its consequences. Society is not a clock so finely articulated that it breaks down even if a smallest part is changed. But neither is it an aggregate of independent components. The persistence of traditional sex roles cannot but cause social disorganization and personal stress in a contemporary society in which the total fertility rate in 1973 stood at a new low level of 1.9 children per woman (Paul C. Glick, 1975: 16), in which the proportion of married women in the labor force reached 42.2 percent (*Statistical Bulletin*, Metropolitan Life, August 1974), and with women comprising almost half of the freshman class in colleges in the United States in 1972.

Indeed, these demographic, economic, and educational changes both reflected and, in turn, triggered other changes. Survey after survey reports increasing awareness of women's problems, changing attitudes towards sex and marriage and towards concep-

tions of femininity and masculinity. A survey by Daniel Yankelovich (1974) shows that the gap between college and noncollege
youth in values related to gender roles has been closing. The
attitudes of noncollege youth in 1973 were just about where the
college population was in 1969. The Women's Liberation Movement in its various forms began to gather strength in the late 1960s
and has had an impact upon attitudes and to a lesser extent, on
institutional practices. Not only professional women, but factory
and clerical workers have brought thousands of complaints of sex
discrimination under Order 11246 of the Equal Employment
Opportunity Act. Children's readers, college curricula, TV shows,
etc., are being studied and monitored for evidence of pernicious
sex stereotypes. Quotations from elementary school readers, such
as "Janey says she might be only a girl, but she isn't stupid," or
"Janey knows girls cannot be doctors so she will be a nurse instead"
are exposed to public view.

To return to the seniors, a considerable proportion experienced
difficulties in fulfilling what they conceived to be the normatively
expected masculine roles in intellectual, sexual, and emotional
relationships with women. The problem of attaining independence from parents was particularly difficult when the total status-
set of young adults was so full of contradictions, with newly
acquired privileges (e.g., sexual permissiveness, early marriage)
and emerging dependencies (e.g., prolongation of professional
training). The role of the citizen during the Vietnam war in 1969
and 1970 presented tormenting problems.

The overwhelming majority of the seniors attributed the strains
in relationships with women to personal inadequacies. In this the
men were similar to women in the 1950s, when only a minority of
women recognized the social roots of their frustrations. This recognition, on the part of men, will be slower in coming than in the
case of women. The very reforms which might alleviate the strains
experienced by the seniors inevitably entail yielding some power
and privileges and few posessors of power can be expected to yield it
lightly. Only a few seniors acknowledged that the rewards of power
and privilege hardly compensated them for the pressures and obligations of masculinity. The vast majority would not wish to change
places with the weaker sex (see pp. 232–33). But vested interest in
masculine superiority was not the only source of resistance to
change. The interviews revealed that the seniors were trapped (as

are the rest of us) in certain dual classifications and were caught on the horns of a false dilemma because they could not conceive of a third option. The only alternative that came to the young men's minds when the traditional sex roles were challenged was simple reversal. One could almost hear them say: "If I am not the one to tell her 'rely upon me, I'll be brave and strong,' must I then say 'I'll rely upon you?' If the husband is not going to be the mainstay, the leader, the dominant partner—will the wife then be the boss? If women are not to be reared to be loving, warm, supportive, will they be hard, competitive and aggressive?" But are courage and warmth, achievement and compassion, moral strength and sensitivity, self-confidence and capacity to love, doing and being—are these antithetical qualities to be neatly allocated to each sex? Must we not, instead, try to rear both little boys and little girls to be warm *and* strong, creative *and* sensitive, able to accept responsibility for themselves and for others?

Ideally these are the attributes which, in various degrees, might be combined in all human beings, played out at different times and in different situations.

Models of egalitarian sexual relationships, especially in marriage, were simply not available in reality or in literature on a scale to shape their imagination and free them of the false dilemma of power. A clearer insight into the possibility of complementary strengths and weaknesses within a marriage was shown in an earlier study by a twenty-eight-year-old taxi driver, with nine years of schooling (Mirra Komarovsky, 1967: 179). Asked who was the boss in his family, he answered: "It is hard to say. We go to pieces differently. She's like a powerful engine that shakes itself to pieces. I'm likely to run down. I make her calm down and she makes me stick together."

We need to present to both men and women more vivid models of egalitarian relationships between the sexes in order to replace the traditional ones so deeply etched in social consciousness. But the agenda for needed reforms is far broader and more radical than this consciousness raising. In order to translate pious equalitarian pronouncements about wider and more equal options for men and women, we shall have to reorganize several institutions in a far more profound way, in my opinion, than would be necessary, for example, to solve the problems of the black minority in the United States.

A major ideological roadblock still remains before serious efforts at institutional reorganization are undertaken. This obstacle may be first illustrated by the attitudes of the seniors in our study. In Chapter 2 we have shown that the seniors have accepted the ideal of sexual equality in public spheres. The vast majority no longer questioned women's rights to equal access to promotions and rewards in the most highly valued occupational and political positions. But this endorsement of equal opportunities coexisted with one traditional principle: "The major responsibility for child rearing is the mother's." For all the cooperation they were prepared to offer, their wives were expected to be the child-rearers and the homemakers.

Some seniors no doubt perceived (and felt relieved thereby) that the withdrawal from work during child rearing would so handicap a woman that she would be unlikely to excel her husband in occupational success and earnings. A few seniors claimed that there were no practical alternatives to traditional sex-role differentiation in families with young children.

It would be too facile to conclude that the men held these contradictory ideals solely out of self-interest. There is some truth in this view and we shall return to it. But self-interest is evidently not the only possible motive because the great majority of American women express a similar contradiction: Sexual equality in access to all occupational, economic, and political rewards but traditional sex-role differentiation within the family.

The evidence of female attitudes comes from a study, in 1970, of a representative (a national probability) sample of ever-married women under the age of forty-five (Karen O. Mason and Larry L. Bumpass, 1975). Ninety-five percent of the total female sample, noncollege and college, agreed that "men and women should be paid the same money if they do the same work," 72 percent agreed that "on the job, men should not refuse to work under women," 56 percent assented to the proposition "women should be considered as seriously as men for jobs as executives or politicians or even president."

Side by side with this thrust towards equality, however, 76 percent of women agreed that "it is much better for everyone involved if the man is the achiever outside the home and the woman takes care of the home and the family"; 71 percent asserted that "a preschool child is likely to suffer if his mother works." On the subject of task allocation within the home the majority had more egalitarian or "modern" views, with 52 percent endorsing the statement that: "Men should share the work around the house with women, such as doing dishes, cleaning and so forth." Forty-four percent of the women thought that there should be free child-care centers so that women could take jobs.

Neither the seniors nor the female national sample, including noncollege women, explicitly perceived that their advocacy of sex equality in the public spheres was undermined by continued adherence to sex-role segregation within the family. This is the case for the great majority of women who wish or need to combine familial and economic roles. Even should social struggle eliminate in time what might be termed direct discrimination in sex typing of occupations, in promotions and pay, equality of opportunities will not have been achieved. Women will continue to suffer from indirect, derivative discrimination as long as traditional sex-role socialization persists together with traditional segregation of sex roles within the family. The sequential pattern of women's work, including the withdrawal from the labor market for child rearing, inevitably relegates women to second-class citizenship in most professions. Of course, makeshift arrangements have enabled a small minority of women today to combine child rearing and demanding careers. In the case of working-class mothers the dual responsibilities of a paid job and homemaking not only create an excessive burden but also leave large numbers of children without proper care and education.

We referred earlier to self-interest as a partial explanation of the seniors' ambivalence in this area. Though a similar ambivalence has been just demonstrated on the part of a sample of women, the same study reveals that college-educated women are more "feminist" in their attitudes than the less-educated women. For example, only 54.7 percent of college women as contrasted with the 76 percent of the total sample of women agreed that "it is much better for everyone involved if the man is the achiever outside the home and the woman takes care of the home and the family." Again, 64.1 percent of the college women wanted men to share in the work around the house as compared with only 52 percent of all the women. Seventy-one percent of the college women but only 46 percent of the total sample subscribed to the statement: "A working mother can establish just as warm and secure relationship with her children as a mother who does not work" (Mason and Bumpass, 1975).

Since there exists a tendency towards educational homogamy in marriage, the seniors in this study will be likely to marry college women whose views will tend to be more feminist than those expressed by the males in this study. Therein lie the seeds of potential conflict, though we are not prepared to estimate the flexibility and the future direction of attitudes on the part of either the males or their future mates.

We have sought to document a basic contradiction implicit in public opinion which upholds sex equality of opportunity outside the home but insists on traditional role segregation within the family. This contradiction derives from the deeply rooted assumption that women must naturally bear the major responsibility for child rearing as well as the recognition of radical changes required in many institutional sectors if this assumption were to be challenged.

The most recent assessment of sex differences in nurturance (Eleanor E. Maccoby and Carol N. Jacklin, 1974: 371) concludes that among lower animals, "the hormones associated with pregnancy and childbirth produce a state of 'readiness' to care for the young. It is not known whether there are similar biochemical elements in human responsiveness to young infants."

During the period of breast feeding the mother's ties to the infant are obviously primary. With the birth rate likely to continue to be low, this period is but a short segment of a woman's life. Even during breast feeding, social rather than strictly biological considerations dictate what infant care can be performed by the father or what occupational constraints breast feeding must impose, e.g., nurseries near places of work would make some occupations compatible with infant care.

Suppose future biological research should reveal that "the hormones associated with pregnancy and childbirth produce a state of 'readiness' to care for the young" among human females? Despite present differences in the socialization of the sexes, the variation in psychological traits within each sex group is greater than the average differences between them. The overlap in the distributions of male and female psychological traits is great even under present conditions; it will be greater with increased similarity in child rearing and in the mode of life of males and females.

Whatever the future biological discoveries, certain reforms are long overdue. The repeated grievance of the seniors about shallow and aloof paternal relationships points to the need for greater paternal participation in nurturant socialization of their children. These largely middle-class sons felt that they had not received enough expressive fathering. Maccoby and Jacklin (1974: 372–73) report that "both men and women take a tougher stand toward children of their own sex." They conclude that, since control and indulgence are both necessary in child rearing, adults of both sexes should be involved in the care of the children. Under such conditions both little girls and boys will receive a balance of discipline on the one hand, and permissiveness and support for independence, on the other, from adult caretakers. As for the full-time mother-homemakers, we can be sure that nature did not decree that mothers exercise their natural talents around the clock, in isolation from other adults, and at the cost of sacrificing channels for self-development and service open to men even in our imperfect society.

The frustrations of young mothers vary from class to class. When, in a study of blue-collar women, the full-time homemakers were asked, "Who has it harder in marriage, a man or a woman?" a significant proportion answered, "A woman—she is more tied down," "Takes care of the kids around the clock." College-educated young mothers with aspirations for professional careers have other frustrations, and working-class mothers who return home after a day's work to a full round of domestic tasks suffer in still other ways.

What, then, are these institutional reforms that would, in fact, provide effective choices for individuals? Minor incremental improvements are reported in the daily press. Some colleges have taken a step forward in considering for tenure part-time teaching staff, who hitherto had no permanent status. One school system has granted paternity leaves to male teachers, fathers of infant children. Some success has been achieved in repealing the nineteenth-century state abortion laws. There appears to be an increasing interest in, but so far only a little experimentation with, modified work patterns for both sexes such as flexi-time, staggered and part-time, the four-day week, and other schedules. The pressure must continue for the development of easily accessible child enrichment centers of high quality, open mornings and afternoons, and available to all economic classes. Incidentally, a full-time homemaker-mother could profit by such centers to relieve the trapped feeling of around-the-clock child care, to say nothing of the educational values such experiences would have for the child.

New housing and neighborhood planning patterns must take into consideration the growing interest in forming closer and more cooperative ties between child-rearing families.

It should be clear from this inventory of some needed reforms that the author's personal view of a good society includes the acceptance of symmetrical role allocation in marriage, with both partners sharing in work, child rearing, and homemaking, making use of whatever innovations may develop to relieve the individual family of full responsibility for housekeeping chores which certainly could be performed more efficiently than they are at present.

This emphasis on parenthood does not imply a denigration of a single status or of childlessness. Whatever the costs of these choices (and every choice has its own price tag), the major obstacle to sex equality will be experienced by women who desire to combine economic and child-rearing functions.

Does the freedom of options, advocated in these pages, include the preference of some women for full-time mothering of young children? Of course it does. The feminist movement has been criticized for its alleged tendency to "deprecate" motherhood. Dr. Benjamin Spock was only one of several writers who urged women to realize that it is "much more creative to rear and shape the personality of a fine, live child than it is to work in an office or even to carve a statue."

Why is it necessary for Dr. Spock to remind mothers of the importance of child rearing? If educated women do not hear this message, it is certainly not for want of repetition.

It is quite true that building bridges, writing books, and splitting the atom are no more essential to society or more difficult than child rearing. But, in my opinion, women cannot be made to believe it unless men believe it too. The appeal to women to realize their full creative potential in child rearing and to find dignity in domesticity is likely to fail as long as our society is saturated with other values.

A dozen times a day events belie the sermons directed to women alone. If our whole society endorsed different values, a nursery school teacher would rate a salary at least equal in hourly rate to the beginning salary of a street cleaner, and the curtailment of social services to children would not be the first economies that politicians felt safe to propose in a period of retrenchment.

If men believed for a moment that the rearing of children is as difficult and important as building bridges, they would demand more of a hand in it too. It would become unnecessary for child and social psychologists to campaign for more active fatherhood. A man could derive prestige and self-esteem from spending time with his children even if this called for a less single-minded dedication to occupational success. The conflict between occupational and family interests would then become a problem also for men, and each would have to strike his own balance between the conflicting interests. One can imagine a male sociologist writing a book to show that, though women are the child bearers, nature did not intend to bar men from the honorable task of educating the young. He would seek to demonstrate that, whenever their environment demands it, men too exhibit psychological insight, and that a good salesman, politician, or psychoanalyst can match any woman in intuition.

To sum up, what defeats our appeal to women to find dignity in domesticity is that the experience of the educated and the gifted housewife flies in the face of the unconvincing assurance that she is doing the most important job in the world. She knows that when her husband says that in rearing their children she is doing something more creative and difficult than anything he can do in a lifetime, he does not quite believe it himself.

But is it likely that side by side with economic success, creative professional achievement, athletic prowess, political power, our society could include esteem for nurturant socialization of the young? Perhaps there is no ready yardstick with which to measure excellence in child rearing. Perhaps even when excellence is achieved it is too invisible to the wide public to serve as a basis for social esteem. Possibly an activity must have an economic reward to be acclaimed in our society. Be this as it may, I doubt that it is possible any longer to maintain a system of values for women only (Mirra Komarovsky, 1953: 290 ff.).

I will not presume to prophesy what, if any, differentiation in the social roles of the sexes will remain in a society which, by incorporating the values and the institutional reforms sketched above, will offer real options to men and women. Should the paternal role in child rearing be given its due importance, and symmetrical marital roles be accepted as an honored cultural alternative, this pattern would likely prove appealing to a great many parents. This presupposes appropriate adjustments in work schedules and assistance in child care through easily accessible child-care centers.

High-powered, exceptionally creative personalities, male or female, ambitious to reach peak positions, will choose a single-minded dedication to their careers. Such personalities may decide to remain childless or to find mates willing to play complementary roles. Are such mates, on the average, more likely to be women? Perhaps, but we cannot be certain, though some writers presume to tell us that science has already closed this case. We have such a long way to go to provide a real equality of opportunities for men and women that it appears premature to center our attention on the possible genetic limits.

The economic, political, and ideological struggle to create a new society will not be an easy one and, in the short run, may exacerbate role strains for both sexes. The reforms that could ease the combination of work and homemaking for women have not kept pace with the increasing number of married women in the labor force, subjecting them to discrimination at work and a double burden of responsibilities. The aspirations awakened by the Women's Liberation Movement will bring fulfillment to some, but will surely increase the frustrations of others in this period of transition. The problems of men attracted to "feminine" occupations may be even more severe than pioneering choices of women. Kelvin Seifert (1974) describes the difficulties of the few men who work in child-care centers. Since "masculine" occupations carry more prestige, power, and higher economic rewards, pioneering choices on the part of women, whatever the struggle, constitute upward mobility. On the other hand, in the present climate of opinion, males entering "feminine" jobs must brace themselves against some degree of scorn and suspicion.

S. M. Miller (1971) in "The Making of a Confused, Middle-Aged Husband" describes insightfully the "lapsed egalitarianism" of his own marriage to a physician-wife with the coming of children. He traces the erosion of his egalitarianism to his drive for occupational achievement and his resentment of the freedom from domestic "distractions" enjoyed by husbands (competitors?) in conventional marriages. A male, he concludes, is not likely to bestow equality—it will have to be won by women.

As for women, even a liberated wife may on occasion experience ambivalences, demanding her husband's participation in domestic tasks but harboring disappointment if he relaxes his drive for success.

If, in the short run, the struggle may create even greater disharmonies, these are the inevitable costs of achieving a more harmonious society, which would release the creative potential of the female half of its citizens and provide a less constricted range of choices for the males to lead lives congenial to their capacities and inclinations.

BIBLIOGRAPHY

Aldous, Joan
  1974 "The Making of Family Roles and Family Change," *Family Coordinator*, July: 231–35.
Balswick, Jack O., and James A. Anderson
  1969 "Role Definition in the Unarranged Date," *Journal of Marriage and the Family* 31 (November): 776–78.
Balswick, Jack O., and Charles W. Peek
  1971 "The Inexpressive Male: A Tragedy of American Society," *Family Coordinator* 20: 263–68.
Barton, Allen H.
  1955 "The Concept of Property-Space in Social Research," in *The Language of Social Research*, Paul F. Lazarsfeld and Morris Rosenberg, eds., Glencoe, Illinois: The Free Press.
Bates, F. L.
  1956 "Position, Role, and Status: A Reformulation of Concepts," *Social Forces* 34, 4: 313–21.
Bayer, Alan E.
  1975 "Sexist Students in American Colleges," *Journal of Marriage and the Family* 37, 2 (May): 391–97. (See also the appended bibliography.)
Bayer, Alan E., Jeannie T. Roger, and Richard M. Webb
  1973 *Four Years after College Entry*, A.C.E. Research Report 8, 1, Washington, D.C.: American Council on Education.
Bell, Robert R., and Jay B. Chaskes
  1970 "Premarital Sexual Experience Among Coeds, 1958 and 1968," *Journal of Marriage and the Family* 32 (February): 81–84.
Benson, Leonard
  1968 *Fatherhood, A Sociological Perspective*, New York: Random House.
Biddle, Bruce J., and Edwin J. Thomas
  1966 *Role Theory: Concepts and Research*, New York: John Wiley and Sons.
Brenton, Myron
  1966 *The American Male*, New York: Fawcett Premier.

Broderick, Carlfred D.
  1966   "Socio-Sexual Development in a Suburban Community,"
          Journal of Sex Research 2 (April): 1–24.
Broverman, Inge K., et al.
  1970   "Sex-Role Stereotypes and Clinical Judgements of Mental
          Health," *Journal of Consulting and Clinical Psychology* 34, 1:
          1–7.
  1972   "Sex-Role Stereotypes: A Current Appraisal," *Journal of Social
          Issues* XXVIII, 2: 59–78.
Cannon, Kenneth L., and Richard Long
  1971   "Premarital Sexual Behavior in the Sixties," *Journal of Marriage
          and the Family* 33 (February): 36–49. (See also bibliography,
          47–49.)
Christensen, Harold T., and Christina F. Gregg
  1970   "Changing Sex Norms in America and Scandinavia," *Journal of
          Marriage and the Family* 32, 4 (November): 616–27.
Cohen, Albert K.
  1955   *Delinquent Boys*, Glencoe, Illinois: The Free Press.
Davis, Keith E.
  1971   "Sex on Campus: Is There a Revolution?" *Medical Aspects of
          Human Sexuality* 5 (January): 128–42.
Dean, Dwight G., et al.
  1973   "Replication and Fallacy: Cultural Contradictions and Sex
          Roles Revisted," paper presented at the annual meetings of the
          American Sociological Association.
Deutscher, Irwin
  1973   *What We Say, What We Do, Sentiments and Acts*, Glenview,
          Illinois: Scott, Foresman and Company.
Erikson, Erik
  1965   "Comment," in J. Mattfield and C. Van Aken, eds., *Women in
          the Scientific Profession*, pp. 239–45. Cambridge: M.I.T. Press.
Etzioni, Amitai
  1968   *The Active Society*, New York: The Free Press.
Farrell, Warren
  1974   *The Liberated Man: Freeing Men and Their Relationships with
          Women*, New York: Random House.
Fasteau, Marc
  1974   *The Male Machine*, New York: McGraw-Hill.
Fernberger, S. W.
  1948   "Persistence of Stereotypes Concerning Sex Differences,"
          Journal of Abnormal and Social Psychology XLIII: 97–101.
Festinger, Leon
  1957   *Theory of Cognitive Dissonance*, Evanston, Illinois: Row Peter-
          son.

Festinger, Leon, and Elliot Aronson
  1968 "Arousal and Reduction of Dissonance in Social Context," in
        D. Cartwright and Alvin Zander, eds., *Group Dynamics*, New
        York: Harper and Row.
Getzels, J. W., and E. G. Guba
  1954 "Role, Role Conflict and Effectiveness: An Empirical Study,"
        American Sociological Review 19: 164–75.
Glick, Paul C.
  1975 "A Demographer Looks at American Families," *Journal of Marriage and the Family* 37, 1 (February): 15–26.
Goffman, Erving
  1967 *The Operation Room: A Study in Role Distance*, cited in Dennis
        H. Wrong and Harry L. Gracey, eds., *Readings in Introductory
        Sociology*, pp. 117–27. New York: The Macmillan Company.
Goldberg, Steven
  1973 *The Inevitability of Patriarchy*, New York: W. M. Morrow.
Goode, William J.
  1960 "A Theory of Role Strain," *American Sociological Review* 25
        (August): 246–58.
Gross, Neal, Ward S. Mason, and Alexander W. McEachern
  1958 *Explorations in Role Analysis: Studies of the School Superintendency Role*, New York: John Wiley and Sons.
Hacker, Helen Mayer
  1957 "The New Burdens of Masculinity," *Marriage and Family
        Living* XIX, 3 (August): 227–33.
Horner, Matina S.
  1972 Toward an Understanding of Achievement-Related Conflicts in
        Women," *Journal of Social Issues* 28, 2.
Hartley, Ruth E.
  1959 "Sex-Role Pressures in the Socialization of the Male Child,"
        Psychological Reports 5: 457–68.
Heilbrun, Alfred B., Jr.
  1965 "An Empirical Test of the Modeling Theory of Sex-Role Learning," *Child Development* 36, 3 (September): 789–99.
Heiss, Jerald S.
  1962 "Degree of Intimacy and Male-Female Interaction," *Sociometry*
        25: 197–208.
Johnson, Kathryn P.
  1969 "A Progress Report on a Study of Factors Associated with the
        Male's Tendency to Negatively Stereotype the Female,"
        Sociological Focus 3: 21–35.
Jourard, Sidney M.
  1961 "Religous Denominations and Self-Disclosure," *Psychological
        Reports* 8: 446. (Reprinted in Jourard, 1971, 53–54.)

1964   *The Transparent Self*, Princeton, N.J.: D. Van Nostrand Company.

1971   *Self-Disclosure*, New York: Wiley-Interscience.

Jourard, Sidney M., and Paul Lasakow

1958   "Some Factors in Self-Disclosure," *Journal of Abnormal and Social Psychology* 56: 91–98.

Kaatz, Gilbert R., and Keith E. Davis

1970   "The Dynamics of Sexual Behavior of College Students," *Journal of Marriage and the Family* 32, 8 (August): 390–94.

Kammeyer, Kenneth

1964   "The Feminine Role: An Analysis of Attitudes Consistency," *Journal of Marriage and the Family*, August: 295–305.

1966   "Birth Order and the Feminine Sex Role Among College Women," *American Sociological Review* 31, 4 (August): 508–15.

Kelley, Robert K.

1974   *Courtship, Marriage and the Family*, New York: Harcourt Brace Jovanovich.

Kendall, Elaine

1965   *The Upper Hand*, Boston: Little, Brown.

Keniston, Kenneth

1965   *The Uncommitted*, New York: Harcourt Brace and World.

1968   *Young Radicals*, New York: Harcourt Brace and World.

Kitay, P. M.

1940   "A Comparison of the Sexes in Their Attitudes and Beliefs About Women," *Sociometry* 34: 399–407.

Knox, Joel, W. E. Kupferer, and H. F. Kupferer

1972   "A Discontinuity in the Socialization of the Males in the United States," *Merrill Palmer Quarterly* 17.

Kohn, Melvin L.

1969   *Class and Conformity: A Study in Values*, Homewood, Illinois: The Dorsey Press.

Komarovsky, Mirra

1940   *The Unemployed Man and His Family*, New York: Dryden Press. Reprinted New York: Farrar, Straus and Giroux, 1972.

1946   "Cultural Contradictions and Sex Roles," *American Journal of Sociology* 52 (November): 182–89.

1953   *Women in the Modern World: Their Education and Their Dilemmas*. Reprinted Dubuque, Iowa: Brown Library Publishing Company.

1967   *Blue-Collar Marriage*, New York: Random House, Vintage Books.

1973a   "Cultural Contradictions and Sex Roles: The Masculine Case," *The American Journal of Sociology* 78, 4 (January): 873–84.

1973b "Presidential Address: Some Problems in Role Analysis," *American Sociological Review* 38, 6 (December): 649–62.

1974 "Patterns of Self-Disclosure of Male Undergraduates," *Journal of Marriage and the Family* 36, 4 (November): 677–86.

Leik, Robert K.
1963 "Instrumentality and Emotionality in Family Interaction," *Sociometry* 26: 131–45.

Lemert, Edwin M.
1951 *Social Pathology*, New York: McGraw-Hill.

Lennard, Henry L., and Arnold Bernstein
1966 "Expectations and Behavior in Therapy," in Bruce J. Biddle and Edwin J. Thomas, eds., *Role Theory: Concepts and Research.* New York: John Wiley and Sons.

Levine, Adeline, and Janice Crumrine
1973 "Women and the Fear of Success: A Problem in Replication," presented at the annual meetings of the American Sociological Association.

Lipset, Seymour Martin, ed.
1967 *Student Politics*, New York: Basic Books.

Luckey, Eleanore B., and Gilbert D. Nass
1969 "A Comparison of Sexual Attitudes and Behavior in an International Sample," *Journal of Marriage and the Family* 31, 2 (May): 364–79.

Maccoby, Eleanor E., and Carol N. Jacklin
1974 *The Psychology of Sex Differences*, Stanford, California: Stanford University Press.

Macklin, Eleanor D.
1974 "Cohabitation in College," *Psychology Today*, November: 53–59.

Mason, Karen O., and Larry L. Bumpass
1975 "U.S. Women's Sex-Role Idology, 1970," *American Journal of Sociology* 80, 5 (March): 1212–19.

McKee, John P., and Alex C. Sherriffs
1957 "The Differential Evaluation of Males and Females," *Journal of Personality* 25 (March): 356–63.

1959 "Men's and Women's Beliefs, Ideals, and Self-Concepts," *American Journal of Sociology* 64 (4): 356–63.

McKinley, Donald G.
1964 *Social Class and Family Life*, New York: The Free Press.

Merton, Robert K.
1957 "The Role-Set: Problems in Sociological Theory," *British Journal of Sociology* 8 (June): 133 ff.

1968 *Social Theory and Social Structure*, New York: The Free Press (rev. ed.).

Merton, Robert K., and Elinor Barber
 1963 "Sociological Ambivalence," in E. A. Tiryakian (ed.), *Sociological Theory, Values and Sociocultural Change*, pp. 91–120. New York: The Free Press of Glencoe.
Miller, S. M.
 1971 "The Making of a Confused, Middle-Aged Husband," *Social Policy*, July-August: 33–39.
Mirande, Alfred M.
 1968 "Reference Group Theory and Adolescent Sexual Behavior," *Journal of Marriage and the Family* 30 (November): 572–77.
Mirande, Alfred M., and Elizabeth L. Hammer
 1974 "Premarital Sexual Permissiveness: A Research Note," *Journal of Marriage and the Family* 36, 2 (May): 356–58.
Moss, J. Joel, et al.
 1971 "The Premarital Dyad During the Sixties," *Journal of Marriage and the Family* 33 (February): 50–69.
National Norms for Entering Freshmen
 1972 Annual reports for Fall 1970, 1971, 1972, 1973, Washington, D.C.: American Council on Education.
Newcomb, Theodore M., et al.
 1967 *Persistence and Change: Bennington College and Its Students after Twenty-Five Years*, New York: John Wiley and Sons.
Parelius, Ann P.
 1975 "Emerging Set-Role Attitudes, Expectations and Strains Among College Women," *Journal of Marriage and the Family* 37, 1 (February): 146–53.
Parsons, Talcott
 1951 *The Social System*, Glencoe, Illinois: The Free Press.
Parsons, Talcott, and R. F. Bales
 1955 *Family, Socialization, and Interaction Process*, New York: The Free Press.
Perlman, Daniel
 1974 "Self-Esteem and Sexual Permissiveness," *Journal of Marriage and the Family* 36 (August): 470–73.
Pleck, Joseph H., and Jack Sawyer, eds.
 1974 *Men and Masculinity*, Englewood Cliffs, N.J.: Prentice-Hall.
Podell, Lawrence
 1966 "Sex-Role Conflict," *Journal of Marriage and the Family* 28, 2.
Preiss, Jack J., and Howard J. Ehrlich
 1966 *An Examination of Role Theory: The Case of the State Police*, Lincoln: University of Nebraska Press, 229–82.
Reiss, Ira L.
 1967 *The Social Context of Pre-Marital Sexual Permissiveness*, New York: Holt, Rinehart, and Winston.

1970 "Premarital Sex as Deviant Behavior: An Application of Current Approaches to Deviance," *American Sociological Review* 35, 1 (February): 78–96.

1973 *Heterosexual Relationships Inside and Outside of Marriage*, Morristown, N. J.: General Learning Press.

Rosenberg, Morris
1965 *Socity and the Adolescent Self-Image*, Princeton, N.J.: Princeton University Press.

Rosenkrantz, Paul, et al.
1968 "Sex-Role Stereotypes and Self-Concepts in College Students," *Journal of Consulting and Clinical Psychology* XXXII, 3: 287–95.

Seifert, Kelvin
1974 "Some Problems of Men in Child Care Center Work," in *Men and Masculinity*, edited by Joseph H. Pleck and Jack Sawyer. Englewood Cliffs, N. J.: Prentice-Hall.

Spence, J. T.
1974 "TAT and Attitudes towards Achievement in Women: A New Look at the Motive to Avoid Success and a New Method of Measurement" *Journal of Consulting and Clinical Psychology* 41, 3: 427–37.

Steinmann, Anne, and David J. Fox
1966 "Male-Female Perceptions of the Female Role in the United States," *Journal of Psychology* 64: 265–76.

Stratton, John R., and Stephen P. Spitzer
1967 'Sexual Permissiveness and Self-Evaluation: A Question of Substance and a Question of Method," *Journal of Marriage and the Family* 29 (August): 434–47.

Straus, Murray A.
1968 "Communication, Creativity, and Problem-Solving Ability of Middle- and Working-Class Families in Three Societies," *American Journal of Sociology* 73: 417–30.

Tiger, Lionel
1969 *Men in Groups*, New York: Random House.

Treiman, Donald J.
1966 "Status Discrepancy and Prejudice" *American Journal of Sociology* LXX: 651–64.

Tresemer, David, and Joseph H. Pleek
1974 "Sex Role Boundaries and Resistance to Sex Role Change," *Women's Studies* 2: 61–78.

Turner, Ralph
1966 "Role," *International Encyclopedia of the Social Sciences* 13: 556.

Udry, J. Richard
1966 *The Social Context of Marriage*, New York: Lippincott.
Vener, Arthur M., and Cyrus S Stewart
1974 "Adolescent Sexual Behavior in Middle America Revised: 1970–1973," *Journal of Marriage and the Family* 36, 4 (November): 728–35.
Waller, Willard
1938 *The Family*, New York: The Cordon Co.
Wallin, Paul
1950 "Cultural Contradictions and Sex Roles: A Repeat Study." *American Sociological Review* XV, 2: 288–93.
Winick, Charles E.
1968 *The New People: Desexualization in American Life*, New York: Pegasus.
Yankelovich, Daniel
1974 *The New Morality: Profile of American Youth in the Seventies*, New York: McGraw-Hill.
Zelnick, Melvin, and John F. Kantner
1972 "The Probability of Premarital Intercourse," *Social Science Research* 1 (September): 335–41.

Index